'An extraordinarily gifted composer of prose . . . [a] teller of
memorable stories . . . It isn't often that a writer of superlative
skills knows enough about flying to write well about it;
Saint-Exupéry was one; Salter is another'
New York Times Book Review

'He can bestow a powerful aura of glamour and heightened
significance to even the most casual encounter . . .
entertaining, sharply observed . . . pure and ravishing'
Nation

'[His] account of air combat in Korea . . . stands as
a masterpiece of battle writing in this century . . .
His prose is in flight'
Los Angeles Times Book Review

'A dazzling book . . . so full of splendid writing that at times
the overwhelmed reader may blink like a sleeper awaking
to hard light'
Philadelphia Inquirer

'No man who is even remotely honest with himself can read
Burning the Days without envy; no woman of similar truthfulness
will fail to find Salter's life deeply romantic'
John Irving, *Toronto Globe and Mail*

'A wonderful book by a sensitive author who is romantic,
intelligent, and superbly balanced. It is a serene account of
a surprising diversity of experiences, but it is also
a history of
Joseph

BURNING THE DAYS

JAMES SALTER is the author of numerous books, including the novels *Solo Faces*, *Light Years*, *A Sport and a Pastime*, *The Arm of Flesh* (revised as *Cassada*), and *The Hunters*; the memoirs *Gods of Tin* and *Burning the Days*; the collections *Dusk and Other Stories*, which won the 1989 PEN/Faulkner Award, and *Last Night*, which won the Rea Award for the Short Story and the PEN/Malamud Award; and *Life Is Meals: A Food Lover's Book of Days*, written with Kay Salter. He lives in New York and Colorado.

JAMES SALTER

BURNING THE DAYS

RECOLLECTION

PICADOR

First published 1997 by Random House Inc., New York,
and simultaneously in Canada by Random House of Canada Limited, Toronto

First published in the UK 1997 by The Harvill Press

First published by Picador in paperback 2007

This edition published 2014 by Picador
an imprint of Pan Macmillan Ltd, a division of Macmillan Publishers Limited
Pan Macmillan, 20 New Wharf Road, London N1 9RR
Basingstoke and Oxford
Associated companies throughout the world
www.panmacmillan.com

ISBN 978-1-4472-5070-8

With deepest gratitude

to my wife, Kay, and Bill Benton

for their invaluable help

Portions of this book, often in slightly different form, have been previously
published in *Esquire, Grand Street,* and *The Paris Review.*

Grateful acknowledgment is made to New Directions Publishing Corporation
for permission to reprint seven lines from "Lament for Ignacio Sanchez Mejias"
from *The Selected Poems of Federico García Lorca* by Federico García Lorca,
translated by Stephen Spender and J. L. Gili. Copyright © 1955 by
New Directions Publishing Corp. Reprinted by permission of
New Directions Publishing Corporation.

Contents

Certain names in this book have been changed to avoid possible embarrassment to individuals living or dead. The altered names are: (Chapter One) Faith; (Chapter Three) Anita; (Chapter Four) Miss Cole, Demont, Neal, Paula, Leland, O'Mara; (Chapter Five) Brax, Miles; (Chapter Six) Garland; (Chapter Nine) Ilena, Miss Bode, Edoardo; (Chapter Ten) the widow Woods, Sis Chandler.

Preface

This book is, to some extent, the story of a life. Not the complete story which, as in almost any case, is beyond telling—the length would be too great, longer than Proust, not to speak of the repetition.

What I have done is to write about people and events that were important to me, and to be truthful though relying, in one place or another, on mere memory. *Your language is your country*, Léautaud said, but memory is also, as well as being a measure, in its imprint, of the value of things. I suppose it could be just as convincingly argued that the opposite is true, that what one chooses to forget is equally revealing, but put that aside. Somehow I hear the words of E. E. Cummings in *The Enormous Room: Oh, yes, Jean,* he wrote, *I do not forget, I remember Plenty . . .*

Apart from my own memory I have relied on the memories of others, as well as on letters, journals, and whatever else I could find.

If you can think of life, for a moment, as a large house with a nursery, living and dining rooms, bedrooms, study, and so forth, all unfamiliar and bright, the chapters which follow are, in a way, like looking through the windows of this house. Certain occupants will be glimpsed only briefly. Visitors come and go. At some windows you may wish to stay longer, but alas. As with any house, all within cannot be seen.

I was led to write this book by my editor, Joe Fox, who had read a kind of personal essay—not conceived of as a chapter—called "The Captain's Wife" in *Esquire* in 1986, and urged me to write more. After some hesitation, I began.

I found it difficult, more perhaps than will be apparent, to write about myself. I had, as will be shown in the second chapter, come to believe that self was not the principal thing, and I lived that way for a long time. Also, to revisit the past was like constantly crossing a *Bergschrund*, a deep chasm between what my life had been before I changed it completely and what it was afterwards.

As a result, the writing was slow. Wearied by self-revelation, I would stop for months before starting in again. The sad part is that near the last, Fox, who had stood by loyally the entire time, died before seeing the concluding pages. It is to him that the book owes its existence.

In the past I have written about gods and have sometimes done that here. It seems to be an inclination. I do not worship gods but I like to know they are there. Frailty, human though it may be, interests me less. So I have written only about certain things, the essential, in my view, the world as it was, at least for me.

In youth it feels one's concerns are everyone's. Later on it is clear that they are not. Finally they again become the same. We are all poor in the end. The lines have been spoken. The stage is empty and bare.

Before that, however, is the performance.

The curtain rises.

J. S.

BURNING THE DAYS

PRONAOS

THE TRUE CHRONICLER of my life, a tall, soft-looking man with watery eyes, came up to me at the gathering and said, as if he had been waiting a long time to tell me, that he knew everything. I had never seen him before.

I was in my fifties. He was not much older but somehow seemed an ancient figure. He remembered me when I was an infant riding in a horse-drawn carriage on Hope Avenue in Passaic. He named my birthday, "June tenth, 1925, am I right? Your picture was in *The New York Times* when you were a captain in Korea and had just shot down three planes. You married a girl from Washington, D.C. You have four children."

He went on and on. He knew intimate details, some a bit mixed up, like a man whose pockets are filled with scraps of paper. His name was Quinton; he worked in a post office and was called, I learned later, the Historian, derisively, as if his passion were useless and even embarrassing. As if it were an attempt to try to be of some importance. "You went to Horace Mann," he said. "The football coach was Tillinghast."

In fact, the football coach was a bandy-legged, graying man named Tewhill. Tillinghast was headmaster. I felt it was a minor error.

There is your life as you know it and also as others know it, perhaps incorrectly, but to which some importance must be attached. It is difficult to realize that you are observed from a number of points and the sum of them has validity.

His wife was begging him to leave me alone. I was astonished at what he knew. "Forty-four State Street. That was your grandmother's house, right? She served you lentil soup and steak when your father brought you to visit—he hired a cab once a month."

The run-down frame house on the corner with cement steps going into the yard, and the unvarying meal of which I was fond, on a square table in the kitchen, followed by the hour afterwards when, with nothing to do, I sat on the back steps while my father talked to his mother, telling her of things he was doing and comforting her, I suppose. The driver sat silently waiting in the cab.

My father and I made these journeys together. My mother never came. Up the West Side of Manhattan along the river, vacant Sunday morning, looking out the window, the endless drab apartment buildings on one side and in the distance, gleaming, the new George Washington Bridge. Cigar smoke, fragrant and sickening, fled past the top of the glass near my father as he sat musing, sometimes humming softly to himself. Over the driver's radio came the impassioned words of the fervent anti-Semitic priest who broadcast every Sunday, Father Coughlin. His repeated fierce phrases beat against me. These were lean times. The driver was earning five dollars for the trip, including waiting for two hours before taking us back. It was a different driver always, the cab hailed on the street and quickly hired.

We passed beneath the great fretted tower at the east end of the bridge, always significant to me since the time my father said a restaurant had been planned for the very top of it. There was an elevator within the steel framework and we had once gone up in it, perhaps in my imagination, even the Olympian view.

The Hudson was the river of my youth, the river of sunset and wedding cake dayliners, my own river though I never so much as felt a drop of its water on my hand or brow. I had walked across the bridge more than once, leaning over the railing to look down at the dark water an infinite distance below, sometimes lucky enough to see a white excursion boat plow past, its sunny upper deck filled with chairs like an auditorium with the roof gone. Once a year in a long line towards the sea the fleet lay at anchor, cruisers named for distant cities and broad battleships later sunk at Pearl Harbor. From somewhere along the shore, launches took you out to visit them. I had gone several times, climbed the steel ladders and stood beneath the tremendous guns. The crew in their white, wide-bottomed trousers, the manly officers, the wooden decks—it was something of which to be proud, the sole defense of the innocent and unarmed republic in which I was born.

On the far side, above the green bulk of the Palisades, was another landmark, a nightclub called the Riviera—a gambling club I had heard, Le Corbusier–like and modern—that at one time burned to the ground and was rebuilt. It was related through its owner to an order of earlier, legendary places, the Silver Slipper, Cotton Club, and others.

By roads then familiar we drove on, through grim Sabbath neighborhoods, my father towards the end telling the driver how to proceed, exactly where to turn, until we drew up beside the familiar two-story house. My grandmother, thin-faced and sad but for the moment smiling, came to the kitchen door. She lived with my great-grandfather, a fearsome old man in his eighties from the *shtetls* in Poland, unshaven and foul-smelling—it was probably incontinence—who mostly remained upstairs. Jacob Galambia was his name, probably a concoction given to him by an immigration officer. Columbia, the neighbors called him. He and my grandmother had come down from Canada, and she had gone to night school to learn English after her marriage and the birth of her children. What her father's livelihood had been I don't think I was ever told. He was too ancient to be affectionate and the cruel scratch of his beard burned my face. My father was polite but paid him small notice.

I am speaking offhandedly of a great span of time. This great-grandfather had been born in about 1850. I was taken, a small boy who knew nothing of him, to visit. I may eventually look with some wonder upon a grandchild born in the year 2000 or after. A hundred and fifty years. Worlds have disappeared . . .

There was also, on this side of the family, a divorced husband— my grandfather—and an aunt, my father's sister, named Laura. It was at her funeral, years after the monthly visits to my grandmother had ended, that the bard, let me call him that out of respect, confronted and overwhelmed me with his recital of my years. I had watched him being led away from me, like a saddened child.

In old age my mother and her sister, widowed and living together, sorted the past, their girlhood in Washington, D.C., where they were born, as their mother had been, the house on Upsher Street, their strict father, the relatives who became rich, the suitors. Major Sledge, who had been in love with Selma, the oldest sister, before the First World War. He was on the White House staff, a major *in peacetime,* they emphasized. He wanted to marry her and take her to Chicago. Their parents would not give permission. What became of Major Sledge? Neither of them knew.

Of the four sisters, Mildred, my mother, was the most beautiful, also the youngest and most willful. She had a lively girlhood—the dreariness came later—the dances at the country clubs, the embassies, she went to all of them; the Argentine embassy was the best.

"French," my aunt corrected.

"No, the Argentine."

They begin talking about the family again, identifying branches

6

on the tree of kinship. Their father had two brothers and a sister. One of the brothers was—

"A photographer," says my aunt.

"No, a dentist."

"I thought he was a photographer."

My aunt, the second youngest, was blonde and liked to laugh. She had been married twice, for a long time to an unsuccessful lawyer who was my favorite uncle. She shined his shoes and made sure he had a haircut. His clientele was impoverished. Counselor, they called him. He drew up contracts and leases, occasionally he handled a divorce. Some of his business was trying to collect rents.

"Who's there?" they would shout through the door.

When he told them they would yell, "Get out or I kick your ass!"

Short, a bit heavyset, expert at cards and tricks, he also played the piano and wrote songs. His hair was dark and thinning. His fingers were stubby, the backs of them and his forearms rich with silky black hair. He had gone to dental school—it was there he had met my aunt, at the college clinic, while fixing her teeth—but eventually he switched to another field of extraction.

His patience and playfulness made me love him. He and Frances had no children. I was their substitute. My mother and I would take the Weehawken ferry, wide with curved galleries for passengers on either side, the smell of tar and brine in the air, the deck rhythmically rising and falling. My uncle would be waiting for us on the far side in his car, a secondhand sedan. In those years there were factories along the river and farther up, perched on the heights, the sturdy framework of a great roller coaster in the center of an amusement park. We never went to the park but instead to one or another in a series of apartments in buildings of dark brick, often along a steep street. On a couch in the living room I sat entranced as coins which had disappeared with a twist of the fingers into thin air were pulled from behind my ear and aces rose magically to the top of a well-shuffled deck. The piano bench was stuffed with his songs and the magazine rack, I once discovered, had nudist magazines hidden by the *Saturday Evening Post*.

This marvelous uncle, when I was no longer a child and had gone off to school, came home one day complaining he was dizzy and was put to bed. He was sent to the hospital—"I don't think they operated," my aunt said vaguely—and a month or so later he ran off with his secretary. My mother, telling me the news, explained that he was ill, had a brain tumor, and had been taken to an asylum. In fact he and the secretary were in his mother's house on the shore, though not long afterwards, perhaps in some way close to the invented story, he died. I do not know where he is buried.

Families of no importance—so much is lost, entire histories, there is no room for it all. There are only the generations surging forward like the tide, the years filled with sound and froth, then being washed over by the rest. That is the legacy of the cities.

"You know what Poppa's father was?" my mother asks.

"He had a linen factory," replies my aunt.

"He was a brewmaster."

No, no. They argue on about him and the uncle, the dentist or photographer, who came to visit in the early 1900s but didn't like America and went back to Europe.

"To Frankfurt," my aunt says.

"Moscow," corrects my mother.

The tree is only dimly outlined, the *arbor consanguinitatis*. Their father as a youth lived with his grandmother because his parents were divorced, and he was sent to America because of some business with the serving girl. And so, blindly, he escaped the wars and the wave of unparalleled destruction that came with them. In America he married a woman whose mother, my great-grandmother, had been married to a Polish prince named Notés.

"A prince?"

"Maybe he was a general," my mother concedes. "Anyway he was important." In her seventies she was still handsome and haughty, woe to the unsuspecting waiter or shopgirl. A stylish charcoal portrait done when she was in her forties—fine features, faint rings below the eyes, long graceful neck—was still very close to her appearance. She read the newspaper every day, including all the advertisements. Each day she walked two miles.

My mother first saw my father, a photograph of him, at any rate, in the newspaper. She was eighteen. Later, entirely by chance, they were introduced. Her parents liked him very much, her mother especially. They were married in Baltimore in 1924. It was in the morning. They came back to Washington and had lunch and the new groom left for New York to go back to work. He returned a month later.

I was the only child, born early on a June morning of the hottest day imaginable and delivered by a doctor who I later fantasized might have been William Carlos Williams—the time and location are about right—but who was in fact named Carlisle. The evening brought relief from the heat in the form of a terrific storm. I would like to think I somehow remember it and that my love of all storms proceeded from that first one, but more likely I was sleeping, wearied from the passage, my young mother—she was twenty-one—weary too, but immensely happy for everything that was over and all that lay ahead. Thunder shook the windows, the rain rattled down. The year was 1925, the hospital, Passaic General.

Among my other uncles, one owned a factory that made acoustic materials. This uncle, Maurice, was tall and sardonic and had a waxed moustache. At one point he also had a racy convertible, a Cord, parked, in my memory, at an angle to the curb on the street in New York where we lived, a crosstown street, then as now exceptionally wide. He was an engineer of some kind. He and my aunt Sylvia had met in Atlantic City, but the factory, which failed in the Depression, was near Philadelphia and it was there that they lived. They had a house, a maid, cars. They went away every summer. The sisters never visited, they hated him so.

"He never really did anything after 1932," my aunt said of him.

"A lowlife," my mother commented.

In old age, widowed, Sylvia went mad. In her daughter's house she would rise in the middle of every night to pack, and in the end got on a train alone at three in the morning. She was settled afterwards in a small apartment but people were robbing her there, she complained. A woman had gotten in and stolen everything, her money, checkbook, keys. She had once again called the police.

"How did she get in?" my mother asked.

"She got in."

"But the door was locked and just had a new lock put on."

"She came through the ceiling," Sylvia explained calmly, "the thieving whore."

The money and keys were found stuffed under a sofa, together with underclothes. The checkbook was wedged behind the back leg of a chest.

They went walking for an hour afterwards. Sylvia was calm and lucid. She had the vast patience of the insane. Her daughter refused to look after her. Her sisters, by means of long bus rides, took over the task.

———

We lived in New York from the time I was two years old, first in a rented room in some woman's apartment on Ninety-eighth Street, then a few blocks away in our own apartment on West End Avenue, a wide, faceless street of middle-class families. My father had built some houses, without much profit, in New Jersey. In New York his ambition found its place.

In the city that first took shape for me there were large apartment buildings stretching as far as one could see in either direction. On the side streets were private houses, many of which had been divided into rooms. Along Riverside Drive stood unspoiled mansions, stranded, as if waiting for aged patriarchs to die. In the bleak back courtyards men with grinding wheels sometimes still appeared, ringing a bell and calling up to housewives or kitchen maids for knives and scissors to sharpen. Nature meant the trees and narrow park along the river, and perhaps one of the rare snowstorms, with traffic in the streets dying and the silence of the world wrapping around. Newsboys, so-called though they were men, often walked along late in the day shouting something over and over, *Extra! Extra!*, someone murdered, something collapsed or sunk. A block away, around the corner, the police suddenly formed in front of a brownstone and sealed off the street expecting a gunfight with a famous criminal they had cornered, Two-Gun Crowley.

Still, I was allowed to walk to school alone, beginning with the first or second grade, and to play outside afterwards. The classrooms were presided over by invincible white-haired women: Miss Quigley—perhaps it was she who taught me to read—Miss McGinley.

We sat in rows according to merit, the best pupils in front. Marks were given monthly in both schoolwork and conduct. We were made, a little later, to stand and recite poems from memory. A kind of anthology was thus provided and from it one learned the heroic language.

Much of childhood remains everlastingly clear, the first telephone number, the name (Tony) of the feared elevator man, the pure sound—when I lay in bed bored and sick—of the key in the apartment door, which meant my mother was returning at last with the book, mostly pictures, I so wanted.

Looking back, it can be seen that my life was an obedient one. I was close to my parents and in awe of my teachers. I had no crude or delinquent companions. The tyrannical doormen, Irish and Italian, together with the superintendents, undershirted men with strange accents, were my only enemies. There was no heaven but there was a nether region with dark basement corridors and full ashcans where I feared to go. I was a city child, pale, cared for, unaware.

I barely remember that first apartment, in which we lived for years. The streets outside are clearer to me, the children's group I was enrolled in, run by a young woman whose pleasant features I cannot quite make out and who was called Mademoiselle, the friend named Junior who lived in what I could see were lesser circumstances on the side street but who owned something unthinkable, a huge dog, a German shepherd.

We had neither dog, cat, nor family gatherings. My father had friends, usually one or two at a time, and I remember them, the homely, bald-headed builder with steel-rimmed glasses, the city judge, and others, large, jovial men with crushing handshakes and a confident air. Some owned cars. Usually when I saw them they were on their way to or coming back from playing golf.

My mother had friends, as well, Ann, Harriet, Eileen, Rose. Afternoon women. Perhaps they went to lunch. All of them were married, but their husbands, with one or two exceptions, I rarely saw. The women were warm and easy, pleasant to be around. They were still in their twenties, with silken legs and bright smiles. Perhaps they went dancing in the evening. My parents never did and seldom went to parties.

I knew nothing, really, of the lives of these women. I was a little boy, a kind of pet. I did not even know, in most cases, where they lived. I was sometimes put together with their children, but friendships did not result.

In New York in those days, the endless days, you were shaved each morning in a barbershop; suits and shoes came from De Pinna, and mistresses from women who worked in the office or the garment district. At least this was how my father and his closest, lifelong friend, a cousin, Berry, lived. Handsome though completely bald, Berry was a bachelor who had been a boxer in the navy. He lived in a residential hotel near the corner of the park and unselfconsciously wore a beret. Seated at my father's funeral, expressionless and faithful, he had unexpectedly burst into tears as the coffin was lowered, crying my father's name. "George," he sobbed, "George . . ."

My father was rising in the world. He was usually in a good mood, singing a song as he dressed—"*Otche Chornia*" was one he particularly liked, "Dark Eyes." He made up words of his own, knowing only the first few, "*Otche chornia, I prekrasnia . . .*" Often he was gone in the evening, on business. There were arguments. With me he was friendly, affectionate, but not in any true sense intimate. Childish things were beneath him, and he was indifferent to athletics. I never felt the absence of love, only of his interest. My mother may have felt the same.

As long as I can remember he was self-involved. Even as he walked down the street he was seeing only occasional things while thinking. One thing he was certain of: he would succeed. Pieces were already falling into place, he was gaining a reputation and meeting important men. He introduced me once to Jack Dempsey, the dark-jawed champion who in those days was the image for the sport, stalking, lean. My father had arranged a lease for him and they were on good terms. Dempsey must have been in his early forties when I met him and more popular even than he had been in the ring when, humming a deathsong to himself and punching powerfully to its rhythm, he had brought down giants, Willard and Firpo, in fights that became legend. He was big, with the cheekbones of an Indian. His hands were enormous and strong. I was ten or eleven years old and remember him towering above me. I would be bigger than Dempsey, my father told me when we walked away. I would have a left like his. Pal, he used to call me. Then his mind went off to other things, various prospects and dreams.

He had dealings with someone named Lignante, a charming man with European manners who had married a judge's daughter. Lignante was building Hampshire House, a gleaming edifice on

Central Park South, and my father lent him a large amount of money, seventy-five thousand dollars, with no collateral but against a promised share in the completed building. This was in 1929. The crash ruined Lignante, who eventually died in Italy. The money, a huge sum at the time, was never repaid. There were to be other calamities but none of such proportion.

In my father's papers when he died there was still the promissory note, almost the exact size of a check, that Lignante had signed. It was like the bundles of rubles I once saw in the bedroom trunk of a schoolmate, Azamat Guirey, whose mother was a Georgian princess and whose parents had fled Russia after the revolution. Despite all one knows, something clings to paper that once had value.

—————

As a boy I knew none of this. In the summer we went to the beach, Atlantic City, and stayed with my maternal grandparents: my mother, cousins, aunts, and I. Across the bright flatlands and bridges, the earth of the roadside losing its color, we drove, children in a separate compartment, the rumble seat, in back, hair blowing, arms waving in happiness. There was sea smell in the air and sun in the bedroom windows. The rhythm of life was set by adults but the carefree joys were ours.

We played all day in the sand, down where it was smoothest, the green sea hissing at our feet. Not far offshore was the black wreckage of a small coastal steamer. We were unable to go near it but it is stuck there in memory, the sea swelling over it and then pouring away, the water dropping in sheets from its sides. A few years later, but not when we were there, the *Morro Castle,* a cruise ship, burned on the horizon nearby with great loss of life.

The taste of early things lives on. In my mouth I feel the freshness of farm tomatoes and salt, the scrambled eggs my grandmother made, the unexpected gulps of sea. In my heart there remains childish love for those cousins, whom I saw only seldom and who later drifted away entirely.

In the summers that followed I was sent to camp. Cordial men, the owners, brought a movie projector to the apartment during the winter to show baseball games, hilltop dining halls, and small boys diving from a six-meter board. With an unheard click of a switch the boys magically left the water, feet first, sailing up to stand on the board again. "We teach that, too."

The camps were always on a lake, a lake with leeches. The grass was worn and dry, the counselors not reluctant to fix character with praise or a fatal nickname. One night a week the flat wooden benches were arranged in a rectangle—the boxing ring—with spectators' benches behind. You were chosen to fight once or twice during the summer. There in the opposite corner, skinny arms ending in oversized gloves, was the grim opponent. Sometimes the outcome was already revealed in his face, victory or certain defeat. Three rounds amid the yelling, the corner shouting instructions. The sting of the blows, especially in the face, brought shameful tears to the eyes.

At High Lake, the first camp I went to, the most feared fighter was a husky boy with one arm. The right one was missing below the elbow. He would rush in and swing the rounded stump. I have forgotten his name, Miller, I think, but not the way the flesh was rolled tight at the empty end. It was like being hit with a club.

At a second camp, in New Hampshire, where I went for three or four years, I was matched against my closest friend who had a temper, I knew. Royal Marcher was his name. He also had a glamorous red-haired mother and a younger sister whom we scorned but who made a surprising, sensual entrance into my dreams a few years after. Agile, assured, a few pounds lighter than I was, he sat in the other corner with a cold expression. When our eyes met it seemed he did not recognize me. The bell rang.

We moved towards each other, large gloves raised, jabbing

lightly, staring at each other from behind a right hand held close to the cheek. The jabs were from too great a range. They barely brushed the skin. Once in a while there was one more solid. I was watching for his possible anger as much as anything. I saw only a lean, inexpressive face.

Between rounds, close to my ear, the counselor who was my second instructed, "Use your left hook. He's carrying his guard low." I nodded. It was the summer when the first soft pubic hair was beginning to appear but childhood had not ended.

The bell rang for the second round. Armed with expert advice I circled slowly to the right, poked out my left hand once or twice, and then swung a great looping blow with it. It landed with unexpected force squarely on his jaw. I saw him stagger, bewildered. "Again! Again!" I could hear them cry. I jabbed a few times and then hooked, hitting him solidly once more. He hid behind his gloves. Blood, forgetful of friendship, rushed to my head. I felt triumph but also betrayal. Royal kept away from me until the end of the round.

In the third round, coached himself, more cunning, he held his right hand higher and threw some hooks of his own which I danced away from. The judges, aware of the verdict's significance, called the fight a draw. We each had our pride and he, his temper.

There were secret societies—honor societies, they were called—their proceedings unrevealed. Selection came at night, after taps. We lay in bed and watched the shielded flashlights move in an eccentric way around the bunk until, our hearts all beating, they stopped and someone was tapped, told to rise. There were no requisites to being chosen; it was according to some form of popularity, incalculable, really. That was a distinction beyond all others, even the medals and awards given out at the end of the summer. Certain boys were popular. They were the true avatars.

It was at camp that one held in one's palm the dainty red newts found in beds of thick moss, learned filthy songs pure from young mouths, heard strange viewpoints, and discovered the stars. There was the feel of rough wool blankets in the chill mountain night, the comfort of the simple unifying prayer *Now I lay me down to sleep* . . . , the bugle calls, competition, and raising and lowering of the flag on a tall wooden pole painted white. We took hikes of ten or twelve miles, arranged to end at a general store where there were cold bottles of a bitter New England drink called Moxie, and penny candy.

There were abandoned farmhouses with fifty-year-old newspapers yellow on the floor, three-day canoe trips on vast northern lakes, and color week with its stirring songs taken from operas, *Parsifal* and *Aïda*, "Ten thousand strong, we sing a song, men of Orange . . . ," and concluding campfires with huge, crackling pyres of wood sending sparks swirling upwards, the camp having been divided from top to bottom into two groups that competed fiercely for the championship.

There were phonographs and records, cameras shaped like a shoebox, sacred peeled sticks, and one weekend when cars came up the stoney road carrying parents for a visit. My father's bathing suit had a striped top and he seemed a lone figure on the wooden dock when we went swimming together. He asked me nothing about baseball, where, one of the worst players, I stood in exile in right field, occasionally seeing tremendous fly balls soar up from the distant batter, reach their zenith and then, increasing their arc and speed, small, white, and deadly, begin to descend as I ran desperately back over the clumpy ground. He and my mother both urged me to learn to play tennis, though without great conviction since they did not play themselves. They sometimes, in later years, went out together onto the golf course.

Names from childhood—they were from camp and grammar school—were Dickie Davega, George Overholt, Neil Wald, Jamie Falk, and Larry Sloan, whom I recognized later in the pages of *Marjorie Morningstar* and whose sister was a showgirl, leggy and superior, moving haughtily past us.

We had moved to the East Side, to a large building, the Croydon, cleft by two deep courts along Madison Avenue. Here we occupied first one, then another apartment, remaining for years.

We had moved out of simple necessity, that of finding someplace less expensive, pausing for temporary stops in Atlantic City and a hotel on Central Park South owned by some acquaintances of my father.

My new school, one of the most highly regarded in the city, was just across the street, an old red-brick monument, since torn down but still visible, so to speak, in the form of London train stations. The neighborhood was well-to-do, the silk-stocking district, it was called, with a poorer section over towards the river, Yorkville, largely German and Irish. The school's principal, white-haired and shapeless, was Emily Nosworthy, a woman of a kind that was once numerous—educated, unswerving, very likely unmarried. There were no schoolyard fights or scuffles in the hall, and the women beneath her were equally to be feared.

A schoolmate and I, in his apartment one afternoon, were making drawings of what an undressed girl might be like. Neither of us had ever seen one, or even a drawing in a book. Picasso's etchings came much later, Rodin's *Iris*, naked trunk, one leg askew, and we had never heard of Courbet. The art of photography was nascent.

There was another, closer friend who lived one block away and whose life was in large part governed by his mother's career, a mother I rarely saw. She was a pianist and gave concerts at Carnegie Hall. Her son, Alec, was blue-eyed and somewhat rumpled, the tongue of his belt hanging down. We played alone in his room. Everyone was invisible in that family: Nadia, his mother, closed off and practicing behind curtained glass doors; his older brother, who was already in college and had a regime to strengthen the lungs—four steps inhaling while walking, four steps breathing out, then the next block, five, and so forth.

Alec's room was at the rear of the apartment. We wrestled on his bed in the late afternoons, the door closed, the sound of the piano disregarded and faint. The room looked out on a courtyard seven or eight stories below and faced other dull, anonymous windows. One ordinary afternoon as the light was fading we noticed a figure in another apartment not far away, a floor below and close by because the building was in the shape of a "U." It was a young woman, quite alone. The room in which she moved back and forth—a bathroom—was brightly lit and the top half of the window was down. In our room the lights had not been turned on, and concealing ourselves to watch, we sank to our knees.

She slipped the sweater she was wearing over her head, passed from sight and a moment later returned, unfastening her brassiere. I recall the incredible brilliance of her flesh, the blinding nakedness, and the despair when she passed from view. We said not a word to one another. We waited in absolute silence. It was the hour of twilight. That empty box of illumination was more compelling than any stage. As if in obedience she returned. I simply could not see her enough nor, I knew from the first instant, retain what I had seen.

No hunter at dawn, no assassin or searcher, ever felt greater joy. She walked before us, turned, tied back her hair. She leaned forward slightly to remove the last of her clothing and then stood, sacred and incomplete, looking down at something, probably a scale. I cannot imagine the weight of that immortal substance. It had no weight. It was made of glory. Then, abruptly, she stepped away to an invisible shower or tub. She departed, that is, from this earth. I had never, till then, faced the paradox of a dream vivid to the point of ecstasy yet destined to vanish.

Dazzling as it was, it was also commonplace. Everyone knew of it, as we did then for the first time.

———

From a woman who was selling them door-to-door in about 1930, my mother had bought a six-volume set called *My Bookhouse*. The covers were dark green and tortoisey, with a large inset illustration, a beautiful lady in white, perhaps, with long hair and a crown of yellow and golden water lilies. I had other children's books but none I devoted myself to more. The reading was graduated from volume one through six, and though I disfigured the first two, by volume three I was treating them with respect. I knew many of the stories by heart, "The Fisherman and His Wife" by the Grimm brothers, and "The Honest Woodsman" who was offered first a gold, then a silver ax-head to replace the one he had lost but refused them, saying his was only steel, and was rewarded with all three.

There was Dickens, Byron, the Bible, Tolstoy, folktales from many nations, and poems. The texts may have been somewhat modified, softened—I think I realized it even then—but only as regards those things too brutal for young readers. The word "out," for instance, was omitted from a sentence in which a cruel woman cut out a sparrow's tongue, leaving the sensitive child with the impression that the tongue had been slit. The books were richly illustrated. In volume four or five was Kipling's "Ballad of East and West." It was four pages long. I knew every word, and every detail of the illustrations. The hero of the poem, the colonel's son, slender and dashing, wore a pith helmet with a white cloth wrapped around it and had a lanyard on his pistol. He may have been confused in my imagination with the Prince of Wales, who was the darling of the times.

The ballad centered around an epic hoof-drumming chase. A colorful outlaw—I met him later in Tolstoy's *Hadji Murat,* lame and untamable—with a band of men has stolen a horse from the British garrison on India's northeast frontier. The horse, moreover, a mare, is the colonel's favorite. The colonel's son, a troop commander, sets off in hot and lone pursuit. In a treacherous pass he at last catches sight of the mare with the bold thief, Kamal, on her back and a relentless race begins. *He has fired once, he has fired twice, but the whistling ball went wide* . . . even Tolstoy later described bullets' gay sound. Day fades. Hooves pounding, they ride through the night. His horse nearly spent, the colonel's son falls at a water jump and seeing this, Kamal turns back, knocks the pistol from the fallen rider's hand, and pulls him to his feet. There, face to face they stand and, after exchanging threats, confess to the bond that is now between them, rivals who have given all. Their code is the same, and the qualities of manhood they admire. They take a sacred oath as brothers and Kamal dispatches his only son to serve henceforth as bodyguard to his foe. *Belike they will raise thee to Ressaldar,* he predicts, *when I am hanged in Peshawur.*

I did not invent any games for the poem or pose before the mirror as one of its figures; I only stored it close to my heart. In the end, I suppose, I found the poem to be untrue, that is, I never found an adversary to love as deeply as a comrade, but I kept a place open for one always.

Of the cardinal virtues, it was fortitude the poem held high, perhaps with a touch of mercy. Fortitude, I saw, was holy. My life was too meager for me to know if I possessed it. I was white-skinned, sheltered. In the street I ran from gangs of toughs. Tunney, Dempsey's most famous opponent, soaked his fists every day in brine to make them invulnerable, my father had told me, to toughen them, and it was in some sort of brine that I hoped to steep myself.

———

It was my father who handled my sexual education. He did this by taking me to the family doctor, who had an office on Park Avenue with two exposures and an impressive desk. We sat, the three of us, and the doctor began by asking me—he wanted an honest answer, he said—if I played with myself. I did not understand. He then elaborated somewhat. "No," I said, which was true. He seemed almost disappointed but nevertheless undertook to describe how life was created. The egg, he explained, could not produce a baby chick all by itself. Something else was needed. I sat listening though not certain what he was talking about. He had a rugged face and silvery, Airedale hair. My father—I remember him always as having a comfortable double chin—was dutifully listening too.

The other thing that was necessary, the doctor continued, was a sort of kick to get the process started. He asked me if I knew what delivered this kick. He waited but I had no answer. The rooster, he explained.

With this, for me, improbable picture now in place he proceeded, with great discretion, wearing surgical gloves, as it were, to describe the principle of the kick as it related to humans. I more or less understood but did not find it intriguing.

I don't recall what my father said as we left. He may have asked me if I had any questions I hadn't wanted to ask in the office. I am certain my reply would have been no. With that, my father would have felt he had done what was expected of him.

At birthday parties, sitting in a circle, we played spin the bottle. A boy spun it and the girl it pointed to he kissed, usually with embarrassment. I bent awkwardly across towards Regina, the dark-haired daughter of the Greek florist, or Gisela, frail and blonde. The kisses meant nothing. The girls were of an age when only their long hair and instincts distinguished them from us.

In the last year of grammar school, a bright, curly-haired friend one afternoon asked me the same introductory question the family doctor had. This time I lied.

"How many times?" he asked.

Oh, I couldn't count them, I said, and gave the first figure that came to me, modest but not, I felt, inconsequential, "Twelve or thirteen." I was rewarded with a stunning revelation. "You know Faith?" he said.

"Yes."

"I did it with her."

"You did?"

"In her parents' apartment," he said. He added an indelible line, "She spread her legs so nice."

The brazen courage of it. It was unimaginable. He lived over near Third Avenue. She lived in a great, respectable building on Madison, a fortress. To this day it remains to me a kind of land-mark. Over the years the city becomes filled with them, certain side streets, apartment houses on corners, hotels.

What he had done with Faith, though I was amazed at the au-dacity, did not make me envious. I had no real appreciation of it. I saw its daring but I was unable to imagine its pleasure or even to fill the blank of what had led up to it. How did he happen to be in her apartment? In her room? What had he said to lead her—I could picture only abrupt refusal—to the act?

Months later one noon, looking through the magazines in a cigar store, I came across a pamphlet with blue paper covers. Someone had placed it there, concealed behind a magazine; it was not part of the stock. The provocative title I have forgotten, but as I began to read I underwent a conversion. Within, described straightforwardly, was everything the doctor and my friend had failed to clarify, the method, the exact details, the physical sensa-tion. The door had suddenly opened, barely, to be sure, but my in-volvement was intense. Holding the booklet down where no one could see it I read the pages again and again, and fairly trembling with discovery, like someone who has found a secret letter, I hid the precious thing where I had found it and left the store. I was going to try certain things, and all that I had read, in time, I found to be true.

Years afterwards, at a luncheon, I sat next to a green-eyed young woman, a poet, who declared loftily that you learned nothing from books, it was life you learned from, passion, experience. The host, a fine old man in his seventies, heard her and disagreed. His hair was white. His voice had the faint shrillness of age. "No, everything I've ever learned," he said, "has come from books. I'd be in darkness without them."

I didn't know if he was speaking of Balzac or Strindberg or even John O'Hara, to whom his sister had been married and from whose books one can learn a great deal, much of it unsettling, but in no particular order I tried to think of books that had instructed me, and among them, not insignificant, was the anonymous twenty-page booklet in blue covers that had described the real game of the grown-up world.

———

Then as now, the best weeks of the year were at Christmas. In the corner of the living room was the dark tree beneath which, early in the morning, the presents could be found, unhoped-for things, a green electric train, huge and perfect, with doors to the long passenger cars that could be pushed open and a massive engine exactly like ones dwarfing the people on the platform at Penn Station.

When I was older, thirteen and fourteen, we went to Washington at Christmas. There were the great vaults, filled with icy breath, of Union Station, the stone columns of the long façade, the wide avenues, and the Capitol swimming in light. My older cousin, who was a chess champion, and my uncle, large, broad-featured, and bald, were there to meet us. The house, in a modest neighborhood, was small but it was a *house*—there was a basement, a yard—which alone made it exciting. Snow was falling, the lawns were white, the brows and shoulders of statues, the roofs of snug homes. Snow was slanting through the air, the snow of the holidays with their many parties, at which I would be the youngest but somehow accepted by being an out-of-town visitor.

Harold, my cousin, was sixteen, a thrilling age: it meant that he could drive. The family car was a Plymouth. Off we went in the night to exciting addresses on streets he knew. We were from ordinary families but his schoolmates were from wealthy ones, some of them at least: boys who would be taken into large family businesses, and ravishing girls. There was one velvet-skirted brunette with whom I was infatuated. Gloria was her name. That first night she smiled at me. I could not believe I was talking to her or that a night or two later she remembered. I finally gave in to my cousin's taunts and telephoned her. I was meant to ask her out. In a warm voice, No, she couldn't, she said, she had already been asked, but would I call her again? I was ecstatic. I felt it was a triumph.

There was sledding on a hill near the house, where we fell in with the just-blooming daughter of a Marine officer who lived nearby. Soon we were sharing a sled. I sat behind her, arms around her waist as we sped down to crash in the snowbanks, my hands having moved higher as if by accident and the two of us lying there for a minute before rising to hurry back up. Delirious rides, repeated again and again.

Do you think she . . .? I asked my cousin uncertainly. Yes, he said, but seduction, despite the plans we made, proved beyond me. Instead, she and I drank hot chocolate in the kitchen, and when it was revealed there was no one else in the house, suddenly become cautious, she fled.

The pleasure one might, all innocent, have had. The bare, chilly bedrooms of those years, the nights of aching in darkness. Was it meant to be otherwise? Not really.

Colored by those Christmases, perhaps, others have all seemed to me exciting, like some glamorous invitation. It is romantic Christmas that seems to reign, Fifth Avenue Christmas with all the stores, faces shining in the cold, office-party Christmas with its abandon, Christmas in Paris in a postage-stamp hotel near Notre Dame, Christmas in Chamonix and the brightly lit casino, all of them somehow descended from the crowded young parties of 1938 and 1939.

———

My teachers had all been women. In prep school they were men, born towards the end of the nineteenth century and graduates, largely, of Eastern colleges and universities. They were men of strong principles and prejudices. The Latin teacher, he and his subject both feared, was Mr. Nagle, a demanding, wry bachelor with gingery hair, inflexible habits, and a green fountain pen the cap of which he would ceremoniously unscrew to make a note. His humor, laced with scorn, and lofty standards made him a favorite. Automatic failure, he warned, for mispelling Nagle.

History was a required course for all six years, and the American history teacher was a Mr. Martin, another titan, white-haired, commanding, with chalk dust on a habitual blue suit. He was in the habit of correcting term papers while listening to the radio. It would be hard to say exactly what one learned from him. In addition to history he instructed in a version of anthropology, personal hygiene, and morals. "Never swallow it" was one of his admonitions—he was speaking of phlegm, but the wiser boys in back tittered. This brought up what he knew was a constant preoccupation. "Keep your mind off the subject as much as possible" was his droning advice; "disease isn't worth it. The worst thing is the books," he cautioned. "They're much worse than the pictures." His classroom was on the side of the building facing the athletic field where early in the morning, before class, we played a game without rules, often damaging to clothes, called rip-ball, one against all, one darting hare against the trailing pack until he was exhausted or brought down. It was the field on which I recall Kerouac in shoulder pads and cleats, stocky and hard-running in games against Peddie and Blair. In football uniform, short-legged, he seemed a kind of thug. He would drop back to handle punts and, catching them, go like the wind.

The school, Horace Mann, was in Riverdale, the northern suburbs of the city. Its tone was essentially Anglo, there were only boys, and the overriding ethic was that we were responsible for our own destiny and for fulfilling our obligations to society. There was none of Büchner's or Ibsen's determinism, the doctrine that acts have resistless causes. We were not what unknown forces made of us but rather what we made of ourselves. In the mornings, in the auditorium, we sang "Men of Harlech"—"would you win your name in story?"—and, as the school was affiliated with Columbia, "Roar, Lion, Roar."

What effect this had, I cannot say. I was a decent student and lagging athlete, an unknown at track and substitute on the football team. I remember a youth of friendship and no foreboding, though miles away, in Europe, war had already started. Not far from where we lived, in Yorkville, they were showing German propaganda films, *Sieg im Westen,* and later, *Feldzug in Polen,* and women in the lobby of the theater held out cans collecting for German War Relief. *Battle's distant sound.* We sympathized with the British, naturally, and read with excitement, in newspapers that no longer exist, of the trapping by British cruisers of the pocket battleship *Graf Spee* in a South American estuary. Inspired, we invented our own warship game, brilliant as only schoolboys could make it, with complex rules for movement, engagement, damage, and resupply, maneuvering fleets of slender model ships on the bare wooden floors of apartments in endless fights, often with diagrams and accounts written up afterwards, word of it passing down, so that years after, people who had never seen but only heard of it asked to have it described.

Kerouac was only one of the postgraduate students, "ringers," brought in every year to man the school teams. Older, less fine, with faces already showing the shadows of manhood, they were the heroes of the school and at the same time outsiders. I never spoke to any of them; there was nothing to say. A year or two ahead of us, they drank beer, carried their books carelessly in one hand, and knew how to drive. Kerouac astonished us by submitting stories to the literary magazine, for a ringer an utterly unconventional act. He never came to the magazine's offices, however. That would have been too out of character.

The athletes had girlfriends, usually back in the small towns they had come from. We had girlfriends ourselves or, rather, knew girls. Some attended the sister school, Lincoln, some were their friends, a loose coterie of New York girls, well-off for the most part, closely watched over by their parents. They lived in the Seventies, Eighties, or Nineties, some more distant, one beauty in a building with an iron fence in the West Sixties. At school dances in the city on Saturday night a portion of them were likely to appear, and there were parties on Park Avenue with fruit punch in the dining room, the rug rolled back, and parents out of sight in a distant bedroom or at a movie.

The ennui of those parties, the schoolboy sophistication and dancing in darkened rooms. There were no passionate moments or slamming of doors. We did not have love affairs at that age. There were no notes from fifteen-year-olds that said, *I love you. I will give you anything.* Such notes as there were were teasing or clever. As boys we dreamed of the prescription *quantum vis,* "as much as you please," but there was never that. Nor were there many real couples. It was all too formalized and familiar.

I carry within me, however, the memories of those girls, the last of a breed, their freshness and animation, their refusal to be lured. I pass the buildings where they lived, where they live, those who went away, who married, the one who didn't, the one who went insane.

Among those schoolmates who achieved some notoriety there is Julian Beck. Foppish and unathletic, he was the object of ridicule behind his back and was probably aware of it—he followed Cocteau's dictum, whatever you are criticized for, intensify it. Bony-wristed, he floated through schoolboy theatrical productions, a long-nosed, fruity Hamlet, and fifteen years later, having abandoned a try at painting, he was director of an underground theater, metamorphosed into a visionary bringing a vivid and disturbing play, *The Connection*, to the stage. The theater was makeshift, up a narrow flight of stairs. I was astonished by the coolness of a play about drugs and failed to recognize its foresight, but it shone like a diamond. I met Beck several times afterwards but the level was superficial; in a real sense he declined to talk. He had stepped over me and was unwilling to be confronted on the old terms.

With Kerouac, though I never saw him again, it was the same. I recognized his photograph, sensitive down-turned face, in a bookstore window on the jacket of a thick first novel. It was *The Town and the City.* I read reviews of it after, filled with praise. By then I had tried to write a novel myself and failed. His was lyrical and repetitive and, to me, crushing. What he had done staggered me.

In an interview read later I saw the side of him that had been so unsuspected. He was asked about haiku and enthusiastically said, Yes! Then, before one's eyes, he proceeded, like a man peeling an apple in one unbroken strip of skin, to compress an incident—a leaf blown onto the back of a tiny sparrow in a storm—into three succinct lines through trial and error, crossing out words in midair, so to speak. I remembered sitting in the classroom while a favorite teacher tried to kindle our interest in the haiku and its seventeen syllables, but the essence of it, large things evoked by small, was beyond us.

Richard Wooster was the teacher's name. He was young and

had a wide, unnerving smile. Kerouac did not know him nor did Wooster, I think, know the swaggering Lowell boy. Among the teachers, Mr. Wooster was the one to whom I felt closest. When he went into the navy during the war he wrote to me as if to an equal. In the life after, I went to see him when I had published a novel. He was married by then and had four or five children. He was gray but still smiling. We sat in the living room of the large, disorderly house he no doubt had dreamed of. I meant him to see that his faith in me had been confirmed, but I am not sure what he saw—his smile was one of not quite remembering. His children had replaced me and life now crowded in. As if the school years had been a vine and something cut them and they fell.

———

My first duck I tasted in the dining room of a silvery apartment off Fifth Avenue. Across from me, aware of nothing remarkable, sat my friend. At the head of the table was his stepfather, Jonas Reiner, a large, humorous man who owned underwear factories, and at the far end my friend's blonde mother, Ethel.

Of the mothers of friends, she was the most glamorous. She had the most aplomb and style. She was the daughter of a doctor who, when October 1929 came, called and asked, "Are you broke?"—she was twenty-five years old, married to her first husband, with two small children. She had five thousand dollars to her name and her bill at Bergdorf's was four thousand eight hundred. "Yes," she said, "are you?"

"Um, but I've been broke before and I hope to be broke again," her father told her.

She was a regal figure to me, affected but smiling, her ash-blonde hair heaped on her head, the silk of her dresses whispering. I never saw her in the kitchen—there was a cook—or with a vacuum cleaner in her hand or even changing a shoe, legs crossed, slipping it off and putting on another. Perhaps there were weekend mornings when, in a peignoir with fur cuffs she might scramble eggs to put on a breakfast tray and carry down the hallway to her husband. She suggested the sumptuous.

Her son, Wink, was my friend. As young boys, groups of us used to gamble in his room, playing cards. He sometimes brought out five- or ten-dollar gold pieces to prove that he was good for any run of bad luck. I had never seen a gold piece or known they existed. They were prophetic. In time, he became a stockbroker and had a seat on the exchange. Money rolled in. He had a beautiful, extravagant wife and a house in Westchester. That was after the war. We were, strengthened by roots that reached far back, close friends. I was at his wedding and later, godfather to his first child. The money I had in the 1950s he doubled and tripled for me, and I felt myself rising with him, though in a smaller way.

In years that followed there came the life of men, evenings in uptown bars, confiding everything. I knew about his wife, his brother-in-law, his partners. We went to football games and to Mexico together. The welterweight championship of Mexico was being fought in a huge, ramshackle arena somewhere on the outskirts of Mexico City. We were in the second row with a woman we had met, a blonde who said she was the girlfriend of an ex–Chicago Bears football player. Had he lost a leg or been stricken with cancer? I don't seem to recall. I do see the vast, surrounding sea of blackest hair, all of it male. There was not another woman in the place and, a little drunk, the one we were with shone like a beacon. The naked calves of the fighters danced level with our eyes and blood flew from cut faces in what seemed to be sheets. From the balcony, beer was being thrown and lighted newspapers. It was round five or six. The chaos was mounting.

"I have to go to the ladies' room," she said. We were packed close. The empty aisle rose towards the rear between banks of men. "I have to go to the ladies' room," she said again. "Who'll come with me?"

Neither of us stirred. I watched as she made her way alone up the aisle, on high heels, her hips speaking clearly, it seemed, beneath the dress. She was the emblem of it all. Row by row every face turned to watch. I was sure we were not going to see her again.

We walked the dark streets afterwards, however, looking for a cab with her, few lights anywhere and unseen dogs barking.

At the cockfights we were drinking tequila and licking salt from the back of our hands. Wink had given up looking at the roosters as they were carried proudly around. He read the odds instead, written on pieces of board men bore through the darkness. He held out bunches of money, which they took nodding. It was pesos, it didn't matter. The cabs were in pesos, the hotel, the wide boulevards skimming past. We were breathing the Latin air, drunk on altitude. The city was a galaxy. The girls came into the room and lined up, smiling. Their teeth were mostly bad. One was Cuban. I had never been to Cuba. We went there, the palms, her bare room with shutters, the pale streets at dawn.

Perhaps it all still exists. I have never been back. We drove to Cuernavaca, then to the sea. The beach was shadowed by the first great hotels. White-legged we walked along it. There was a slender brown woman in a black bikini; she could have been Mexican but was not. We sat and talked. She was a friend of the English playwright John Osborne and had a gold cigarette case with a persuasive inscription engraved in his own hand.

She may have had some of his money, as well, or perhaps someone else's. She had bought a motorboat for the Mexican boy with whom she was living, so he could have a water-skiing business. We went to remote inlets in it and ate in beach shacks where there were only three or four plates but from somewhere were produced icy bottles of beer. We met in the evenings as well. The Mexican boy was always silent.

I caught sight of her several times afterwards in New York, once in the Veau d'Or with the cigarette case on the table near her plate. She appeared very urban and expensive, a long way from barefoot life. That period was ended. I wanted to know more about her, about Osborne and the past, but all of that she declined to reveal.

My friendship with Wink seemed indestructible and my attachment to his mother grew. It became love, not the love felt for my own mother but something grown-up and apart. It would be truer to say I returned her love, the warmth had first come from her.

During the war she lived in New York, where I often saw her while my own family was in Washington. Later she moved to an estate in Ossining. I forget the sequence of divorce from her husband and his becoming ill, but he grew gaunt and died. In Ossining she came in from the sunlight with a garden trowel in one gloved hand. There was a swimming pool, a sunken living room, a dog. Had I read *Tales of the South Pacific*, which had just been published, she asked? I *must*, she said. The war was over. We'd driven up to Ossining in a new car, perhaps Wink's. His mother had had difficulty in forming his tastes and was turning her efforts towards me.

She also had a nephew, her admired sister's son, Peter, who grew up more or less alongside us, plump and deceivable. His mother hoped he would go into medicine, but he had another ambition. After college he confessed it to Ethel: he wanted to have a gallery, he dreamed of art. She took him to dinner at the house of a famous dealer she knew, where Peter sat silently as the impossibilities of his choice were explained to him in detail, the near certainty of his not succeeding, and the sure disappointment of his mother. At the end he summoned his courage to say, "I'm not Dorothy's son, I'm Ethel's. I have the right to fail," he added.

There was a moment's silence and the dealer said, "I'll sponsor you."

I had two prints, a yellow Chagall marked *hors commerce,* and a Picasso bought from Peter when his gallery, in a town house off Fifth, with pure white walls, was thriving. I longed for a Matisse but hadn't the money.

———

In the summer of 1941 my father, who had been a lieutenant more than twenty years before, was called back into the army as a major. He was stationed in Atlanta in the Office of Engineers. I forget from which field we took off but I had my first airplane flight in a great silver ship with a tailwheel, going down to visit him. We toured munitions factories along the Tennessee River, near Huntsville, and the Coosa River, in Alabama. On a narrow wooden bridge in the country somewhere, a mule lay on its side—it had been pulling a wagon that was hit by an army truck and had a broken leg. It lay there patiently, as patiently as it had lived its life, a worn, gray animal waiting for the lean-faced man who had gone to fetch a gun.

My alluring image of war had been mainly formed by a book we had with a gray cloth cover on which the title was printed in dignified black letters and which had a dedication so stirring that I knew it by heart: Erich Maria Remarque's *All Quiet on the Western Front,* the archtestament, with its stark ordeal, of the First World War. I was unprepared to see real acts, even as part of an obscure overture.

There was a shot. The sound stood apart. I was sickened by it, as if by the impact of a plummeting body. The mule lay there, without existence, with no name. After a few minutes we were able to drive on.

My father, though he wore the insignia of a major, did not seem authentic. Perhaps it was because he was not in command of men, something he was probably ill suited for. In a matter of months he was transferred to Washington, and for three years my mother lived there while he was eventually sent on, to India and England. For some of these years no one knew what the outcome of the war would be, and printed orders to go overseas and join this unit or that, carrying with them the weight of the unknown, were of greatest importance. Some might be death warrants, though usually not for staff officers.

He became a colonel and began to imagine he might go higher, but that turned out to be the good fortune, as he saw it, of lesser men. He had the admiration, even love of subordinates but it is those above who are important.

The war ruined him. When it was over he was never able to fit in again. Everything had changed, he said. The vice presidents of banks were no longer able to turn pieces of property over to you to work on, and there were no old widows who owned hotels and wanted the sale of them arranged. He went to work for large companies in New York and Chicago but things never were right. It was the grandiose that attracted him. He was operatic. He lived on praise and its stimulus and performed best, only performed, when the full rays were shining on him.

The bald-headed friend and builder, Secoles was his name, had urged my mother to get a divorce and marry him. My father was a nice guy, he confided, but he would never amount to anything. He, Secoles, would.

It was a prophecy my father never heard, but gradually—it was also bad luck, two or three big hands, so to speak, that he failed to win; promises that were broken—his belief in himself faltered. He was given to grand predictions. "Mr. Brady, I believe in destiny. I told you we'd build a town together down here and, by God, we will." To make it ring true takes aplomb, and slowly that drained away. Money went with it. Contrary to the advice of Mr. Micawber, it seems to me that those in life who spend freely are better for it, and those who are tightfisted are worse. There is at least one exception: my father.

In the fall of 1957 the bank called his loan on some airline bonds. He had bought them at 120—they were at 62. He'd lost seventy thousand dollars in the market. He had nothing left. He'd have to give up the apartment, he said, he couldn't pay the rent. He had a close friend, a successful lawyer with a Phi Beta Kappa key and confident tone. "Could you tell him what your situation is and ask for help?"

"No."

"Why not?"

"He'd have nothing more to do with me."

He was lucky, my father said, not to own a gun. If he had, he'd shoot himself.

Finally, ashamed to be seen, he would lie in bed for hours, unable to summon the energy to go to work. His expensive shoes, all polished, were lined up in the closet, his many suits. The contents of his pockets were on top of the bureau beside his exhausted checkbook, his gold wristwatch, money, a few cigars. His hair was white, his jawline slack. He was finished.

Herman Melville's father, his import business having failed, became a bankrupt. *He gave up the struggle, became mentally ill and died.* Melville was thirteen years old. I was thirty-one when my father performed the same unforgettable act. He was like a spent horse. We tried to urge him on. He was just lying down for half an hour, he said. We sat in the living room, my mother and I, crushed by finality while he lay in bed in the city he had meant to triumph in, in the afternoon, traffic blaring in the street, the tall buildings shining their dead windows, gulls sitting on the water.

I remember that during those days he said two things in sad summation: "They'll never forget me" and "I'm dead." Both were true.

Soon he was in the hospital. As a final blow, two days before he died the buyer of an apartment complex the sale of which he had negotiated was killed flying in to New York to sign the contract.

This happened at La Guardia Airport. The icy waters—it was January—covered everything.

———

Decades, ages, later I wake at night with a strange feeling in my chest on the fateful side—can it be my heart? It is a feeling I have had before, a commonplace feeling, like a cramped muscle, which will probably go away as it always has, except this is four in the morning and my thoughts somehow turn to my father. We could not encourage him, we could not make him go on. It was cruel to keep trying. He wanted it to end. "In this world there are few enough people who ever care what becomes of you," he said. My mother long after said that the marriage had been wrong, that she had known it early but had been without the courage to act. She remained loyal to the end.

I think of the hopeless visits to psychiatrists, the shock treatments and aimless drives in the country to somehow get away. I think of him walking along the street, preoccupied, the pale wake of cigar smoke following, the blind strolls while his mind sorted through impossibilities, over and over.

———

Ethel Reiner, in her forties, decided upon the theater. She had a brief, exciting apprenticeship under a veteran producer named Saint Subber and then set out to produce on her own. After a few voyages in shallow water, as it were, she boldly took command of a ship of the line in the form of a huge musical production of *Candide* with Leonard Bernstein as its composer and the book, as it is curiously called, by another formidable figure, Lillian Hellman, with whom it was inevitable she would clash.

Candide was a triumph and a catastrophe, in that order. Its out-of-town tryouts, before it came to New York, were dazzling. To bring it to perfection there were final little changes, and something unidentifiable went wrong. The spring had been wound one turn too many. There was the party at Sardi's, a transistor radio pressed to someone's ear to hear the eleven-thirty flash report. It was disastrous, and the millions that had been invested were lost.

In her apartment that night the distraught producer had hysterics and some months later—the humiliation was too great—she retreated to England, temporarily, until the time was right to return.

She had lost confidence and whatever reputation she had built up, but not her style. At the crowded reception following her son's second marriage she was regal in black and as eye-catching as the seductive Dutch girl, an airline stewardess, who was the bride. "My dear," Ethel said to her, not unkindly, "I'll probably see very little of you during this life, but tell me"—she was holding a small velvet box that contained a pair of diamond earrings, each one a single brilliant stone the size of a tooth—"are your ears pierced?" The earrings were her gift. To her credit, the untested daughter-in-law the following day wrote a note of appreciation which read, in its entirety, *Dear Ethel, Thank you for the earrings. Barbara.*

As it happened, I saw more of her afterwards in Europe. She had found a man, English, divorced, who shared her tastes. He had no money but was knowledgeable and even-tempered. He helped her to begin again, or at least pick up the pieces.

He looked sturdy in his trunks at Eze-sur-Mer, well-knit. He had three bullet wounds from the war but they had almost disappeared. I remember the day because of its great calmness, the horizon as if rubbed away. He walked some distance into the sea, then swam, far out. She put on a white bathing cap, her fingers sliding under it to let her stretch it down, and swam after him. For a long time, the only figures in sight, they played together in the soft, rolling water. We watched until slowly, emerging from it like a photograph, they came out.

They were living on her money, as she frequently reminded him, but it was worth it. Eventually they married. She became Mrs. Bezencenet. He was ten years her junior.

They traveled—these were the Aegean years, the purifying light. I saw them in London and Paris. The idea of doing something, a play or film, remained in her mind.

In Spain—it was the late 1960s—her legs began to swell. Then her ankles; they filled with fluid. Finally she went to the hospital. At length, with treatment, the fluid drained away but in its wake came something more terrible. It was scleroderma, a hardening of the skin and the tissue beneath. One gradually became petrified. They went back to England, where, as it happened, the world specialists were, but the doctors could do little and promised nothing.

I went to see her. She had bought a village house in Denham, about forty minutes from London. I took the train from Marylebone Station on a Sunday morning, the compartments sunstruck and empty. It was mid-October. I went down the long path, past meadows, from the station to the village and then down the quiet street to the house.

She came into the room, stately and shuffling. There were tears in her eyes. We sat in the library, which looked out upon a broad garden, and drank champagne, but after one taste she declared, "This isn't good."

"Darling, it's what we always drink," her husband said. He withdrew the bottle from the silver bucket to show her the label, Peiper-Heidseck.

"Come and feel my leg," she said to me.

I put my hand on it and my heart grew weak. It was like a mummy's leg, the lid of a wooden chest. Within this she was encased for life. Her coffin, more macabre than most, had already been made. It was in the shape of a body: her own. She could not get out of a chair by herself. It was that far advanced.

Over the months I came back. We had dinner in the bedroom. A friend, a pianist who was visiting, cooked it. We ate on a pink cloth with fresh, stiff napkins, gleaming glasses, wine. She lay, propped by pillows, in bed. It was as if we were in St.-Moritz and she had, perhaps, twisted her knee. As an hour passed she seemed, in a frightening way, to change. Her face altered, it melted away to a mask of exhaustion and death. The midnight bells were tolling.

She would dine no more at fine restaurants, sometimes asking to borrow the waiter's glasses to read the menu, or gamble drunk at the White Elephant, or be driven back from London late in her Rolls.

It was at about this time that her nephew, Peter, died of a heart attack in a hotel in Munich, where he was on a buying trip. It was completely unexpected, though perhaps not by him. He'd felt pains in his left arm for months.

She took the news stoically. After a bit she remarked that her first recollection in life had been of her own mother in her coffin. Ethel had been four.

A year later, in Barbados for the last time, she died.

We had sat, as boys, by the windows, the light streaming in, she and her husband spiritedly playing board games with us. Later she had tried to guide me, to be a true friend, perhaps more. Her New York terrace apartment was available to me anytime she happened to be out of town, and once, a single long telegram somehow found me when I was lying in a state of serious illness in a hospital in France. It was from her.

I did not recall these things, they were merely part of me. I did not drift back to them, they were the vessel itself.

I went back to Denham in the fall. There was the ancient brick wall beside the footpath, leaning, staved by trees. In the distance the fields were speckled with gulls. The leaves lying at the bottom of puddles on the walk were still green.

I passed the Swan, where we often ate, the house called Wrango, uneven-roofed others. At last I came to Hills House, hers. Through the blinds, in the morning sunlight, I could see an empty table.

The house had been sold. She was next door, in the churchyard, intruder among old families, the Barretts, Tillards, and Wylds with their gravestones head and foot, fading in the earth. Newer than these, destined to be less visited, was a marble plaque in the wall beside the cottage garage. There was her name, *Devoted Mother, Loving and Beloved Wife*. At the bottom, *1904–1971*. She had been born the same year as my mother.

———

There is the immortal city—Grant's Tomb domed and distant in the early days, the great apartment buildings with their polished lobbies, the doormen and green awnings reaching out to the curb. The Metropolitan Museum flanked by worn grassy spaces where we could play beside it, and the wide second-story ledge onto which one could go far out and sit, feet dangling, to watch parades. The mansions and town houses the significance of which, as boys, we did not know.

We were shown the broad past, the Egyptian Wing with its reconstructed tombs and murals of stiff walking figures with almond eyes, and, across the park at the Museum of Natural History, the bones of whales and dinosaurs. I was only rarely taken to the theater and never to concerts.

And so I grew, born to the city and thus free not to love it. I knew the streets, the subways, the steam issuing from the lower parts of buildings, the stores with their proprietors, the movie houses, all the sounds. I felt deadened by the intimacy. I was unaware as yet of the invisible city—the sexual one, its geography forever fixed in memory by acts of love, Greenwich Avenue, Third, Eleventh Street, the Chelsea, the Beaux-Arts—and I was drawn away to what I imagined lay in the world beyond.

In 1948, in the Marianas as a member of an aircrew, I cut my leg on a coral reef and the wound refused to heal. Blood poisoning—septicemia—gradually set in. We had flown on to China and

Peking. My upper leg was covered with sores, my khaki pants stuck to it in half a dozen places. A European doctor, an Italian, in Peking offered to treat me for fifty dollars gold, by which was meant U.S. dollars. There was roaring inflation in China at the time. Huge bundles of bills, tied with string, were only enough for a meal.

I didn't have the fifty dollars. We flew back to Shanghai. By then I was feverish, and heading homewards in the slow droning plane hung far above the sea, I listened to the unearthly music of delirium.

In Hawaii, in the hospital, in the sunlight and silence, I sometimes fell asleep with a book forgotten in my lap. The book was dense and overwritten, though perhaps I did not see it as such; the pages were like slabs and the dialogue often artificial, but the closing lines, when I finally reached them, made the blood come to my face. It was *You Can't Go Home Again,* the last of a series of thick novels in which the barely disguised author, Thomas Wolfe, talented and misunderstood, stormed through life in search of glory, love, and fame.

It was in New York, the seething city, that the unconquerable writer, his brilliant editor, and rich, married mistress carried on their lives in hypnotically repeated sentences. I lost myself in the book and the possibilities it described. I let its size and force sweep over me. That it was essentially banal and too earnest did not affect me. It was like spending three nights on a train with a disheveled stranger—Wolfe was in fact a gigantic man, a kind of Southern Pantagruel who wrote while standing up, on top of the refrigerator, it was said, with pages falling in disorder to the floor—who never stops talking and is able to make all you had formerly known dissolve. Foxhall Edwards was the name of the fabulous editor whose character was based on that of Wolfe's actual editor, Maxwell Perkins, and a woman named Aline Bernstein was known to be the model for the book's Esther Jack.

It had been more than five years since I had been, except for brief visits, home, to Manhattan, and now, brazen and overdrawn, it was before me again, the skyline not of the city of my boyhood but of one that might be. I did not feel the urge to return to it but rather recognized that it was authentic, that having been a boy there was an advantage, one that I might even make use of. Wolfe wrote with the envy and excitement of an outsider. I was, though exiled, a native.

Now it is snowing, one of the terrific storms that first mute and then obliterate the sky. The snow sweeps down, making the buildings seem like liners at sea, muffling everything with silence. The streets become white, all the ledges and trees, the sleeves of overcoats, the marquees. Soon snow has blanketed the earth and hour after hour still down it comes. The cars with their headlights are drifting through the whiteness, the buses and bundled figures struggling home. All night it snows. The city has never been more intimate, more prodigious.

In the morning the snow goes on. The avenues have disappeared, the traffic lights on long unblocked vistas shift without meaning from red to green and back again. There is a sole, breathtaking architecture: white lines.

This is essentially the city, less certain towers, my father and grandfather knew. I know many things about my father's life—not the house he lived in as a boy or the school he went to—but almost nothing of my grandfather's. He had a sister who had married well, and he was part owner of a hotel near Saratoga, my mother says, a wooden hotel in the Greek Revival style—it being her father-in-law's, she is vague concerning the details. I spent the summer there as a child. I can dimly see the broad veranda—perhaps the memories are not genuine—wicker chairs, the glass in the doors, brass spittoons, and stuffy, unwholesome smell.

It was the summer of 1928. In the distance, though no one heard, was the faint sound of a great watershed, the mist rising from it. Events—the Crash—seem to have wrenched the hotel from my grandfather's hands. Why hadn't he sat me down, even at five or six, and, re-creating the place with his hands, told the epic story? I don't know. In truth I don't remember the hotel, I barely remember the grandfather. Whatever he knew, whatever any of them knew, is lost. A few shreds of what their lives meant may have come down to me but the real things, spirit and character, ambitions, marital relations, difficulties, the fate of friends—of all that I have nothing.

We know at first hand, as witnesses, perhaps five generations, most brilliantly of course our own; in one direction those of our parents and grandparents, in the other, children and grandchildren. In my own case much was lopped off. The past is haphazard. I think of the remark of the English cabinet member who was retiring to the seventeenth-century Cornwall farmhouse that had always been in his family. It is the men without roots, he said, who are the real poor of this century.

At the same time there is the exultation of knowing that history begins with one's childhood, that everything around you, the buildings, park, mansions, museums, are all a kind of decor, the background for something far more important: one's own existence. This existence, this starring role, is what the city in fact is made of—it is the true city, the city of memory and triumph, enduring, indifferent to tears. The derelict hotel on the hillside, abandoned long ago or torn down, the weedy tennis courts, the fallen fences, all this has no significance. It foretold nothing and bent not a single strand of one's fate.

YOU MUST

My FATHER, hair parted in the middle, confident and proud, had been first in his class. A brilliant unknown with a talent for mathematics and a prodigious memory, he graduated just ahead of a rival whose own father had been first in 1886.

The school was West Point, and he had also been first captain, though that was harder for me to imagine. In any case, the glory had slipped away by the time I was a boy. He had resigned his commission after a few years and not much evidence had remained. There was a pair of riding boots, some yearbooks, and in a scabbard in the closet an officer's saber with his name and rank engraved on the blade.

Once a year on the dresser in the morning there was a beautiful medal on a ribbon of black, gray, and gold. It was a name tag from the alumni dinner at the Waldorf the night before. He liked going to them; they were held towards the end of the winter and he was a persona there, more or less admired. *George Horowitz, '19*, the white card encased at the top of the ribbon read. His first name, Louis, he disliked.

When I was older he took me to football games, which we left during the fourth quarter. Army was a weak but gritty team that came to Yankee Stadium to play Notre Dame. Behind us, the stands were a mass of gray, hoarse from cheering, and a roar went up as a third-string halfback, thin-legged and quick, somehow got through the line and ran an incredible slanting eighty yards or so until he was at last pulled down. If he had scored, Army would have won.

In the end I went to the same school my father did. I had never intended to. He had arranged a second alternate's appointment and asked me as a favor to study for the entrance exam—it was the spring of 1942. I had been accepted at Stanford and was working for the summer on a farm in Connecticut, sleeping on a bare mattress in the stifling attic, dreaming of life on the Coast, when suddenly a telegram came. Improbably, both the principal and first alternate had failed, one the physical and the other the written, and I was notified that I had been admitted. I knew what my father, more than anything else, wanted me to do. Seventeen, vain, and spoiled by poems, I prepared to enter a remote West Point. I would succeed there, it was hoped, as he had.

In mid-July up the steep road from the station we walked as a group. I knew no one. Like the others I carried a small suitcase in which would be put the clothes I would not see again for years. We passed large, silent buildings and crossed a road beneath some trees. A few minutes later, having signed a consent paper, we stood in the hall in a harried line trying to memorize a sentence to be used in reporting to the cadet first sergeant. It had to be spoken loudly and exactly. Failure meant going out and getting back in line to do it again. There was constant shouting and beyond the door of the barracks an ominous noise, alive, that flared when the door was opened like the roar of a furnace. It was the din of the Area, upperclassmen, some bellowing, some whispering, some hissing like snakes. They were giving the same commands over and over as they stalked the nervous ranks that stood stiffly at attention, still in civilian clothes, already forbidden to look anywhere but straight ahead. The air was rabid. The heat poured down.

I had come to a place like Joyce's Clongowes Wood College, which had caused such a long shiver of fear to flow over him. There were the same dark entrances, the Gothic façades, the rounded bastion corners with crenellated tops, the prisonlike windows. In front was a great expanse which was the parade ground, the Plain.

It was the hard school, the forge. To enter you passed, that first day, into an inferno. Demands, many of them incomprehensible, rained down. Always at rigid attention, hair freshly cropped, chin withdrawn and trembling, barked at by unseen voices, we stood or ran like insects from one place to another, two or three times to the Cadet Store, returning with piles of clothing and equipment. Some had the courage to quit immediately, others slowly failed. Someone's roommate, on the third trip to the store, hadn't come back but had simply gone on and out the gate a mile away. That afternoon we were formed up in new uniforms and marched to Trophy Point to be sworn in.

It is the sounds I remember, the iron orchestra, the feet on the stairways, the clanging bells, the shouting, cries of *Yes, No, I do not know, sir!*, the clatter of sixty or seventy rifle butts as they came down on the pavement at nearly the same time. Life was anxious minutes, running everywhere, scrambling to formations. Among the things I knew nothing of were drill and the manual of arms. Many of the other new cadets, from tin schools, as they called them, or the National Guard, knew all that and even the doggerel that had to be memorized, answers to trivial questions, dictums dating back to the Mexican War. How many gallons of water were in the reservoir, how many names on Battle Monument, what had Schofield said, what was the definition of leather? These had to be rattled off word for word.

All was tradition, the language, the gray woolen cloth, the high black collars of the dress coats, the starched white pants that you got into standing on a chair. Always in summer the Corps had lived in tents out on the Plain, under canvas, with duckboard streets— Summer Camp with its fraternal snapshots and first classmen lounging against tent poles; this was among the few things that had disappeared. There was the honor system, about which we heard from the very beginning, which belonged to the cadets rather than to the authorities and had as its most severe punishment "silencing." Someone who was guilty of a violation and refused to resign could be silenced, never spoken to by his classmates except officially for the rest of his life. He was made to room by himself, and one of the few acknowledgments of his existence was at a dance—if he appeared everyone walked from the floor, leaving him, the girl, and the orchestra all alone. Even his pleasures were quarantined.

West Point was a keep of tradition and its name was a hallmark. It drew honest, Protestant, often rural, and largely uncomplicated men—although there were figures like Poe, Whistler, and even Robert E. Lee, who later said that getting a military education had been the greatest mistake of his life.

I remember the sweating, the heat and thirst, the banned bliss of long gulping from the spigot. At parades, three or four a week, above the drone of hazing floated the music of the band. It seemed part of another, far-off world. There was the feeling of being on a hopeless journey, an exile that would last for years. In the distance, women in light frocks strolled with officers, and the fine house of the Superintendent gleamed toylike and white. In the terrific sun someone in the next rank or beside you begins to sway, take an involuntary step, and like a beaten fighter fall forward. Rifles litter the ground. Afterwards a tactical officer walks among them as among bodies on a battlefield, noting down the serial numbers.

Bang! the door flies open. We leap to our feet. Haughty, sway-backed, wearing white gloves, a cadet sergeant named Melton saunters into the room. He glances at us. "Who are you misters? Sound off!" he commands. He turns to the wall lockers on which we have worked for hours preparing for inspection. Everything has its shelf and place, the folds are clean and sharp, the undershirts like pads of paper, the neat linen cuffs, the black socks.

"Whose locker is this?" he asks with disdain. Not waiting for an answer, he sweeps the contents of a shelf to the floor. "It's a mess. Are these supposed to be folded? Do it over again." Shelf after shelf, one locker after another, everything is tumbled out. "Do it right this time, understand?"

Implacable hatred floods upwards. "Yes, sir!"

———

One of my first roommates was the son of a congressman. He was twenty. In Chicago, he revealed, he'd been living in an apartment with two prostitutes. As a sort of proof he smoked, walked around in his underwear, and marveled at nothing. We were, for the most part, fingerlings, boys in our teens, and his swagger seemed the mark of an enviable thing with which he was already familiar: dissipation. We ran up and down the stairs together but in formation stood far apart. There I was next to a tall, skinny boy who had a cackling laugh and astonishing irreverence. He was a colonel's son and had come from Hawaii, crossing the continent in a Pullman and spending the night with a woman in a lower berth as she moaned over and over, "My son, my son." His name was Horner; in time he introduced me to rum, cards, and as a last flourish, poison ivy.

The most urgent thing was to somehow fit in, to become unnoticed, the same. My father had managed to do it, although, seeing what it was like, I did not understand how. I remembered him only strolling in a princely way; I had never seen him run, I could not imagine him in the exhausting routine of each day.

But it was also hard to be nothing and no one, to be faceless in ranks and unpraised. In still another line, this one in the Cadet Store, where we were being measured for winter uniforms, one of the tailors, a Mr. Walsh, frail and yellowish-haired, noticed my name and asked if I was the son of the honor man in the class of 1919. It was the first feeling I had of belonging, of having a creditable past.

What you had been before meant something—athletic ability mattered, of course—but it was not always enough to see you through. The most important quality was more elusive; I suppose it could be called dignity, but it was not really that. It was closer to endurance.

Downstairs was the former second-string quarterback for Boston College who had a wristwatch he'd gotten for playing in the Sugar Bowl. It had letters instead of numerals circling the dial, *S, U, G, A, R*, etc., and there were small diamonds between the words, as I recall. Nash had come to play football. The days of players who truly came out of the Corps, mostly with unspectacular results, were ending and the war had made winning a matter of great concern. Nash had an Irish face and an unspoiled nature. He had seen something of the world and his enthusiasm for cadet life was limited. He braced with his neck pulled in reluctantly, like a tortoise. More and more he was above such childishness, and annoyance showed in his face. "Stand up straight, Mr. Nash, pull your shoulders back!"

One day as he was being tormented, he did the inconceivable: he simply stopped obeying. The effect was galvanic—they swarmed around him, almost dancing with rage. In the noon formation he marched calmly to the mess hall, at ease towards it all, with the detached air of a condemned man. He was beyond punishment. The year-end ceremony which marked the end of plebe status was called recognition. The word passed in unbelieving whispers: *Nash has recognized himself.*

That, of course, was impossible—he was found unfit and left

soon afterwards. My last memory of him is on the top floor of barracks where our rooms were, on a hellish afternoon. There was a form of punishment for general delinquency; it had a benign name, clothing formation, and was held once or twice a week. The list of those to attend was read aloud at formation: at such and such a time the following named fourth classmen would report to the sinks of the Xth division. Sinks was the name for the basement, the engine room with pipes, lockers, and storage. There, in the nearly windowless dark, with the showers turned full hot to create steam and make it more unbearable, a program of steady exercise went on, interrupted only by an announcement: everyone had exactly five minutes to go back to his room and return in a different uniform. Up the stairs we fled to change frantically and run down to begin again. It was like the recruits being drilled to "change trains" in *All Quiet on the Western Front,* the so-called lesson one never forgets. The various uniforms were described item by item in the regulations book and in addition to everything, amid the confusion, had to be looked up. "Drill D!" was the desperate cry, racing up the last stairs, thirty seconds gone already.

In the hallway, seated on a banister in an undershirt, doubly forbidden, was Nash with the Blue Book of regulations in his hand. He was smoking a cigar and calmly reading out the particulars, repeating them on demand while we flung clothes wildly off and on. Good luck, he called, as we ran down the stairs. It was his farewell performance.

Had Nash repented and borne the consequences, he might that year or the next have trotted onto the field to become famous, but there are men born to be impetuous, to live by a gesture and keep their pride.

———

You were never alone. Above all, it was this that marked the life. As a boy I had had my own room, and though familiar enough with teeming hallways and schoolboy games, these existed only temporarily. Afterwards there was home with its quiet, lights in the evening, the rich smell of dinner.

There was nothing of that at West Point. We brushed shoulders everywhere, as if it were a troopship, and waited a turn to wash and shave. In the earliest morning, in the great summer kiln of the Hudson Valley, we stood for long periods at strict attention, dangerous upperclassmen drifting behind us sullenly, the whole of the day ahead. Over and over to make the minutes pass I recited lines to myself, sometimes to the bullet-hard beat of drums, *The time you won your town the race* . . . Buried and lost, but for the moment by myself, wrapped in words.

I was an unpromising cadet, not the worst but a laggard. Among the youngest, and more immature than my years, I had neither the wisdom of country boys, who knew beasts and the axioms of hardware stores, nor the real toughness of the city. I had been forced to learn a new vocabulary and new meanings, what was meant by "polished," for instance, or "neatly folded." For parade and inspection we wore eighteenth-century accessories, crossed white belts and dummy cartridge box, with breastplate and belt buckle shined to a mirrorlike finish. In the doorway of the room at night, before taps, we sat feverishly polishing them. Pencil erasers and jeweler's rouge were used to painstakingly rub away small imperfections, and the rest was done with a continually refolded polishing cloth. It took hours. The terrible ring of metal hitting the floor—a breastplate that had slipped from someone's hand—was a sound like the dropping of an heirloom.

———

At the end of the summer, assignment to regular companies was made. There were sixteen companies, each made up of men who were approximately the same height. Drawn up in a long front before parade, the tallest companies were at each end, grading down to the shortest in the middle. The laws of perspective made the entire Corps seem of uniform size, and as it passed in review, bayonets at the same angle, legs flashing as one, it looked as if every particle of the whole were well formed and bright. The tall companies were known to be easygoing and unmilitary in barracks, but among the runts it was the opposite. To even pass by their barracks was perilous. This was not only fable but fact.

The stone barracks were arranged around large quadrangles called Areas. Central Area was the oldest, and on opposite sides of it were South and North Areas, and a small appendix near the gym called New North. They were distinct, like provinces, though you walked through several of them every day. Beyond and unseen were the leafy arrondissements where West Point seemed like a serene river town. In mild September with classes about to begin, it settled into routine. There was autumn sun on the playing fields but the real tone was Wagnerian. We passed by the large houses, all in a long row, of the colonels, heads of academic departments, some of them classmates or friends of my father's, old brick houses to which I would one day be invited for Sunday lunch.

My new roommates were from Texas and Michigan, the one wide-jawed and springy-haired, the other handsome and Teutonic. Bob Morgan was the Texan. I am trying to recall if he smoked but it was surely the other roommate who taught me that. Morgan came from a small town, Spur, a dot on the map, and the sun and dust of Texas had paled his eyes.

We had clean slates. All demerits from the summer had been removed and we were as men paroled. Demerits were a black mark and a kind of indebtedness. The allowance was fifteen a month. Beyond that, there were punishment tours, one hour for each demerit, an inflexible rate of exchange. The hours were spent on the Area, walking back and forth, rifle on shoulder, and with this came a further lesson: at the inspection which took place before the tours began, demerits were frequently given out. For shoes with a scuff mark accidentally made or brass with the least breath of tarnish you could receive more tours than you were there to walk off.

We had learned the skills of a butler, which were meant to be those of gentry. We wore pajamas and bathrobes, garters for our socks. Fingernails were scrubbed pink and hair cut weekly. We learned to take off a hat without touching the bill, to sleep on trousers carefully folded beneath the mattress to press them, to announce menus, birthdays, and weekend films with their casts. Like butlers we had Sunday off, but only after mandatory chapel.

There was an exception to this. On Friday evenings in an empty theater, twenty-five or so of us sat on folding chairs in Jewish chapel, including one of the most respected men in my company, a yearling named Sohn. After an hour of services, eternal and unconnected to the harsh life we were leading, we marched back to barracks where everyone was studying or preparing for the next morning's inspection. I felt uncomfortable about having been gone. Though no one ever said a word, I felt, in a way, untrue. In the end I dropped out and went to chapel with the Corps.

Of course, you cannot drop out—you may perhaps try—and I became part of neither one group nor the other, but it seemed to me that God was God, as the writings themselves said, and what essentially distinguished me was an ingrained culture, ages deep, which in any case I wanted to put aside.

Three times a day through three separate doors the entire Corps, like a great religious order, entered the mess hall and stood in whispery silence—there was always muted talk and menace—until the command "Take seats!" With the scrape of chairs the roar of dining began. Meals were a constant terror, and as if to enhance it, near their close the orders of the day were announced, often including grave punishments awarded by the regimental or brigade boards. At the ten-man tables upperclassmen sat at one end, plebes at the other. We ate at attention, eyes fixed on plates, sometimes made part of the conversation like an amusing servant but mostly silent or bawling information. At any moment, after being banged on the table, a cup or glass might come flying. The plebe in charge of pouring looked up quickly, hands ready, crying "Cup, please!" It was a forbidden practice but a favorite. A missed catch was serious, since the result might be broken china and possible demerits for an upperclassman. It was better to be hit in the chest with a cup, or even in the head.

"Sit up!" was a frequent command. It meant "Stop eating," the consequence of having failed to know something—passing the wrong dish, or putting cream in someone's coffee who never took it that way—and might result in no meal at all, though usually at the last permission was given to wolf a few bites. Somewhere, in what was called the Corps Squad area, the athletes, plebes among them, were eating at ease.

Like a hereditary lord's, the table commandant's whim was absolute. Some were kindly figures fond of teasing and schoolboy skits. Others were more serpentlike, and most companies had a table that was Siberia, ruled by a stern disciplinarian, in our case an ugly Greek first classman, dark and humorless. In the table assignments you made your way downward to it and there, among the incorrigibles, even felt a kind of pride.

It was the year of Stalingrad. One Saturday evening following a football victory when we were eating at ease, a waiter I had come to know, an older man whose feet gave him trouble, showed me a clipping from his wallet. From an English newspaper, fragile and forgotten, it was the notice of his having been awarded, at Passchendaele, the Victoria Cross. Yes, he had gotten it, although more important at the time, he remembered quietly, was what he had gotten with it, a tin of cigarettes. He spoke with a slight accent; he was Belgian. How he had ended up, a civilian with worn heels waiting on tables, I forget. Above our heads, covering an entire wall, was a mural of the great captains of history and beneath, unnoticed, shuffled one of their own.

The hour before dawn, everything silent, the air chill with the first bite of fall. The Area empty, the hallways still.

The room was on the second floor at the head of the stairs, the white name cards on the door. I waited for a moment, listening, and cautiously turned the knob. Within it was dark, the windows barely distinguishable. At right angles, separated by desks, were the beds. Waters, a blue-jawed captain, the battalion commander, slept in one. Mills, a sergeant and squad leader, was in the other. I could not hear them breathing; I could hear nothing, the silence was complete. I was afraid to make a sound.

"Sir!" I cried and shouting my name, went on, "Reporting as ordered, ten minutes before reveille!" A muffled voice said, "Don't make so much noise." It was Mills. His quilt moved higher against the cold and as an afterthought he muttered, "Move your chin in."

I stood in the blackness. Nothing, not the tick of a clock or the creaking of a radiator. The minutes had come to a stop. I might stand there forever, invisible and ignored, while they dreamed.

It was Mills who had ordered me to come, for some misbehavior or other, every morning for a week. He was my squad leader but more than that was famous, known to everyone, as king of the goats.

The first man in the class was celebrated; the second was not, nor any of the rest. It was only when you got to the end that a name became imperishable again, the last man, the goat, and it was with well-founded pride that a goat regarded himself. Custer had been last in his class, Grant, nearly. The goat was the Achilles of the unstudious. He was champion of the rear. In front of him went all the main body with its outstanding and also mediocre figures; behind him was nothing, oblivion.

It was a triumph like any other, if you were not meant for the classroom, to end up at the very bottom. Those with worse grades had gone under, those with only slightly better were lost in the crowd. Mills had a bathrobe covered with stars. Each one represented the passing of a turn-out examination, the last, all-or-nothing chance in a failed subject—his robe blazed with them. He had come to this naturally; his father had made a good run at it and been fifth from last in 1915. Mills knew the responsibilities of heritage. He had fended off the attacks of men of lesser distinction who nevertheless wanted to vault to renown. Blond and good-looking, he was easy to admire and far from ungifted. A well-executed retreat was said to be among the most difficult of all military operations, at which some commanders were adept. It meant passing close to the abyss, skirting disaster, and surviving by a hair. It was a special realm with its tension and desperate acts, men who would purposely spill ink over their drawing in engineering on the final day when nothing else, no possibility, was left.

Mills was also a good athlete. He had come from South Carolina and gone to The Citadel for a year. There was a joy of life in him and a kind of tenderness untainted by the merely gentle.

Nothing more had been said to me. I stood in silence. There was neither present nor future. They were unaware of me but I was somehow important, proof of their power. I began to feel dizzy, as if the floor were tilting, as if I might fall. I had lost track of how long I had been there; time seemed to have stopped when from the distance came a single, clear report: the dawn cannon.

Immediately, like a demonic machine, the sounds begin. Outside in the void, drums explode. Someone is shouting in the hallway, "Sir, there are five minutes until assembly for reveille! Uniform, dress gray with overcoats! Five minutes, sir!" Music is playing. Feet can be heard overhead and on the stairs. The hives of sleeping men are spilling forth. The drums begin again.

In the room, not a movement. It is still as a vault. Four minutes

until assembly. They have not stirred. The plebes are already standing in place with spaces between them that will be filled by unhur-
rying upperclassmen. The drums start once more. Three minutes.

Something is wrong. For some reason they are not going to the
formation, but if I am late or, unthinkable, miss it entirely . . . The
clamor continues, bugles, drums, slamming doors. Two minutes
now. Should I say something, dare I? At the last moment a bored
voice murmurs, "Post, dumbjohn."

I hurry down the steps and into the cold. Less than a minute remains. Hastily making square corners I reach my place in ranks
just as two figures slip past, overcoats flapping, naked chests beneath: Waters and Mills. Fastening the last buttons, Waters arrives
in front of the battalion as the noise dies and final bells ring. He
appears instantly resolute and calm, as if he had been waiting patiently all along. In a clear, deep voice he orders, "Report!"

I did not exist for Waters, and for Mills, barely. We marched,
early one Saturday, down to the river, where the Corps boarded a
many-decked white dayliner to sail to New York. At the football
game that afternoon, jammed in the halftime crowd, Mills was
coming the other way, by chance behind a very beautiful girl, just
behind her, with an expression of innocence on his face. As he
passed me, he winked.

His class graduated early, that January of 1943, hastened by the
war. There was a tremendous cheer as he walked up to receive his
diploma, and for some reason I felt as they did, that he was mine.
I thought of him for a long time afterwards, the ease and noble
face of the last man in his class.

In the safety of that autumn, I foundered. The demerits began
again—unpolished shoes, dirty rifle, late for athletics, Blue Book
misplaced—there were fifty the first month. One night in the
mess hall a spontaneous roar went up when it was announced that

at the request of a British field marshal—I think it was Field Marshal Dill—all punishments were revoked. According to custom, a distinguished visitor could do that. The cheers passed over my head, so to speak, but the amnesty did not; I had thirty-five tours erased, seven weeks of walking.

Still I was swept along as if by a current. I felt lost. There were faces you did not recognize, formations being held no one knew where, the pressure of crammed schedules, the formality of the classrooms, the impersonality of everyone in authority from the distant superintendent to the company tactical officers . . . it was plain to see why they called it the Factory. It was a male world. In the gym we fought one another, wrestled one another, slammed into one another on darkened fields battling for regimental championships and came raw-knuckled to supper. There were no women except for nurses in the hospital and hardened secretaries, but there was the existence of women always, outside. An upperclassman had his laundry come back with a note pinned to the pajama bottoms, which had gone out with a stiffened area on them. A girl who worked in the laundry had written, *The next time you feel like this, call me.*

The hospital was a narrow granite building that stood edge to the road like a town house. There you met other convalescents and formed brief, intense friendships that were overwhelming. I remember a tough, handsome face from the other regiment. We sat in the white-tiled washroom for hours and talked. There is a little tendril now that quivers to make me wonder why he found me so admirable—he was in some sort of nameless trouble—but I was unquestioning, feverish and recovering from the flu. His brothers had been killed in the war, he told me. For a few days he seemed the perfect comrade. Afterwards he disappeared.

We were inmates. The world was fading. There were cadets who wet the bed and others who wept. There was one who hanged himself. I sometimes thought of boyhood friends with whom I had

spent countless hours. I saw that we were separating; I would not
find them again.

In a leather-dark room in the gym we stood with boxing gloves
on in facing lines while a bird-legged ex-champion gave instruction. His voice was hoarse and street-accented. It was as if the
chalk of the prize ring had given his skin a permanent ashen tone.
He moved along the line and stopped in front of me. We had been
practicing jabs. "Hit me," he ordered. I hesitated. "Go ahead," he
commanded. He was standing close.

I jabbed. He leaned back, fluent and spry. "Again," he said. I
tried harder. "Go on," he said, "hit me this time." I stepped forward, missed again, and something solid crashed into the side of
my head. I stood with my ear ringing as he explained my error—I
had let my right hand slip down as I jabbed. He shuffled like an
old pensioner but his fists were like cement.

In the gloom of the sallyports were lighted boards where grades
from classes were posted at the end of the week. Morgan was already failing in mathematics and I was in difficulty in languages.
"Don't worry," the professor, a major, had said, "it'll get tougher."
We stayed up after taps studying with a flashlight, exhausted and
trying to comprehend italicized phrases in the red algebra book. I
was trying to explain them and have Morgan solve problems; he
was stubborn, it seemed, in his inability to do it. "Let's rest for a
few minutes." Kneeling side by side on the cold wooden floor we
dozed with only our upper bodies on the bed. Often we studied
past midnight in the lavatory.

———

The field marshal's gift was soon squandered. My name appeared
on the gig sheet three or four times a week; I was walking tours and
coming back to the room at dusk, dry from the cold and weary,
putting my rifle in the rack, taking off my crossbelts and breastplate,
and sitting down for a few minutes before washing for supper.

Punishment had a moral, which was to avoid it, but I could not. There was something alien and rebellious in me. The ease with which others got along was mysterious. I was losing hope.

In the first captain's room in the oldest division of barracks there were the names of all those who had once held that honor. I wanted to see it, to linger for a moment and find my bearings, as had happened long ago in the Cadet Store line. Late one Sunday afternoon, telling no one, I went there—nothing forbade it—and stood before the door. I nearly turned away but then, impulsively, knocked.

The first captain was in his undershirt. He was sitting at his desk writing letters and his roommate was folding laundry. He looked up. "Yes, mister, what is it?" he said.

Somehow I explained what I had come for. There was a fireplace and on the wall beside it was a long, varnished board with the names. I was told to have a look at it. The list was by year. "Which one is your father?" they asked. I searched for his name and for some reason missed it. My eye went down the column again.

"Well?"

It was inexplicable. I couldn't find it; it wasn't there. I didn't know what to say. There had been some mistake, I managed to utter. I felt absolutely empty and ashamed.

My father, in a letter, was able to explain. His class, in wartime, had graduated early and had come back to West Point after the armistice as student officers. As highest-ranking lieutenant, the result of his academic standing, my father had been student commander. He called this being first captain, and I realized later that I should never have brought it up.

When he came from Washington to visit we walked on the lawn near the Thayer Hotel in winter sunshine. Bits of the wide river glittered like light. I wanted him to counsel me and, looking moodily at the ground, recited from "Dover Beach." What was I struggling for and what should I believe? It would be more clear later, he finally said. He had never forsaken West Point. He believed in it and would in fact one day be buried near the old chapel. He was counting on the school to steady me, fix me, as the quivering needle in a compass firms on the pole, a process he did not describe but that in his case had been more or less successful.

It was a school not of teachers but of lessons, many unspoken, few forgotten, and some I have made an effort to forget. There was the idea that one could be changed, that West Point could make you an aristocrat. In a way it did; it relied on the stoic, outdoor life which is the domain of the aristocrat: sport, hunting, hardship. Ultimately, however, it was a school of less-privileged classes with no true connection to the upper world. You were an aristocrat to sergeants and reserve officers, men who believed in the myth.

It was a place of bleak emotions, a great orphanage, chill in its appearance, rigid in its demands. There was occasional kindness but little love. The teachers did not love their pupils or the coach the mud-flecked fullback—the word was never spoken, although I often heard its opposite. In its place was comradeship and a standard that seemed as high as anyone could know. It included self-reliance and death if need be. West Point did not make character, it extolled it. It taught one to believe in difficulty, the hard way, and to sleep, as it were, on bare ground. Duty, honor, country. The great virtues were cut into stone above the archways and inscribed in the gold of class rings, not the classic virtues, not virtues at all, in fact, but commands. In life you might know defeat and see things you revered fall into darkness and disgrace, but never these.

Honor was second but in many ways it was the most important. Duty might be shirked, country one took for granted, but honor was indivisible. The word of an officer or cadet could not be doubted. One did not cheat, one never lied. At night a question was asked through the closed door, "All right, sir?" and the answer was the same, "All right." It meant that whoever was supposed to be in the room was there and no one besides—a single voice answered for all. Absences, attendance, all humdrum was on the same basis and anything written or signed was absolutely true. Even the most minor violation was grave. There was an honor committee; its proceedings were solemn; from its judgment there was no appeal. The committee had no actual disciplinary power. It was so august that anyone convicted—and there were no degrees of guilt, only thumbs up or down—was expected to resign. Almost always they did. Inadvertence could sometimes excuse an honor violation, but not much else. Word traveled swiftly—someone had been brought up on honor. A few days later there was an empty bed.

————

At Christmas that year, apart from the few upperclassmen who for one reason or another had chosen not to take leave, we were alone. Morgan was failing and in the end was turned out. He was by then resigned to it. He had wanted to play football, as he had in the districts of West Texas with their rickety grandstands, but never had the chance; math had barred the way. I knew his plain but honest dreams, his muscular torso, his girlfriend's temperament and name (it was Nona).

He did not pass the reentrance exam. He joined the paratroops with the uncertain prestige of having failed at West Point, and eventually earned a battlefield commission. I received occasional letters written in pencil and with words like "bucko" in them. He was wounded in Italy and deserted the hospital to rejoin his unit, which by then was fighting in France. He was in reconnaissance, which took heavy casualties, and one day a letter came—it was the first I ever received from Paris; he was there on leave in the fall of 1944 for four days, he had the most beautiful girl in the entire city, she had a fur coat that cost ten thousand dollars. It was, I think, the last letter. I lost track of him. I was engaged in urgent things myself. The wires went dead.

In the winter there were parades within the barracks area rather than on the Plain—the band, the slap of hands on rifles, the glint of steel, the first companies sailing past. One of the earliest, in the rain, was for the graduation of the January class. They were walking along the stoops afterwards in the brilliance of their army uniforms, Roberts, Jarrell, Mills, all of them. The wooden packing boxes stenciled with their names and new rank were waiting to be shipped off, the sinks strewn with things they had no use for, that in the space of a single day had lost their value, cadet things they had not given away or sold, textbooks, papers. The next morning they, the boxes, everything was gone. It was like a divorced household; with them somehow went a sense of legitimacy and order. The new first class seemed unfledged—it would always exist in the shadow of the one gone on.

———

One afternoon near the end of winter we ordered class rings. The ring was a potent object, an insignia and reward. Heavy and gold, it was worn on the third finger of the left hand, the wedding finger, with the class crest inwards until graduation. After, it was turned around so the academy crest would be closest to the heart. Engraved within was one's name and "United States Army." I had decided I wanted something more, perhaps not the *Non serviam* of Lucifer, but a coda. Someone, I knew, somewhere would take this ring from my lifeless finger and within find the words which would sanctify me. The line moved steadily forward, the salesman filling out order blanks and explaining the merits of various stones. Could I have something else engraved in my ring, I asked? What did I mean, something else? I wasn't sure; I hadn't decided, and I had the feeling I was taking up too much time. Finally he wrote "To follow" in the space for what was to be engraved.

Unknown to me, all this was overheard. That evening in the mess hall before "Take seats," a cadet captain was ferreting his way between the tables, here and there whispering a question. I had never seen him before. He was looking for me. I saw him come around the table and the next moment he stood beside me. Was I the one who didn't want "United States Army" in his ring, he asked in a low voice? I didn't have a chance to reply before he continued icily, "If you don't think the U.S. Army is good enough for you, did you ever stop to think that you might not be good enough for the U.S. Army?" On the other side of me another face had appeared. They were converging from far off. "Did you ever make a statement that you would resign just before graduation?" someone said. It was true that I had. "Only facetiously, sir." I could feel the sweat on my forehead. "Did you ever say you came here only for the education?" "No, sir!"

Their voices were scornful. They wanted to get a look at me, they said, they wanted to remember my face, "Mister, the Corps will see to it that you earn your ring." It was useless to try to explain. Who informed them, I never knew. Later I realized it had been a classmate, of course. The worst part was that it all took place in front of my own company. I was confirmed as a rebel, a misfit.

Incidents form you, events that are unexpected, unseen trials. I defied this school. I took its punishment and its hatred. I dreamed of telling the story, of making that my triumph. There was a legendary book in the library said to have been written by a cadet, to contain damning description, and to have been suppressed, all copies except one destroyed. It was called *The Tin Soldier* and was not in the card file, nor did anyone I asked admit to having heard of it. It was a kind of literary mirage, though the title seemed real.

If there was no such book, then I would write it. I thought of its power all that spring during endless hours of walking back and forth on the Area at shoulder arms. Pitiless and spare, it would be published in secret and read by all. Apart from that, I was indifferent and tried to get by doing as little as possible since whatever I did would not be enough.

At the same time, kindled in me was another urge, the urge to manhood. I did not recognize it as such because I had rejected its form. *Try to be one of us,* they had said, and I had not been able to. It was this that was haunting me, though I would not admit it. I struggled against everything, it now seems clear, because I wanted to belong.

Then in sunlight the music floated over us and when it ended— the inachievable last parade as plebes—we turned and in a soaring moment, having forgotten everything, shook hands with the tormentors. They came along the ranks at ease, seeking us out, and with self-loathing I found myself shaking hands with men I had sworn not to.

So the year ended. I have returned to it many times since. The river is smooth and ice clings to its banks. The trees are bare. Through the open window from the far shore comes the sound of a train, the faint, distinct clicking of wheels on the rail joints, the Albany or Montreal train with its lighted cars and white table-cloths, the blur of luxury from which we are ever barred.

At night the barracks, seen from the Plain, look like a city. All of us are within, unseen, studying determinants, general orders, law. I had walked the pavement of the interior quadrangles interminably, burning with anger against what I was required to be. In the darkness the uniform flags hung limply. In a few minutes it would be taps, then quickly the next day. Ten minutes to formation. What are we wearing, I ask, where are we going? Bells begin to ring. People are vanishing. The room, the hallways, are empty. Dressing, I run down the stairs.

II

That summer, after leave, we went into the field and to a camp by
a lake, wooden barracks, firing ranges, and maneuver grounds of
all kinds. Yearling summer. In the new and sunny freedom, weedy
friendships grew. We fired machine guns and learned to roll cigarettes by hand. In off-hours I lay on my bed, reading. I knew lines
of Powys's *Love and Death* by heart and reserved them for a slim,
witty girl who came up from New York on several weekends. She
was the daughter of a famous newspaperman. We danced, swam,
and went for walks in permitted areas, where the sensuous
phrases fell to the ground, useless against her. I was disappointed.
The words had been written by someone else but I had assumed
them, they were my own. I was posing as part of a doomed generation. *They shall not grow old as we who are left grow old . . .* She
did not take it seriously. "Kiss the back of your letters, will you?" I
asked her. Such things were noticed by the mail orderly.

There is a final week of maneuvers before we return to the post,
of digging until exhausted and then being told abruptly that we are
moving to different positions; and deeper, they say, dig deeper.
There is the new, energetic company commander with wens on his
face who seems to like me and for whom, exhilarated, I would do
anything. His affection for me was probably imagined, but mine
for him was not. He was someone for whom I had waited impatiently, intelligent, patrician, and governed by a sense of duty—
this became a significant word, something valuable, like a dense
metal buried in the earth that could guide one's actions. There
were things that must be done; there were faces that would be
turned towards yours and rely on you.

That year we studied Napoleon and obscure campaigns around
Lake Garda. There were arrows of red and blue printed on the
map but little in the way of thrilling detail, the distant ranks at
Eylau, the fires, the snow, the wan-faced emperor wearing sable,

the obscure horizon and arms reaching out. We studied movement and numbers. We studied the Civil War and sometimes in the mess hall it was reenacted, as on the birthday of Robert E. Lee, with the plebes of one table singing "Dixie" and others a few feet away "The Battle Hymn of the Republic," louder and louder, veins swelling in their necks and the table commandants urging them on, red with fury. We analyzed the battles of the First World War and what was accurately known of the Second. We studied leadership, in part from German texts, given to us not so much to know the enemy but because of their quality, with nothing in them of politics or race.

There was one with the title *Der Kompaniechef*, the company commander. This youthful but experienced figure was nothing less than a living example to each of his men. Alone, half obscured by those he commanded, similar to them but without their faults, self-disciplined, modest, cheerful, he was at the same time both master and servant, each of admirable character. His real authority was not based on shoulder straps or rank but on a model life which granted the right to demand anything from others.

An officer, wrote Dumas, *is like a father with greater responsibilities than an ordinary father.* The food his men ate, he ate, and only when the last of them slept, exhausted, did he go to sleep himself. His privilege lay in being given these obligations and a harder duty than any of the rest.

The company commander was someone whom difficulties could not dishearten, privation could not crush. It was not his strength that was unbreakable but something deeper, his spirit. He must not only have his men obey, they must do it when they are absolutely worn out and quarreling among themselves, when they are at the end of their rope and another senseless order comes down from above.

He could be severe but only when it was needed and then briefly. It had to be just, it had to wash things clean like a sudden, fierce storm. When he looked over his men he was conscious that a hundred and fifty families had placed a son in his care. Sometimes, unannounced, he went among these sons in the evening to talk or just sit and drink a beer, not in the role of superior but of an older, sympathetic comrade. He went among them as kings once went unknown among their subjects, to hear their real thoughts and to know them. Among his most important traits were decency and compassion. He was not unfeeling, not made of wood. Especially in time of grief, as a death in a soldier's family at home, he brought this news himself—no one else should be expected to—and granted leave, if possible, even before it was asked for, in his own words expressing sympathy. Ties like this would never be broken.

This was not the parade-ground captain, the mannequin promoted for a spotless record. It was not someone behind the lines, some careerist with ambitions. It was another breed, someone whose life was joined with that of his men, who had reached the peak of the human condition, *admired, feared, and loved,* someone hardened and uncomplaining upon whom the entire struggle somehow depended, someone almost fated to fall.

I knew this hypothetical figure. I had seen him as a schoolboy, latent among the sixth formers, and at times had caught a glimpse of him at West Point. Stroke by stroke, the description of him was like a portrait emerging. I was almost afraid to recognize the face. In it was no self-importance; that had been thrown away, we are beyond that, stripped of it. When I read that among the desired traits of the leader was a sense of humor that marked a balanced and indomitable outlook, when I realized that every quality was one in which I instinctively had faith, I felt an overwhelming happiness, like seeing a card you cannot believe you are lucky enough to have drawn, at this moment, in this game.

I did not dare to believe it but I imagined, I thought, I somehow dreamed, the face was my own.

I began to change, not what I was truly but what I seemed to be. Dissatisfied, eager to become better, I shed as if they were old clothes the laziness and rebellion of the first year and began anew.

On the back of the door, which an inspecting officer never saw since it was flung open upon his entrance, I taped a declaration of faith, drawn from recollection of an article I had once read, that the officers who poured into the army during the First and Second World Wars brought to it the great gifts of the American people (I wrote unenthusiastically), but that West Point gave it standards of duty and performance that were as precise as the Hoke measurement blocks in a machine-tool factory. Other officers might sometimes lie or cheat a little, but the whole army knew that a West Pointer was as good as his word, without exceptions or reservations. Other officers might sometimes take a reasonable line of retreat, but a West Pointer always tried to do exactly as told, even though he and his command were wiped out. One morning I watched as the tactical officer, at the end of his inspection, apparently having heard of it, pushed the door closed and stood in silence reading what was on the back. He was a cavalry officer, moustache and uniform perfect. His face was expressionless. There was a regulation against anything on the walls or door, but when he was finished he left without saying a word.

I was undergoing a conversion, from a self divided and consciously inferior, as William James described it, to one that was unified and, to use his word, right. I saw myself as the heir of many strangers, the faces of those who had gone before, my new roommate's brother, for one, John Eckert, who had graduated two years earlier and was now a medium bomber pilot in England. I had a photograph of him and his wife, which I kept in my desk, the pilot with his rakish hat, the young wife, the clarity of their features, the distinction. Perhaps it was in part because of this snapshot that I thought of becoming a pilot. At least it was one more branch thrown onto the pyre. When he was killed on a mission not long after, I felt a secret thrill and envy. His life, the scraps I knew of it, seemed worthy, complete. He had left something behind, a woman who could never forget him; I had her picture. Death seemed the purest act. Comfortably distant from it I had no fear.

There were images of the struggle in the air on every side, the fighter pilots back from missions deep into Europe, rendezvous times still written in ink on the backs of their hands, gunners with shawls of bullets over their shoulders, grinning and risky, I saw them, I saw myself, in the rattle and thunder of takeoff, the world of warm cots, cigarettes, stand-downs, everything that had mattered falling away. Then the long hours of nervousness as the formation went farther and farther into enemy skies until suddenly, called out by jittery voices, high above, the first of them appear, floating harmlessly, then turning, falling, firing, plummeting past, untouchable in their speed. The guns are going everywhere; the sky is scrawled with smoke and dark explosions, and then it happens, something great and crucial tearing from the ship, a vast flat of wing, and we begin to roll over, slowly at first and then faster, screaming to one another, going down.

That was death: to leave behind a photograph, a twenty-year-old wife, the story of how it happened. What more is there to wish than to be remembered? To go on living in the narrative of others? More than anything I felt the desire to be rid of the undistinguished past, to belong to nothing and to no one beyond the war. At the same time I longed for the opposite, country, family, God, perhaps not in that order. In death I would have them or be done with the need; I would be at last the other I yearned to be.

That person in the army, that wasn't me, Cheever wrote after the war. In my case, it was. I did not know the army meant bad teeth, drab quarters, men with small minds, and colonels wearing sunglasses. Anyone from the life below can be a soldier. I imagined campaigns like Caesar's, the sun going down in wooded country, encampments on hilltops, cool dawns. The army was that; it was like a beautifully dressed woman; I saw her smile at me and stood erect.

The army. They are playing the last songs at the hop, the sentimental favorites. I am dancing with a girl named Pat Potter, blonde and elegant, whom I somehow knew. There are moments when one is part of the real beauty, the pageant. They are playing "Army Blue," the matrimonial and farewell song. A hundred, two hundred, couples are on the floor. The army. Familiar faces. This immense brotherhood in which they bend you slowly to their ways. This great family in which one is always advancing, even while asleep.

The stern commandments had become my commandments, the harder thing than triumph, in the poet's words. Long afterwards, in Georgia, as a captain, I was getting off an airplane behind a lame man. We paused at the bottom of the steps. "Remember me?" he asked. It was then I saw who he was, the son of a friend of my father's, whom I had recognized as an underclassman. "What happened to you?" I said. "You're not still in the army?"

He'd been retired, he said, but it was strange, he often thought about me.

"What do you mean?"

I began to recall it as he told me. He had played football as a plebe although he was small. He was a quarterback. The following fall he had come to me for advice: Should he continue to try and make the team—there was only the slightest chance—or drop it and go out for manager? There was an assistant's opening; he was from Atlanta, and the manager of "A" Squad was traditionally a Georgian. It was a wonderful spot and he would be in line to inherit it.

The manager was someone to be envied, I agreed, but not admired. Even if he was only a third-string quarterback, he would be on the team, and his moment might come in the twilight of some epic game. Unsoiled and slender, he might come off the bench to lead them to victory.

It sounded like advice of mine. He had taken it, and the week afterwards his leg was broken in practice, he said. He was in the hospital for more than a month and fell so far behind in his studies that he never caught up, graduating much farther down in his class than he would have, so though he had wanted the Engineers, he got the Infantry instead. In Korea he was hit by a mortar shell that shattered his legs and was given a medical discharge. His career had ended.

"I'm sorry to hear that," I told him.

"I owe it all to you," he said.

The truest man I knew was dark, with skin almost sallow, a high forehead, and Asia-black hair, Kelton Farris—Nig, as they called him, or Bud. He was from a town called Conway, not far from Little Rock, and all plebes from Arkansas were expected to know an apocryphal speech made in the legislature when it had been proposed to change the name of the state, or at least its unique pronunciation. "Mr. Speaker, Mr. Speaker, Goddamnit," it began—I forget its many outrages though I knew them then. "When I was a boy at the age of fourteen, I had a prick the size of a roasting ear and could piss halfway across the Ouachita River. 'Out of order, out of order!' You're Goddamn right it was out of order, if it wasn't, I could have . . . ," and so forth. The performers were popular, like mimics or banjo players. Let's have the Arkansas poop, upperclassmen called, as if summoning a favorite fool. But it was not something as homespun as this that made Farris stand out. It was not something you could memorize.

Looking back I see that later, as officers, in Salt Lake City, Manila, Hawaii, wherever we went among strangers, he was picked out as the one they wanted to know. He did it by his appearance, which was masculine and which somehow set itself as a standard. As I think of him he has a luster like something made of wood, something durable and burnished. But there was also his behavior; he was completely unselfconscious, like an animal. If I use the word "animal" to describe him it is not only in tribute to his ease but to natural responses which in him were unimpeded. He was without flamboyance or the kind of eagerness that repels. Even now I sometimes enter a room thinking of him doing it, imperturbable, assured, drawing people's interest, their admiration. Heads might not turn but some equilibrium changed, as in a solution when an electrolyte is added.

I have tried to know what it was that created this. I can see him stand, walk, smile, but, as with a woman you are afraid of, I do not know what he is going to say, only that it will be something I envy, probably for its candor. You could be with him constantly, even bored with him, and be no closer to discovery. Intimacy did not betray him, no examination could reveal his magic. It was like the glitter on the sea, which, scooped up, vanishes. Something priceless had been given him, the power to attract, to be trusted. You could not imagine him dead—whatever happened, he would get through. That was written on him. It was the promise of nature herself.

Irresistible to women, of course, and with a normal interest in them. They, on the other hand, were more intent. Though not yet married, and placid in his desire to be, he bore the mark of family: brothers, uncles, in-laws, a world in which family was accepted as everything—women recognized it immediately as the thing in him that was genuine and desirable. Alone with them, I am sure, he behaved naturally, by which I mean without needless constraint. A girl once told him, I knew you were a West Pointer from the way you folded your pants over the back of the chair. I imagine it being afternoon as he did this, with the light slipping through the blinds.

I remember that a few years later, having come back to Conway for it, he called off his wedding at the last minute. He told his fiancée it was no good, he didn't really know her, though they'd been thought of as a couple since high school. She protested. She hadn't changed a bit since then, she said; it had been seven years. Well, if she hadn't, he said, he knew damn well he had.

Though we were in the same company it was not until flying school or down in Texas the summer we graduated, with the khaki-colored airplanes baking in the sun like abandoned cars, that we became friends. In Salt Lake City, waiting to be sent overseas, we flew together over the great, desolate lake and snowy ground. Rising from damp beds in Manila at four in the morning with cocks crowing somewhere, we drove through rancid streets to Nichols Field for the early run to Japan, transport pilots, fallen to that in the aftermath of the war, and later we were stationed together in Honolulu, living in old wooden bachelors' quarters, the sort of building that in the South sits on short stacks of bricks. I had a new yellow convertible that had been shipped over on the Lurline. Farris had a room paneled in cedar which he had found, sawed, and nailed up expertly board by board, but he was a country boy and knew how to do anything. One of his favorite words was "silly." It could apply to anyone or anything and was deflating. He once handled a surly, troublesome soldier by threatening to write a letter to his mother.

He, himself, the son of an insurance agent, was a born soldier. He had learned it walking down a muddy road to his house half a mile from where the paving ended, and driving in the summers, seven miles in a horse-drawn wagon with his brothers, to work fifty acres of rough farmland that his father had bought near the river. He was an original, a native, like his father, both of them, a flaring of America. Uncounted days had shaped them, as water does stone. The things they knew they had no doubts about, and they were the important things. There were officers in the First

War who strolled out calmly under fire in an advance, walking to death as though it were to lunch or adjutant's call. It was thrilling to see men with disdain like that. As much as you tried, however, you could not imagine Farris in the role. His strength was in his sanity, his straightforwardness. Beneath the palms one night we walked up the smooth stone steps to a masquerade at the Hickam Club. A girl I was very attracted to at the time came over. She was wearing a torn, low-cut blouse, stiletto heels, and mesh stockings, with a rose in her hair. Behind her, pirates, cowboys, and Cleopatras were passing. Farris greeted her, "Hi, Carol," and, taking in her outfit, "I thought this was supposed to be a costume party."

Then we were separated. I went to Washington and he was sent to Europe. Paris was all that anyone ever said it was, the showgirls don't believe in wearing clothes, he wrote. I visited Europe for the first time in the winter of 1950 and found him comfortably lodged in rainy Wiesbaden in the best surviving hotel—thick carpets, once-white curtains; it had been requisitioned by the occupation forces. Around it were houses that had been flattened. Cities, like women, are tender to the victors. Wiesbaden was shabby but everyone—chambermaids, drivers, shopkeepers—was deferential and hardworking. They should have been on our side, Farris told me; they had wanted to join us at the end and fight the Russians together, not a bad idea. Did he really mean that? I asked. We'd be doing it eventually, he told me. I wondered, did he have a German girlfriend; there was none in evidence.

In the old-fashioned plush rooms we drank with women officers and secretaries, and towards the end of the visit I borrowed his car and drove to the south of France, my ignorance such as to make me think it would be summery there. From the empty Hotel Martinez I looked out on gray sea and tried to talk to the barman in French.

I was going to come over again in July or August; we would go to London or down to Greece. The glorious, vacant summers of youth. I never went; more important things came up, I forget of course what they were. I saw him about two years later in South Carolina when I had returned from the Korean War. He was still in Troop Carrier and I may have even worn a ribbon or two, feeling they would be admired. I had the idea I had done something he had not.

Sometimes you are aware when your great moments are happening and sometimes they rise from the past. Perhaps it's the same with people. From those days his seems to be, above all others, the face that remains. He rose to be a brigadier general and died unexpectedly, of a heart attack, soon after he retired. With it, something passed out of the soul of the class for me. Occasionally on the street or in an audience, a crowd, you see a person who has died, the replica—nature has made a second version. I have never seen Farris, however. I had never known anyone like him nor would I again. We old first captains, Pershing is supposed to have said to MacArthur, must never flinch. He never would have flinched, I was sure of that.

As to what he was made of, what rare element, perhaps in the end I'll know, perhaps he'll tell me in the obscurity, the shade where he has gone. We will stroll aimlessly, as by rivers in France beneath the trees with their huge flat leaves, or along the Rhine, freed from desire and time, like patients in some hospital, never to leave; he'll tell me what he remembers and I will finally understand.

———

Images remain, Army-Navy games in Baltimore and the morning's staticky excitement, the first snow falling on the Plain, the voices of the choir angelically rising from the dark Area at Christmas. I remember the long walk back from the Thayer, half-run as it drew close to midnight, the walk to classes, to the old cemetery, the stadium, to everywhere. The geography of West Point was the sum of its distances. We could not be married, drink, or have a car, though we were permitted to drive. One of the school idols was said to have smuggled a girl onto the post in the trunk of a car. She spent the night in barracks and even attended reveille the next morning in a raincoat with her long hair concealed. This was daring of the highest sort, far above mere drinking. One of the few acts I admired more took place in the mess hall and involved a classmate named Benson. He was then a yearling. The table commandant, a first classman, was a Southerner and one of the plebes at the table was black—there was barely a handful of blacks in the Corps. The first classman, speaking as if the plebe were not there, was talking about niggers. If he ever heard of anyone, a yearling particularly, being nice to one, he said, he would see that he was run out of school. Without a moment's hesitation Benson reached across the table to the plebe, "My name's George," he said, shaking his hand. I had heard of few things more instantly brave.

———

There was a special physical examination in the winter of 1944 that included the eyes: aligning two pegs in a sort of lighted shoebox by pulling strings—"Am I good enough for the Air Corps, sir?"—and identifying colors by picking up various balls of yarn. In April, those who had passed, hundreds, that is, including my two roommates and me, went off to flight training in the South and Southwest. Hardly believing our good fortune, we went as if it were a holiday, by train. Left behind were classes, inspections, and many full-dress parades. Ahead was freedom and the joy of months away.

ICARUS

PASSING THROUGH darkened Virginia, lips eager and sticky from Southern Comfort, a girl and I talked intently in the vestibule. She was married, her husband was off in the army. I don't remember where the bottle came from—it was either hers or we'd gotten it from the porter. The floor was trembling beneath our feet, the threshold between the cars creaking. She was from a small town somewhere and was wearing a cotton dress. The train leaned into slow, lurching curves, the metal squealing like a message passed along it. We saw nothing but each other's faces. I was nineteen years old, on my way to primary flight training. The others were in the sleeping cars behind us; most had gone to bed. Soon we were embracing fiercely. A married woman on a train at night, her body tight against mine. "Pete," she moaned, "oh, Pete . . ."

I had told her my name was Peter Slavek—it came from a book by Arthur Koestler. I was linking everything together, fatalism, sex, war. In my imagination I was already a pilot, handsome, freedom reeking from me, winds coiled round my legs. I had no real idea of what lay ahead, vast southwestern skies with their clouds and shafts of light, towns with railroad tracks running through them and Masonic lodges, dejected country with little lakes and fading cabins amid the pines, Bible country, the air pure with poverty and religious broadcasts. It didn't matter, I was going.

Arthur Koestler had also written about an RAF flyer named Richard Hillary, well known at the time. Hillary had been a pilot in the Battle of Britain—grass fields and the insectlike planes bouncing across them, the sky dense with fights. He was nearly killed when the canopy on his burning plane jammed and he could not bail out. I knew his beautiful scarred looks by heart. He had written a book about his experiences called *Falling Through Space*. The chapters often closed with a knell: from this mission Peter Pease, from this mission Rupert someone, from this mission still another, failed to return.

Hillary, Koestler noted, was burned three times—it was only the first when his canopy would not open. They patched him up—his face would be a glossy reminder as long as he lived—and he returned to flying and a second crash, which was fatal. He burned to death. His wish had been that his body be cremated and his ashes scattered in the sea, and to complete the cycle this was done. He was twenty-three when he died. I do not recall whether or not he was married, but there were many moving love letters to a particular girl.

We have long forgotten those girls, doomed to go alone or with their parents down the lane to the village church, girls whose hopes had vanished. They were the fruit that had fallen to the ground. I longed to know these girls but also to bear the guilt for having robbed them, to have my ashes be the cause of their grief.

Then there was St.-Exupéry. He seduced me as well. I had read him, joylessly at first, in French, line by line and forever looking up words. He was a favorite of the French teacher. Eventually I came to like him on my own—it was his knowledge I admired, his wholeness of mind, more than his exploits—and years later my feeling was confirmed by a woman who told me that her youthful love affair with him was the most cherished episode of her life.

She had met him at a reception in New York in about 1941 or 1942. She was good-looking, European. She fell in love instantly, at first sight. He had been in America since a few months after the fall of France in the spring of 1940. I imagine him—these are the dark days of a long war in which he would eventually be lost, fate unknown—as somewhat drab, in a gray double-breasted suit with perhaps an overlooked stain on the lapel. Like an ex-fighter whose career had ended a decade before, he is carrying a bit of weight. Balding but with a face that is smooth and somehow youthful— the clarity of intelligence shines in it—in his buttonhole sits a distinguished dot of red.

She tries to talk to him, she absolutely must, *"Monsieur . . . ,"* but her French is hopeless. She tries English, to no avail. Finally she says outright, *"Wollen Sie mein* telephone number?"

Then she goes home and waits, until late in the evening. The sullen black phone never rings. The next day, however, he calls, and the searing love letters he subsequently wrote she kept for the rest of her life.

There was also his affair on one side of the world or the other, among the palms of California or the forests of East Africa, with Beryl Markham—two ecstatic souls, somehow unjealous of each other. Over the years St.-Exupéry managed to progress, for me, from being a mere figure of culture to one of enviable flesh and blood.

In such footsteps I would follow.

———

Pine Bluff, Arkansas, on a loop of a sluggish, curving river, was where we learned to fly. The field was east of town. The flying school there was run by civilians.

We lived in barracks and were broken up into flights—four students to an instructor—alphabetically, of course, although inexplicably I was together with Marlow, Milnor, and Mahl. Our instructor was an ancient, perhaps in his forties, crop duster from a town in the southwest part of the state, Hope, which he described as the watermelon capital of the world. His name was Basil York. We were probably among scores of young men he had taught to fly, and were reminded of this by a stern warning for the next student to be ready when the plane taxied in from the previous flight. We waited, watching intently for the plane's number and with no chance to question whoever had just come down about what had happened, what had they done in the air and what should we look out for?

Early flights, the instructor in the rear cockpit, the bumpy taxiing on the grass, turning into the wind, tail swinging around, dust blowing, and then the abrupt, wild sound of the engine. The ground was speeding by, the wheels skipping, and suddenly we were rising in the din to see the blue tree line beyond the field boundary and, below, the curved roofs of the hangers falling away. Now fields appeared, swimming out in all directions. The earth became limitless, the horizon, unseen before, rose to fill the world and we were aloft in unstructured air.

Looking over the side of the airplane, I could not believe it, the noise, the clatter of the engine, the battering wind, and the flat country below laid out in large rectangular patterns with dirt roads, the glint of occasional metal roofs, smooth water. They talked meaninglessly about "section lines." In the air these quickly became real.

We passed a thousand feet. I felt as helpless as if sitting in a chair at that height. We climbed higher, to fifteen hundred or two thousand feet, the height of the stalls, the first of the demonstrated maneuvers. The nose soars up into steep blue air, higher, higher still, unforgivingly higher, something sickening is happening, the bottom of the seat feels ready to drop away, and the dry voice of the instructor is explaining it as at the top the plane, almost motionless, suddenly shudders, then starts to fall. Now I am to do this, his matter-of-fact voice directing it: throttle back, pull the nose up, way up, higher, hold it there, hold it . . .

There were spins, jamming the rudder in at the top of a stall and falling, the plane turning around and around like a maple pod. There was the anguish of trying to make proper "S" turns across a road, the wind making one loop bigger than the other unless you steepened your bank.

An hour has passed. All directions have melted away, the earth is too vast and confusing to be able to say where we are. Only later is it clear that the roads run on cardinal headings, north-south, east-west. The world and everything in it, the river, farmers' houses, the roads and lone cars, are unaware of us, droning above. The field is nowhere in sight. Like a desert, everything visible is almost the same when he says, "OK. Take us home." It must be this way, you think, though there is nothing to confirm it. After a few minutes, without a word, he brusquely corrects the heading ninety degrees as if in disgust.

Everything you have done has been unsatisfactory, the stalls not steep enough, the "S" turns uneven, the nose of the plane continually wandering off in one direction or the other when you are told to hold it straight and level, anything that could speed up, slide, or drift away has done so.

In the distance, magically, the field appears and with precision, sometimes explaining what he is doing, he enters the traffic pattern and expertly lands. My flying suit is black with sweat. Face glazed, disheartened, I scramble from the plane as soon as we park. One of the others is standing there to take my place.

———

All was tin, the corrugated hangars shining in the sun, the open-cockpit airplanes, the tin gods. We were expected to solo in a few hours, not less than four or more than eight. If you were not able to take off and land by yourself after eight hours, you were washed out. The days were filled with classes, briefings, flights, the sound of planes, the smell of them. We were mixed in with regular air cadets, some of whom were older and had flown before. We marched with them, singing their songs, the vulgarity of which was disarming, and continued to kick into spins at three thousand feet on every flight and mechanically chant the formula: throttle off, stick forward, pause, opposite rudder . . . Even after three or four flights I still did not fully understand what a chandelle was supposed to be and had only a faint conception of a landing.

Like the first buds appearing, individuals began to solo. Word of who had done it spread immediately. Face scorched red by the sun, in the back cockpit Basil York repeated over and over the desiderata as we entered traffic, "Twenty-fifty and five hundred, twenty-fifty and five hundred." He was referring to engine rpm and traffic pattern altitude. "When you're flying B-17s," he said in his high-pitched voice, "I want you to still be hearing that: twenty-fifty and five hundred." We had begun to execute the landings together, nose up, throttle all the way off, both of us on the stick. I knew his recitation, "Start breaking the glide, ease back on the throttle, start rounding out, all right, that's good, hold it off now, hold it off . . ." The trouble was, I did not know what it all meant.

There was the story I heard later, of the instructor who had a favorite trick with students having difficulty learning to land. After exhausting the usual means, above the traffic pattern somewhere he would shake the control stick from side to side, banging the student's knees—the front and rear sticks were connected—to get his attention. He would then remove the pin holding the rear stick in place and, with the student twisting his neck to see what was happening, wave it in the air and toss it over the side, pointing at the student with the gesture *You, you've got it,* and pointing down. It had always worked. One day for still another lagging student he rattled the stick fiercely, flourished it, and tossed it away. The student nodded numbly, bent down, unfastened his own stick, and ig-

ICARUS

noring the instructor's cries, threw it away also. He watched as the
frightened instructor bailed out and then, fame assured, reached
down for the spare stick he had secretly brought along, flew back
to the field, and landed.

To solve the complexities of the traffic pattern, I had made, for
quick reference, a small card with a diagram of each of the possible patterns drawn on it. Entry was always at forty-five degrees to
a downwind leg, but to work it all out backwards and head straight
for the proper point was confusing, and nothing seemed to annoy
York as much as starting to turn the wrong way. The worst was
when the wind changed while you were away from the field; the
pattern had shifted, and everything you had tried to remember was
useless.

A week passes thus. We fly to an auxiliary field, a large meadow
five or ten minutes away. There is bare earth near the borders
where planes have repeatedly touched down.

"Let's try some landings," he says. Nervously I go over in my
mind what to do, what not. "Make three good ones and I'll get
out."

We come in for the first. "Hold that airspeed," he directs.
"That's good. Now come back on the power. Start rounding out."

Somehow it works. Hardly a bump as the wheels touch. "Good."
I push the throttle forward in a smooth motion and we are off
again.

The second landing is the same. I am not certain what I have
done but whatever it is, I try to repeat it for the third. Almost confidently I turn onto final once more. "You're doing fine," he says. I
watch the airspeed as we descend. The grass field is approaching,
the decisive third.

"Make this a full stop," he instructs. I ease back the throttle.
The airspeed begins to drop. "Keep the nose down," he suddenly
warns. "Nose down! Watch your airspeed!" I feel a hand on the
stick. The plane is beginning to tremble. Untouched by me the

throttle leaps forward, but through it somehow we are falling, unsupported by the roar. With a huge jolt we hit the ground, bounce, and come down again. He utters a single contemptuous word. When we have slowed, he says, "Taxi over there, to the left." I follow his instructions. We come to a stop.

"That was terrible. You rounded out twenty feet in the air. As far as I can make out, you're going to kill us both." I see him rising up. He climbs out of the cockpit and stands on the wing. "You take her up," he says.

This consent, the words of which I could not even imagine. Alone in the plane, I do what we had done each time, taxi to the end of the bare spot, turn, and almost mechanically advance the throttle. I felt at that moment—I will remember always—the thrill of the inachievable. Reciting to myself, exuberant, immortal, I felt the plane leave the ground and cross the hayfields and farms, making a noise like a tremendous, bumbling fly. I was far out, beyond the reef, nervous but unfrightened, knowing nothing, certain of all, cloth helmet, childish face, sleeve wind-maddened as I held an ecstatic arm out in the slipstream, the exaltation, the godliness, at last!

———

At night in the white wooden barracks not far from the flight line we talked of flying, in the clamor of the student mess, and on the battered buses swaying into town. We walked the streets in aimless groups, past lawyers' offices with names painted in gold on the windows. There were tracks through the center of Pine Bluff along which freight trains moved with provincial slowness. There was the gold-domed courthouse and the bulky Pines Hotel, even then middle-aged with a portico entrance, balconies, and mysterious rooms. Of the silent residential neighborhoods with large clapboard houses or lesser ones set on the bare ground, we knew nothing. From the desolate life of the town on many Sundays we returned willingly to the field.

We flew less often with the instructor. It was late spring, the sky fresh and filled with fair-weather clouds—weather, which could mean so much, was already a preoccupation. Late in the day the clouds would become dense and towering, their edges struck with light; epic clouds, the last of the sun streaming through. One afternoon, alone, I caught sight in their tops, far above, of a B-24 moving along like a great liner. Dazzled by its distance and height I turned like a dinghy to follow until it was gone.

On an outlying field two rows of empty peach baskets had been placed at intervals on each side of a wide lane. A cross was marked on the ground halfway down. It was a kind of bull's-eye. If your wheels touched on that spot you got a perfect grade, which is to say zero. Ten feet from it was a ten, twenty feet a twenty, and so forth. The figures were averaged and had to be below some number, I don't remember, seventy or so, to pass. Around and around we flew, a supervisor on the ground in the blowing dust marking scores on a clipboard. Landing stages, this was called.

At noon they were talking about someone's extraordinary grade, one of the regular air cadets with whom we were training. His score had been six. It seemed unbelievable. He was pointed out—suddenly everyone knew who he was—the one with the dark hair. I could see him in the food line, distinct from the others, slim, at ease. He had flown before, it turned out. He already had a pilot's license and sixty hours in a Cub.

The hurdles in primary were soloing and then two check rides with an Air Force pilot given, I believe, after forty and sixty hours of flying time. Don't forget to salute before and after the flight, they said, and be sure you can explain the maintenance form. In the air there would be brief commands to do this or that maneuver and at some inconvenient moment the throttle would be pulled back with the announcement, "Forced landing."

The shakiest students confessed their fears and often did worse because of them, but some failures were unforeseeable, even unimaginable, like that of the dark-haired angel who had scored the six. One day he disappeared. He had somehow failed his forty-hour check and was gone. It made you realize how flimsy your position was and how unforgiving the machinery behind it all. The least promising of us, though we did not know it then, those with the least élan, would go to bombers and attack aircraft, and the others to fighters. That was a year off. Meanwhile, one by one they were dropping away, sometimes the leaders.

We were gone all spring and summer and returned much changed. We marched less perfectly, dressed with less care. West Point, its officer's sashes and cock feathers fluttering from shakos, its stewardship, somehow passed over to those who had stayed.

Among the great firsts: first solo, first breath of outside air, in here belongs first love affair.

I had known her before, in New York, the younger of two sisters in a well-to-do Upper East Side family. She was dark-haired and theatrical and had grown, over a period of more than a year, to become very important, in fact essential, to me. Good-looking and expensively dressed, teeth fine and white, she stood at the entrance to life itself, the things I had yet to know and had sworn not to die before I did. Her father was a stockbroker with loyal, and many European, clients. Her mother, whose role was larger in our intrigue, disapproved of me, which was a stimulus. I was eager to have a past and a heart that longed for me.

From the early football weekends when we drank in hotel rooms and alongside other couples lay in the feverish dark with murmurs and the low rustle of clothing, to weekends when she stayed at the Thayer, above the ground floor of which cadets were forbidden to go, evenings at dances and sometimes afternoons in borrowed quarters, we fell in with one another. I was filled with urges which

she put down skillfully, like insurrections. I was trying to impose
my new-formed self on her, but she had known the previous one
and wavered.

Gradually I prevailed. After many long overtures, occasionally
desperate, something passed between us one New York weekend
at the intermission of a musical called *Panama Hattie*. I can't remember what was said; we casually edged through the crowd on
the sidewalk and crossed the street to the hotel.

She was at last willing, unresistant, we were face to face, she
gleamed in the dark. That hotel is gone now, though the act remains, the unremarkable act which cut life in two, one part falling
to the ground and the other stretching gloriously ahead. The great,
thronged palaces with their countless windows, the Astor,
McAlpin, the Pennsylvania, their dangerous lobbies and corridors
along which we uneasily strolled, their rooms with twin beds and
ominous black phones, became our stage. There was, that year, a
then-irresistible novel called *Shore Leave* with a pair of Navy
wings on its blue jacket, and written in a confident style. It became, at my insistence, our text. The name of its nihilist hero,
gaunt and faithless, was Crewson. He had flown at Midway and in
other battles. The blood baths. Would he remember as an old
man, the author, Frederic Wakeman, wrote, rising at three in the
morning on the third of June? The briefing at four and soon afterwards reports of enemy aircraft inbound. And then on the dense
rippled sea, *the Kaga, steaming upwind at a brisk thirty knots, the
coming-out-of-the-ether feeling when he split his flaps and made an
eighty-degree dive for the red circle on her flight deck . . . the first
hit . . .*—all this was indelible. Those bombs going home freed him
forever from the trivial and mundane. His society girlfriend was
only one of the women who trotted after him like colts.

We shared this book as a Bible might be shared by a devout couple. It was a hymn to the illicit. Emboldened by it we acted as

though we were part of the war. On the inside cover she inscribed it to me, the Crewson of her past. There were many things in it that she could have written herself, she continued, and then, as if granting to a beloved child possession of a favorite plaything, *Keep this book with you, my dearest.* If things had turned out differently, it managed to say; if we had, in the way of all failed lovers, only met years sooner or later . . .

I knew the handwriting well. I had received many letters, for a long time one each morning after class, special delivery, scented, covered with stamps, letters I read sitting with my dress coat unzipped, a torn undershirt beneath it, the insignia of the upperclassman. I thought of her constantly, in the stuporous hours of code class, legs jammed against the table in desire; listening to songs on the phonograph; hearing classmates on Saturday evenings walking to the hop. The question was simple, was I going to marry her?, for marriage was heavy in the air, graduation, the chapel, former roommates and young women they more or less knew passing beneath the flash of crossed sabers and down the steps into a waiting automobile and what was surely life. I was unreliable but she would steady me. I was in uniform but that would be over before long and I would come back to the city to lead an appropriate life. All that was muted but clear. She was only eighteen but sure in her instinct. Besides, she coolly admitted, there was someone else in the picture who had been a year behind me in prep school and was now an enlisted man in Sioux Falls, less glamorous but more sensible, with not even the vaguest idea of staying in the army an hour longer than necessary. His name had been tossed lightheartedly back and forth between us until the point when I received a fateful telegram: Yes or no, it demanded.

Whatever indecisive form my answer took, she responded by doing what she had threatened. She married him just as I was graduating. For a moment it seemed like another bit of teasing, with the impermanence things had in those days. Nevertheless I felt an unexpected, sweet-sad pang. Later I saw it clearly, as I had not then. I had turned my back on three things, marriage, money, and the past, never really to face them wholeheartedly again.

I try to summon her and all the letters with their girlish script, the pleas and admonitions, gossip of friends, endearments, exaggeration. Sometimes it seems that all that has happened since is less vital than what we were, and the luster of her eighteen years, the tawdriness I wanted to immerse them in, to stain their glory and make them immortal. She was, for a season, mine, and I was drunk with it. I had the hussarlike luxury of being bored by the genuine thing, and though places have vanished, where she stands is where she has always stood and I carefully place her story where it belongs, before the rest.

———

In the fall of 1944, amid the battles on the continent, came word of the death of the unrivaled goat, Benny Mills. He was killed in action in Belgium, a company commander. Beneath a shroud his body had lain in the square of a small town; people had placed flowers around it, and his men, one by one, saluted as they passed through and left him, like Sir John Moore at Corunna, alone with his glory. He had fallen and in that act been preserved, made untarnishable. He had not married. He had left no one.

His death was one of many and sped away quickly, like an oar swirl. I could never imitate him, I knew, or be like him. He was part of a great dynamic of which I, in a useless way, was also part, and classmates, women, his men, all had more reason to remember him than I, but it may have been for some of them as it was for me: he represented the flawless and was the first of that category to disappear.

We bought officer's uniforms from military clothiers who came on weekends that next spring and set up tables and racks in the gymnasium. The pleasure of examining and choosing clothes and various pieces of decoration—should pilot's wings be embroidered in handsome silver thread or merely be a metal version, was it worthwhile to order one or two handmade "green" shirts, was the hat to be Bancroft or Luxembourg—all this was savored. Luxembourg, thought to be the very finest, was in fact two tailor brothers surrounded by walls of signed photographs in their New York offices. The pair of them were to the army as Brooks Brothers was to Yale.

Like young priests or brides, immaculately dressed, filled with vision, pride, and barely any knowledge, we would go forth. The army would care for us. We had little idea of how careers were fashioned or generals made. Napoleon, I remembered, when he no longer knew personally all those recommended for promotion, would jot next to a strange name on the list three words: "Is he lucky?" And of course I would be.

Eventually you meet generals, walk beside them, talk, and slowly, as with beautiful women, manage to hold your eyes on them. A few years after graduation I became aide to a general who was moody, dashing, and had a scar like a knife-slash across the bridge of his nose, made by German flak. He was from Savannah, Georgia, class of 1928, fearsome reputation and the face of a leading man. On his starched collar was a single, slightly antique star.

He gave me an initial piece of advice: "As long as you're my aide," he said pleasantly, "you can get away with murder. You'll be able to make bird colonels jump when you speak. They'll think you're speaking for me, but as soon as it's over, when I'm not around anymore"—he made a gesture near his neck—"they'll slit your throat," he told me.

His name was Robert Travis and the stories preceded him,

mostly of his toughness. The very first one I heard was of his simply reaching out and tearing the stripes off a sergeant who had failed to salute him. LeMay himself was said to have been his copilot before the war.

The poker he liked was five-card draw, open on anything, guts, as he said. One night his first bet was forty dollars, which was a lot then. We were flying over the Pacific. The game was table stakes. I looked at my cards; I had two tens.

There were five of us playing. All but one called. The dealer asked, "How many?"

"I'll play these," Travis said.

I had drawn a third ten. He began counting out money. Eighty dollars was his bet.

I was to his left. There was more than a month's pay on the table. It was late at night. "Get out," he said without looking at me. The heaped green of the bills was mesmerizing, the fascination of all that money, the thickness of it folded. "Get out, Jimmy," he said again. This was the game he liked to play, perhaps because it had always favored him. Was he truly advising me? I had three of a kind. "Get out," I heard him warn for the last time.

Youth that I was, I tossed my cards away and with them, unfortunately, the memory of what he had. He won the hand, I remember that. I had bent to power.

We were close. He hid nothing from me, diaries, ambition, desire. He had a notable if ominous charm and had once almost married a movie star, when he was a lieutenant and she a doll-like celebrity, but his family I think objected on the grounds that his career would have been compromised. I see him in Shanghai, forty years old, sitting in the barber's chair in Chiang Kai-shek's bathroom—the house had been offered as a courtesy. We were touring the Far East. For him it was marking time. He was waiting for the chance he had not gotten during the war. Eventually it came.

Was he lucky? Yes and no. The bluish flak had come within an inch of his eyes and he had led some of the most dangerous raids of the war. He was made for that, to dare and command, but he died in an accident a few years later—his plane, fully loaded and with atomic bombs aboard, went down in a trailer park immediately after takeoff and an airfield in California was named for him.

——

At Stewart Field the final spring, nearly pilots, we had the last segment of training. This was near Newburgh, about forty minutes from West Point. We wore flying suits most of the day and lived in long, open-bay barracks. That photograph of oneself, nonexistent, that no one ever sees, in my case was taken in the morning by the doorway of what must be the dayroom and I am drinking a Coke from an icy, greenish bottle, a ritual prelude to all the breakfastless mornings of flying that were to come. During all the training there had been few fatalities. We were that good. At least I knew I was.

On a May evening after supper we took off, one by one, on a navigation flight. It was still daylight and the planes, as they departed, were soon lost in their solitude. On the maps the course was drawn, miles marked off in ticks of ten. The route lay to the west, over the wedged-up Allegheny ridges to Port Jervis and Scranton, then down to Reading, and the last long leg of the triangle back home. It was all mechanical with one exception: the winds aloft had been incorrectly forecast. Unknown to us, they were from a different direction and stronger. Alone and confident we headed west.

The air at altitude has a different smell, metallic and faintly tinged with gasoline or exhaust. The ground floats by with tidal slowness, the roads desolate, the rivers unmoving. It is exactly like the map, with certain insignificant differences which one ponders over but leaves unresolved.

The sun has turned red and sunk lower. The airspeed reads one-sixty. The fifteen or twenty airplanes, invisible to one another, are in a long, irregular string. Behind, the sky has become a deeper shade. We were flying not only in the idleness of spring but in a kind of idyll that was the end of the war. The color of the earth was muted and the towns seemed empty shadows. There was no one to see or talk to. The wind, unsuspected, was shifting us slowly, like sand.

On my mind apart from navigation were, I suppose, New York nights, the lure of the city, various achievements that a year or two before I had only dreamed of. The first dim star appeared and then, somewhat to the left of where it should be, the drab scrawl of Scranton.

Flying, like most things of consequence, is method. Though I did not know it then, I was behaving improperly. There were light-lines between cities in those days, like lights on an unseen high-way but much farther apart. By reading their flashed codes you could tell where you were, but I was not bothering with that. I turned south towards Reading. The sky was dark now. Far below, the earth was cooling, giving up the heat of the day. A mist had begun to form. In it the light-lines would fade away and also, al-most shyly, the towns. I flew on.

It is a different world at night. The instruments become harder to read, details disappear from the map. After a while I tuned to the Reading frequency and managed to pick up its signal. I had no radio compass but there was a way of determining, by flying a cer-tain sequence of headings, where in a surrounding quadrant you were. Then if the signal slowly increased in strength you were in-bound towards the station. If not, and you had to turn up the vol-ume to continue hearing it, you were going away. It was primitive but it worked.

When the time came I waited to see if I had passed or was still approaching Reading. The minutes went by. At first I couldn't de-tect a change but then the signal seemed to grow weaker. I turned north and flew, watching the clock. Something was wrong, something serious: the signal didn't change. I was lost, not only literally but in relation to reality. Meanwhile the wind, unseen, fateful, was forcing me farther north.

Among the stars, one was moving. It was the lights of another plane, perhaps one from the squadron. In any case, wherever it was headed there would be a field. I pushed up the throttle. As I drew closer, on an angle, I began to make out what it was, an airliner, a DC-3. It might be going to St. Louis or Chicago. I had already been flying for what seemed like hours and had begun, weakhearted, a repeated checking of fuel. The gauges were on the floor, one on each side of the seat. I tried not to think of them but they were like a wound; I could not keep myself from glancing down.

Slowly the airliner and its lights became more distant. I couldn't keep up with it. I turned northeast, the general direction of home. I had been scribbling illegibly on the page of memory, which way I had gone and for how long. I now had no idea where I was. The occasional lights on the ground of unknown towns, lights blurred and yellowish, meant nothing. Allentown, which should have been somewhere, never appeared. There was a terrible temptation to abandon everything, to give up, as with a hopeless puzzle. I was reciting "Invictus" to myself, *I am the master of my fate* . . . It availed nothing. I had the greatest difficulty not praying and finally I did, flying in the noisy darkness, desperate for the sight of a city or anything that would give me my position.

In the map case of the airplane was a booklet, *What to Do If Lost,* and suddenly remembering, I got it out and with my flashlight began to read. There was a list of half a dozen steps to take in order. My eye skidded down it. The first ones I had already tried. Others, like tuning in any radio range and orienting yourself on it, I had given up on; something was wrong with that, it wasn't working. I managed to get the signal from Stewart Field but didn't take up the prescribed heading. I could tell from its faintness—it was indistinct in a thicket of other sounds—that I was far away, and I had lost faith in the procedure. The final advice seemed more practical. If you think you are to the west of Stewart, it said, head east until you come to the Hudson River and then fly north or south; you will eventually come to New York or Albany.

It was past eleven, the sky dense with stars, the earth a void. I had turned east. The dimly lit fuel gauges read twenty-five gallons or so in each wing. The idea slowly growing, of opening the canopy and struggling into the wind, over the side into blackness, tumbling, parachuting down, was not as unthinkable as that of giving the airplane itself up to destruction. I would be washed out, I knew. The anguish was unbearable. I had been flying east for ten minutes but it seemed hours. Occasionally I made out the paltry lights of some small town or group of houses, barely distinguishable, but otherwise nothing. The cities had vanished, sunken to darkness. I looked down again. Twenty gallons.

Suddenly off to the left there was a glimmer that became—I was just able to make it out—a faint string of lights and then slowly, magically, two parallel lines. It was the bridge at Poughkeepsie. Dazed with relief I tried to pick out its dark lines and those of the river, turning to keep it in sight, going lower and lower. Then, in the way that all things certain had changed that night, the bridge changed too. At about a thousand feet above them, stricken, I saw I was looking at the street lights of some town.

The gauges read fifteen gallons. One thing that should never be done—it had been repeated to us often—was to attempt a forced landing at night. But I had no choice. I began to circle, able in the mist to see clearly only what was just beneath. The town was at the edge of some hills; I banked away from them in the blackness. If I went too far from the brightly lit, abandoned main street, I lost my bearings. Dropping even lower I saw dark roofs everywhere and amid them, unexpectedly, a blank area like a lake or small park. I had passed it quickly, turned, and lost it. Finally, lower still, I saw it again. It was not big but there was nothing else. I ducked my head for a moment to look down—the number beneath each index line was wavering slightly: ten gallons, perhaps twelve.

The rule for any strange field was to first fly across at minimum altitude to examine the surface. I was not even sure it was a field; it might be water or a patch of woods. If a park, it might have buildings or fences. I turned onto a downwind leg or what I judged to be one, then a base leg, letting down over swiftly enlarging roofs. I had the canopy open to cut reflection, the ghostly duplication of instruments, the red warning lights. I stared ahead through the wind and noise. I was at a hundred feet or so, flaps down, still descending.

In front, coming fast, was my field. On a panel near my knee were the landing light switches with balled tips to make them identifiable by feel. I reached for them blindly. The instant they came on I knew I'd made a mistake. They blazed like searchlights in the mist; I could see more without them but the ground was twenty feet beneath me, I was at minimum speed and dared not bend to turn them off. Something went by on the left. Trees, in the middle of the park. I had barely missed them. No landing here. A moment later, at the far end, more trees. They were higher than I was, and without speed to climb I banked to get through them. I heard foliage slap the wings as just ahead, shielded, a second rank of trees rose up. There was no time to do anything. Something large struck a wing. It tore away. The plane careened up. It stood poised for an endless moment, one landing light flooding a house into which an instant later it crashed.

Nothing has vanished, not even the stunned first seconds of silence, the torn leaves drifting down. Reflexively, as a slain man might bewilderedly shut a door, I reached to turn off the ignition. I was badly injured, though in what way I did not know. There was no pain. My legs, I realized. I tried to move them. Nothing seemed wrong. My front teeth were loose; I could feel them move as I breathed. In absolute quiet I sat for a few moments almost at a loss as to what to do, then unbuckled the harness and stepped from the cockpit onto what had been the front porch. The nose of the plane was in the wreckage of a room. The severed wing lay back in the street.

The house, as it turned out, belonged to a family that was welcoming home a son who had been a prisoner of war in Germany. They were having a party and had taken the startling noise of the plane as it passed low over town many times to be some sort of military salute, and though it was nearly midnight had all gone into the street to have a look. I had come in like a meteorite over their heads. The town was Great Barrington. I had to be shown where it was on a map, in Massachusetts, miles to the north and east.

That night I slept in the mayor's house, in a feather bed. I say slept but in fact I hung endlessly in the tilted darkness, the landing light pouring down at the large frame house. The wing came off countless times. I turned over in bed and began again.

They came for me the next day and I watched them load the wreckage on a large flatbed truck. I rode back with the remains of the plane. In the barracks, which were empty when I arrived, my bed, unlike the rows of others, was littered with messages, all mock congratulations. I found myself, unexpectedly, a popular figure. It was as if I had somehow defied the authorities. On the blackboard in the briefing room was a drawing of a house with the tail of an airplane sticking from the roof and written beneath, *Geisler's student*. I survived the obligatory check-rides and the proceedings of the accident board, which were unexpectedly brief. Gradually transformed into a comedy, the story was told by me many times, as I had felt, for a shameless instant, it would be that night when the boughs of the first trees hit the wings before I saw the second. There was a bent, enameled Pratt and Whitney emblem from the engine that I kept for a long time, until it was lost somewhere, and years later a single unsigned postcard reached me, addressed care of the Adjutant General. It was from Great Barrington. *We are still praying for you here,* it said.

Confident and indestructible now, I put a dummy of dirty clothes in my bed and one night after taps met Horner near the barracks door. We were going off limits, over the fence, the punishment for which was severe. Graduation was only days away; if we were caught there would be no time for confinement to quarters or walking the Area; the sentence would be more lasting: graduating late and loss of class standing. The risk, though, was not great. "Anita is coming up," he told me. "She's bringing a girlfriend." They would be waiting in a convertible at the bottom of a hill.

Anita was new. I admired her. She was the kind of girl I would never have, who bored me, in fact, and was made intriguing only by the mischievous behavior of Horner. In some ways I was in that position myself, his Pinocchio, willing and enthralled.

Anita was the daughter of a carpet manufacturer. She wore silk stockings and print dresses. She had red fingernails and was tall. Her efforts to discipline Horner were ineffective and charming. "Well, you know Jack . . . ," she would explain helplessly. I did know him and liked him, I think, at least as much as she did and probably for longer.

Staying close to the buildings we made it in the darkness to the open space near the fence and climbed over quickly. The road was not too long a walk away. We came over a slight crest and halfway down the hill, delirious in our goatlike freedom, saw the faint lights of the dashboard. One of the doors was open, the radio was softly playing. Two faces turned to us. Anita was smiling. "Where the hell have you been?" she said, and we drove off towards Newburgh to find a liquor store. Jack was in front with her; their laughter streamed back like smoke.

The Anitas. I had more or less forgotten them. Ages later, decades, literally, in the deepest part of the night the telephone rings in the darkness and I reach for it. It's two in the morning, the house is asleep. There is a cackle that I recognize immediately. "Who is this?" I say. To someone else, aside, gleefully he says, "He wants to know who it is." Then to me, "Did I wake you up?"

"What could possibly give you that idea?"

Another cackle. "Jim, this is Jack Horner," he says in a businessman's voice. He was divorced and traveling around. "Doing what?" I ask. "Inspecting post offices," he says. Bobbing around his voice are others, careless, soft as feathers. One of them comes on the phone. "Where are you?" I ask. My wife is sleeping beside me. A low voice replies, "In a motel. About three blocks from you." She adds a burning invitation. In the background I can hear him telling them I am a writer, he has known me since we were cadets. He tries to take the phone again. I can hear them struggling, the laughter of the women, his own, high and almost as feminine, infectious.

That May night, however, we parked near an orchard and went up beneath the trees. We got back to barracks very late. A day or two afterwards I came up to him while he was shaving before breakfast. "Have you noticed anything strange?" I asked.

"Yes. What is it? Have you got it too?" It was a rash. It turned out to be poison ivy covering our arms and legs, a first mock rendering to Venus.

We went without neckties, excused from formation. With blistered skin and unable to wear a full-dress coat, I stood at the window of my room and heard the band playing in the distance and the long pauses that were part of the ceremony of the last parade. There came the sound of the music played just once a year when the graduating class, some of them openly weeping, removed their hats as the first of the companies, in salute, came abreast, officers' sabers coming up, glinting, then whipped downwards.

Far off, the long years were passing in review, the seasons and settings, the cold walls and sallyports, the endless routine. Through high windows the sun fell on the choir as it came with majestic slowness, singing, up the aisle. The uniforms, the rifles, the books. The winter mornings, dark outside; smoking and listening to the radio as we cleaned the room. The gym, dank and forbidding. The class sections forming in haste along the road.

The Area was filled with footlockers and boxes. Everyone would be leaving, scattered, dismissed for the last time, to the chapel for weddings, to restaurants with their families, to the Coast, the Midwest, to the smallest of towns. We were comparing orders, destinations. I felt both happiness and the pain of farewell. We were entering the army, which was like a huge, deep lake, slower and deeper than one dreamed. At the bottom it was fed by springs, fresh and everlastingly pure. On the surface, near the spillway, the water was older and less clear, but this water was soon to leave. We were the new and untainted.

On my finger I had a gold ring with the year of my class on it, a ring that would be recognizable to everyone I would meet. I wore it always; I flew with it on my finger; it lay in my shoe while I slept. It signified everything, and I had given everything to have it. I also had a silver identification bracelet, which all flyers wore, with a welt of metal that rang when it touched the table or bar. I was arrogant, perhaps, different from the boy who had come here and different even from the others, not quite knowing how, or the danger.

As we packed to leave, a pair of my roommate's shoe trees got mixed up with mine and I did not notice it until after we had gone. In a hand distinctly his, *Eckert, R. P.* in ink was neatly printed on the wooden toe block. He was killed later in a crash, like his brother. His life disappeared but not his name, which I saw over the years as I dressed and then saw him, cool blue eyes, pale skin, a way of smoking that was oddly abrupt, a way of walking with his feet turned out. I also kept a shako, some pants, and a gray shirt, but slowly, like paint flaking away, they were left behind or lost, though in memory very clear.

———

One thing I saw again, long afterwards. I was driving on a lonely road in the West about twenty miles out of Cheyenne. It was winter and the snow had drifted. I tried to push through but in the end got stuck. It was late in the afternoon. The wind was blowing. There was not a house to be seen in any direction, only fences and flat, buried fields.

I got out and started back along the road. It was very cold; my tire tracks were already being erased. Gloved hands over my ears, I was alternately walking and running, thinking of the outcome of Jack London stories. After a mile or two I heard dogs barking. Off to the right, half hidden in the snow, was a plain, unpainted house and some sheds. I struggled through the drifts, the dogs retreating before me, barking and growling, the fur erect on their necks.

A tall young woman with an open face and a chipped tooth came to the door. I could hear a child crying. I told her what had happened and asked if I could borrow a shovel. "Come in," she said.

The room was drab. Some chairs and a table, bare walls. She was calling into the kitchen for her husband. On top of an old file cabinet a black-and-white television was turned on. Suddenly I saw something familiar, out of the deepest past—covering the couch was a gray blanket, the dense gray of boyhood uniforms, with a black-and-gold border. It was a West Point blanket. Her husband was pulling on his shirt. How fitting, I thought, one ex-regular bumping into another in the tundra, years after, winter at its coldest, life at its ebb.

In a littered truck we drove back to the car and worked for an hour, hands gone numb, feet as well. Heroic labor, the kind that binds you to someone. We spoke little, only about shoveling and what to do. He was anonymous but in his face I saw patience, strength, and that ethic of those schooled to difficult things. Shoulder to shoulder we tried to move the car. He was that vanished man, the company commander, the untiring figure of those years when nothing was higher, *privations mean little to him, difficulties cannot break his spirit . . .* I was in the snow of airfields again where we dug our wheels free and taxied up and down the runway to let the exhaust melt the ice, in the rime cold of forty-five thousand feet with the heat inoperative, in dawns of thirty below, when to touch the metal of the fuselage was to lose your skin to it.

Together we rescued the car, and back at the house I held out some money. I wanted to give him something for his trouble, I said. He looked at it, "That's too much."

"Not for me," I said. Then I added, "Your blanket . . ."

"What blanket?"

"The one on the couch; I recognize it. Where'd you get it?" I said idly. He turned and looked at it, then at me as if deciding. He was tall, like his wife, and his movements were unhurried. "Where'd we get it?" he asked her. *The ladies who come up in June . . . ,* I thought. They'd been married in the chapel.

"That? I forget. At the thrift shop," she said.

For a moment I thought they were acting, unwilling to reveal themselves, but no. He was a tattoo artist, it turned out. He worked in Cheyenne.

The summer after graduation, the first great summer of my life, passed without a trace. I had one ambition, to degrade myself. I first sped to New York to spend a weekend with a girl I had heard stories about for at least a year. The daughter of a diplomat, she was notorious throughout the regiment, passed from hand to

ICARUS

hand, not particularly beautiful, as I discovered, but unsurprisable
and even witty. I was eager to know what the others had known,
the inner circle, and to be able to mention her casually.

After this came leave in sweltering Washington, indolent days
and nights, and the minimal pleasure that went with them.
Horner was there also. He was living with his mother. At the end
of a month, still enchanted with ourselves, he and I climbed
aboard a B-17 bound for Columbus, Ohio, and lay luxuriously
amid the baggage, Horner strumming on his ukulele while the
crew pulled the props through and prepared for flight. Island
songs were among his favorites, and one called "Standard Gas."
Soon we were in the cool, thin air of altitude, the engines lulling
us to sleep. Thus, rather clownishly, began days of roving. We were
headed eventually for Oklahoma, regular officers, in the comfort
of our status, unaware of the multitudes and their fate.

———

From time to time I would think of Bob Morgan, most often at
year's end, when you look back, sometimes a long way. I once went
as far as to get a telephone number for him from long-distance information but I never called. There among my vague recollections
he never changed, he kept his broad, flat chest, his modesty and
doggedness.

Decades passed, and I happened to be in Texas, though far from
his town. On an impulse I called information again. There were no
Morgans listed in Spur; I had waited too long. There were two
Robert Morgans in Lubbock, a large city not far away that he often
mentioned, but neither was the right one. I finally tried the Veterans Administration. There were countless Morgans on the com-
puter, the man said, including hundreds of Roberts. He suggested
I call Spur, where I talked to the editor of the local paper.

"Morgan?" Speaking to someone else, the editor said, "Didn't
we run an obituary for a Morgan this past fall? I don't know if it

was Robert," he said to me—he had only been there since 1952, he was a newcomer, he admitted. "Wait a minute, here." He was looking at the subscription list, "There's a Bob Morgan who takes the *Texas Spur*. He's in New Waverly, Texas." He read me the postal code. Where New Waverly was, he couldn't say, but I knew at last I had found him, gone but still subscribing to the hometown paper, he and Nona.

In New Waverly a woman answered the phone. Yes, she said, this was Bob Morgan's number. I described who I was, his roommate from long ago if this was the Bob Morgan who was in the army during the war.

"He was in the Air Force," she said.

"The Air Force? Not the paratroops?"

"I think you want his uncle," she said. "*He* was in the paratroops."

"Was he ever wounded?"

"I don't know about that. You might ask my husband; he'd know. He'll be home about four."

Where did the uncle live? I asked. He lived in Plano, she said, outside of Dallas, but she used the past tense.

"He doesn't live there anymore?" I said. She was afraid not; he'd died back here a bit.

I felt a sudden, terrible disappointment. There was no real reason. It was just that a distant piece of the shoreline had dropped away. When had it happened? I asked. She wasn't sure. About 1985, she said. After a moment's pause she added, "He committed suicide."

I wanted to know more, I wasn't sure why, and she gave me the name of his sister, who was visiting a niece in Lubbock. I called there and left a message, which they said they would get to her.

Two days later, early in the morning, the phone rang. It was Bob Morgan's sister. I talked to her about him. I had wanted to call his widow, I said, but hadn't known how. "He wasn't married to her when he died," his sister told me. "He divorced her about three years before and married the girl he always wanted to marry, he said, his high school sweetheart."

"Nona?"

"Not Nona. He married Betty," she said. She told me about his children; there were four, two of them his former wife's that he adopted. "So he had two natural children?" No, she said, there was another adopted one, a girl, from an even earlier marriage to a rancher's daughter in New Mexico.

"Actually," she said, "I think he married her as much as anything because he liked her father. He always formed an attachment to older men, ever since his own father was murdered when Bob was, let's see, he must have been about four. I guess he never did get over that."

Their father was murdered by two men, she said. "They knew he was headed for Amarillo to buy some horses, and of course they never heard of a letter of credit or anything like that. They thought he was carrying a lot of money so they robbed and killed him. Actually, he only had forty dollars on him; it was a lifetime rule never to carry more than that, two twenty-dollar bills folded up. There were five of us," she said. "My mother—she was a remarkable woman, I don't know how she did it—was left with five small children, a ten-thousand-dollar estate and twelve thousand dollars of debt, with the Depression just ahead. That was around 1925. She moved us all into an old house and on her own learned to farm and to break horses."

But what had happened to him, at the end?

There was a pause. "I wish I knew," she said. They had some imbalance in the family, they were very sensitive to medication, she explained. It had taken him a long time to get over the medication they treated him with in Italy when he got wounded. Just years. Perhaps he was on some medication again. She only knew that he got ready to go to work one morning and just went into the bathroom and shot himself. He was buried in Spur, she said, in the family plot.

Afterwards I sat thinking about him. I hadn't seen him for half a lifetime and yet I remembered him clearly. His letters always began in a touching way, *My dear Jim*. He'd been a sergeant in a reconnaissance platoon and had heard the colonel remark, unaware he was nearby, that if a single man was commissioned in the field, he wanted it to be Morgan. He was twenty-one at the time but true manliness arrives early. In one of his letters to me he had written, *I have come a long way since I left you, and I regret every step . . .*

THE CAPTAIN'S WIFE

IN THE LATE SUMMER OF 1945, a second lieutenant wearing wings, I walked into the officers' club at Enid, Oklahoma, with Horner. We had driven half the continent with gas coupons begged from truck drivers, occasionally shooting holes in rural road signs with our new pistols. In the club the jukebox was going. They were playing poker. We were part of the Air Force. It was our turn now. It was to be our story, our broad wake, the immense battering noise of the engines just outside the cockpit window of the B-25s we would soon be flying, roaring past the grain elevators that were close to the field. We were a form of gentleman, the sort that strolls along the beach in summer clothes after the shipwreck, making jokes about capsized lifeboats. Our interest was in the prodigious—riotous nights mainly and the emptiness of mornings when we lounged in wrinkled uniforms, recalling late hours and all we had seen and done.

Horner, who had a face that looked as if he might be reformed, given the time, and that was capable of an expression very close to earnestness, I see with a sheet pulled around him, hair awry, and the furious arm of some girl as she awkwardly throws a bottle at him, damn you! It is in the Gayoso or the Carlton, Memphis or perhaps Dallas. Four A.M. and a knock on the door—the bellboy arriving with the unobtainable fifth under his jacket. Whoever it was who said she didn't do things like this is caught standing in bra and panties. "Why, hello, Miss Cole," the boy says politely.

The scene shifts readily, the artistes walk on and off, some making a single appearance, others demanding more, banging on the door in the early hours with their high heels.

Withal there were moments of something else, decency, perhaps, pure amid the disorder—the two WAVES, and the one I was with, though I never saw her again, who came from a world that coolly rebuked ours. Clean-limbed in blue and white, she seemed prepared to like someone I was not ready to be, and I remembered her long after and her town, Green River, Wisconsin. I didn't mention it to Horner, who would have used one of his familiar words: "heartrending." In these matters, as in others, he was dauntless.

———

The end of the war, though not unexpected, came quickly. We were in Austin at the time and aware that something had happened—people were hurrying down the street and crowding in front of a doorway nearby. It was the doorway of a liquor store, and they were preparing for the greatest celebration of their lives, one which, although joining in, we observed with halfhearted enthusiasm. In one bold stroke we were devalued, like currency, and for nearly six months were transferred from field to field, to bases ever more bleak and—the aircraft mechanics having been demobilized—silent.

Horner and I had been separated. He was stationed in Florida, where, in a sudden conversion, like Pascal's, he got married. I was to have been his best man but couldn't get to the wedding. I knew the bride's name, that was all.

We left for overseas that winter, destined for places with storied names that had now become backwaters—defeated nations, abandoned staging points. We sailed from San Francisco in early 1946, beneath the Golden Gate Bridge, from which hung a huge sign we were unable to read. When our troopship had passed it we went to the rear deck, thrilled by the glory of mission at last though gloomy at the timing, and looked back. Facing the Pacific it read: WELCOME HOME, HEROES. It was the era of flight but not jet flight. The Pacific was endless—it took almost forty hours to fly to Japan and fifteen days to sail to Manila. Horner was in a group sent to Europe.

I had achieved, with assistance, a state of emotional nihilism, or had tried to achieve it. It seemed proper. We were going off for three years to the other side of the world with no real idea of what it would be like other than its great distance from home. This spoke for lack of attachment, even fatalism. At the same time, however, like a man with an unwholesome secret, I was in love.

During the final spring, at one of the last hops at West Point— gold buttons, gray trousers with black stripes, young faces, couples possessing the dream—there had been a moment when the crowd of dancers parted to reveal a girl in a black dress with many small slits, like the eyes in a silhouette, and a flesh-colored slip beneath, a girl with beautiful hair and a brilliant smile. She was leaning back from her partner and talking. It was an illumination. It overwhelmed me. They turned and she was visible on the opposite side of him. From the shadow of the balcony which was the running track, wait, that was not it, from the arched doorway that led to the stairs where the stags lingered on the landing, I stepped forward. I walked onto the floor without hesitation, as if I had received a signal, as if on cue. A hundred couples were dancing on the wide wooden floor. Not knowing her, barely knowing her partner, I said, "May I cut in?"

Fortunately I do not remember what else I said, only the confidence with which I took her in my arms and danced. Everything I was and that I was sure she was seemed clear. This close she was even more stunning, magnificent dark brows, fine arms, a touch of coolness in her level gaze. I was elated—she was so clearly the ideal.

I discovered she was a student at Pratt and came from West Newton, a town near Boston. She was not like the brittle New York girls. Deft with my questions, she was more grave, assessing. Physically she was breathtaking, flawlessly made—you can say all you like about soul—and capable of arousing the greatest desire. Poised and somewhat teasing, she was maddeningly discreet about who had invited her up for the weekend and whom she knew. But I had her name and address and in the rush of those final weeks I wrote to her.

After graduation I was able to come to New York more than once to see her. We went to nightclubs, a football game. That I was still in uniform and would stay in uniform was distracting to her. Her own ambitions lay in art. In a year or two she would be working as assistant to a prominent fashion illustrator, wearing the models' clothes and sunbathing on the terrace when he was out. I said those things to her that come from enthusiasm and complete belief. I was in her thrall. I had hardly done more than kiss her, but that winter, as we prepared to board the troopship, it was she I called from California to say goodbye.

There were three other men sailing who were involved with her. I was aware of only one. I had learned his name, and several days out, having waited for an opportunity, I approached him as uneasily as if I were going to ask for a loan. He was at the railing by himself, a lean, romantic type with a rather elegant surname which I will approximate as Demont—I suspected that he knew her better than I did and perhaps in ways I did not. We looked at the sea for a while. As casually as I could, I mentioned her name.

He nodded his head, showing no sign of surprise. As, with an occasional glance at me, he began to talk, I realized I did not figure in his story, either among memories or rivals. I felt like a spy, one who with the greatest luck finds secret papers lying openly on a desk. He had met Toni when she was fifteen, he told me. She had been visiting a cousin in Charleston, West Virginia, where he was from. As he spoke he seemed like a young man from a good family who had fallen in love with an unknown girl who had been sailing by. "She's always had men running after her in droves," he said matter-of-factly.

"What is she like?" I asked. I had a very good idea of what she was like. I had kissed her. I had felt her against me, touched her neck and waist. Peripheral as these things were, I was certain what lay at the core.

She was ambitious, beautiful, heartless, he told me. A good drinker. One night when he was at Napier Field he had called her long distance and proposed for thirty minutes and then gone on leave to New York and stayed there for ten days, begging. He had managed to read some pages in her diary. He saw that there were others, someone named Beezy. *I love him so!* she had written. There was a telegram from him saying he was flying in from Oklahoma (*Love you like mad*) to see her. *I can hardly wait!* she wrote.

All this had crushed Demont. He had given up. She belonged to Neal now, he said—he'd had her up for June Week. Neal was on the ship, but instinct told me not to talk to him, too. In any case, I had decided: I was going to win her.

It took two years. Her love was slowly given and deeply held. One way or another I was able to come back to New York several times. The surprise of having me call. In a low voice she confessed, "I feel all heavy inside." Down Park Avenue we fled in a kind of delirium, on our way to the theater, in a separate cab from my parents', kissing passionately. I would wait outside the fashion illustrator's apartment house and she would come down after work, young and smiling. Everywhere the city welcomed us. We were its renewal, its lyric. Along cool parkways drenched in green I drove to see her in the country, where she had borrowed for a weekend the house of some friends. It was early summer, the road filled with homeward-bound cars. Chappaqua, Campfire Road. The narrow signs are flashing by, the hour of shadow and the last, stunning light. She is waiting on shaded porches, alone in the house. I am flying along the side road, filled with life. Of course, it did not turn out as I foresaw. This was still in the beginning. Bare-shouldered and seemingly interested in other things—the dinner, how to open the wine—she shied away from me all evening. I did not know enough to take her ear in my teeth, so to speak, to hold tightly and force her to be still.

I sent close friends, when they were home from the Pacific, to see her, Crawford, who was gentle and sincere, Rafalko, the great end of the 1943 and 1944 teams. I did not want her to forget me, and there was also the power of all the letters, of being apart, the denied love that reality cannot equal.

I cannot think of it without sadness. I think of the day-long, intimate hours in her apartment with the same record playing over and over, phrases from it like some sort of oath I will know till the day I die. The intensity, the closeness.

For once only are we perfectly equipped for loving. That was the time; she, perhaps, was not the right person or I was not. It is heartbreaking to remember her pleas and her simple words: *I am waiting.*

There is the fever and afterwards the long white mornings, the blankness of recovery. I was in Washington by then, still on the road that led away from her, and among rivals she did not know. She had stopped begging me to let my true desires and real self live. She had written them off, although when love has been etched so fiercely, the scar remains always.

A few years later she married someone. He was away somewhere when I came to see her, one of the last times. My first book had been published; there was money from the sale of it to the movies and we were going to dinner at the Brazilian restaurant next door to her old apartment, where Greta Garbo, she once told me, liked to go.

She was wearing a blue silk dress. The same dark hair, birch-white skin, full mouth, bright teeth. The same goddess's body. We drank, we talked as we used to, but it was not the same, it had been used up. We spent the night in harmony, like two veteran dancers, reunited but no longer lustrous.

She was married to still another man when she died at forty, beautiful and inachieved until the end. She had never had children or fame. Men had always desired her, some I never knew about. As if obedient to her wishes, I had finally turned to the life she always envisioned for me, but too late for the two of us. The years when we might have joined together had passed.

It is in the blizzards of New England that I see her, the snow, the old houses hidden in it, warm window lights. I drive through her town in winter, oak woods, pale sky, a stone boathouse, memories. I think of her mother, her mother's life, when she brought her children east to live, or was it that her mother stayed in California and sent them to an uncle and aunt in West Newton? No matter, there is the pond, gray and ice-coated, and the railroad bridge that she passed on walks, in her girlhood, in her youth and perfection long ago.

———

In the Pacific the war had ended but its vast, shabby landscape remained. In Manila Bay the water was the color of rust from sunken ships. Unidentified masts and funnels were sticking above the surface. Manila was half destroyed; the tops were blown off the palm trees, the roads were ruined, the air filled with dust. There were still rotting helmets and field equipment to be found on Bataan. The licit had disappeared. Theft was an industry, deserters coming into barracks before dawn to steal what they could.

There were incomplete rosters, slack discipline. Men were threatening to shoot officers who were too conscientious. On Okinawa a corporal was driving a nurse around to the black units in an unmarked ambulance. She lay on a bed in back, naked from the waist down. She charged twenty dollars.

I saw MacArthur in the Manila Hotel on Philippine Independence Day. He was thicker around the middle than I had pictured him and shorter, with hair slicked across a balding head. MacArthur was then still a disputed figure, slandered by many who had been under his command and of less interest to me than the fighter pilots met in the latrines of bars and nightclubs who, weaving on their feet, claimed to have been Richard Bong's wingman or possibly McGuire's. Of less interest also than one of my hutmates at Nielsen Field who every night showered, put on fresh khaki, and went off to an enormous dance hall in a once fashionable district, Santa Anna, returning the next morning soiled, unshaven, missing insignia, and smelling faintly of ammonia, which was the approximate odor of Filipino women. I went with him finally. It was a place as big as a field house, seething and crowded, with a full band on a stage at each end and a thousand sergeants, petty officers, and girls sitting at tables.

We were at last sent to squadrons where a few languid oldtimers reigned, secure figures who were on intimate terms with the supply sergeant and knew how everything was done. The fighter pilots went to remote fields in Korea, Japan, and Okinawa. With fifteen or twenty others I was sent to transports and stayed on for a while in Manila, living in corrugated-iron huts that the last of the wartime flyers had abandoned, leaving behind among other things amateur photos of nude Australian girls and addresses scribbled in pencil on the back of instrument cards.

It was not long before, like the onset of a disease, the winnowing began. Word of mouth brought the news—someone had seen someone, someone had heard . . . Men began to disappear. One by one there came the names.

Did you hear about McGranery? they said. Spun in on Palawan in a P-51. Gassman was killed there, too. Jack Ray, always smiling, was killed on Okinawa. Woods crashed in a coral pit on takeoff there and died. The planes had to be flown correctly or they were treacherous; they would stall, one wing dropping abruptly, like a horse stumbling. At low speed, on a go-around, suddenly opening the throttle could make them roll onto their back, the controls unable to prevent it.

Schrader was dead, we heard. MacDonald. Like drops of pelting rain they were exploding in the dust. Averill got killed in Korea, going around in a P-38. Domey was killed; Joe Macur. Cherry got killed; Jim Smart, the streamers curling from his wingtips as he went into the sea.

The accidents. They were the stark trees in the forest that stood alone, at the foot of which nothing thereafter grew. The wreckage of the cities would be cleared away but never the oil slick on the sea that was all they found of Smart. For me, however, it was a siren song—the fierce metal planes with their weathered insignia, the great noise as they launched, the distant runways at Negros, Yontan, Cebu. The danger of it was a distinction which nothing else could afford. It would not happen to you, of course, it would never happen to you, and also, as has been pointed out, you could discover death as quickly by fleeing from it, be stung the soonest.

Mahl, with whom I had flown in primary, was dead in Europe, his funeral was in Paris; Joe Martin, split-"S"ing from fifteen hundred feet in a P-47; Dabney, a unique figure, killed in a crash in Italy, the local people cut the finger from his corpse to get his ring.

Who had been killed—it was that for years. I flew in many funeral formations, timed to pass over the chapel as the officers and wives, the widow among them, emerged, two flights of four, tight as nails, roaring past with one ship conspicuously missing. In the evening the piano is playing at the club. They are rolling dice at the bar. You are surviving, more than surviving: their days have been inscribed on yours.

———

In July 1946, five of us, Farris and I among them, went on to Hawaii. For more than a year I remained, flying transports.

Honolulu in those days was not much changed from the town James Jones described in *From Here to Eternity*. The war had filled it with money and strangers but the social structure and pace were those of a colonial domain, untroubled, remote. Visitors came by sea, on the Matson Line, and usually stayed for a couple of weeks at one of the two big hotels that were on the beach at Waikiki, the Moana or the famous Royal Hawaiian, which during the war had virtually belonged to naval officers on leave. There was a fountain in the lobby that gave forth pineapple juice and musicians strolled beneath the windows in the fragrant darkness. Close by was the private Outrigger Club, a few restaurants and shops, and beyond that the low, sunstruck façades of the tropics.

Hawaii was in many ways a distant province of California and its reputation so romantic that they said, as they did of Tahiti, you left it either crying or drunk. Movie stars were part of its lore. I had a navigator, part Hawaiian, whose beautiful sister had run off to the other side of Oahu with one, hoping to get into the movies in the time-honored way, and their mother had made him follow and humiliatingly retrieve her. He had been a beachboy, this navigator, at the Outrigger, an envied position something above a caddy and beneath a tennis pro. He told me that before the war when the old *Matsonia* sailed they would go from stateroom to stateroom, drinking and saying goodbye, and when the gangplank was raised they would still be aboard. As the ship passed the breakwater they would dive, fully clothed, heaped with leis, from the stern, *aloha*.

Apart from this misty and alluring nonsense there were the little farming communities, the military posts, the expensive homes
out by Diamond Head and up in the hills, the outer islands, and
the sea. The Navy and the Army still possessed some of their
wartime prestige. The brass still mingled with society, which was
beginning to fluff its feathers again after chaotic years.

Sometimes, when visiting Los Angeles, in the vast, mild nights,
I feel the flavor of it again—dancing under the palms, drinks on
the lanai, boxing matches, idleness, summer clothes.

———

It was in Honolulu that I fell hopelessly in love with another
woman. She had a wide mouth and good-looking legs. She'd been
a page at the Ak-Sar-Ben Ball when she was six years old, dressed
in a white satin tunic, long white stockings, and a fez with ostrich
plumes—there was a photograph of it, the costume oddly provocative, in her living room. She told me she'd been brought up by
nursemaids, girls straight off the Nebraska farm who were addressed as "mademoiselle."

We were attracted to one another instantly. We ridiculed one
another and adored one another. She was high-spirited and careless. People always told her they liked the way she talked. She used
words like "heavenly," "intense," "lechers," and "god-awful." Years
later she would quit a job by smiling sweetly and saying to the
boss, "I'll bet I can make you say 'shit,' Mr. Conover." She was a
year older than I was, but at that age it made no difference. She
was also married. Her husband was a captain in the Air Force. He
was to be my best friend.

We had been in the same company at West Point, Leland and
I—that wasn't his name. He was a couple of classes ahead of me,
which is to say worlds. Lighthearted and not very studious, he was
slender with black hair and white skin. He'd been raised in the
army—his father was a general—and they'd lived in Hawaii before

the war. One of his sisters who had died just before her wedding
was buried there, in fact. At the funeral they had played island
songs—*calling to the wanderer to return* . . .

Like a minister's son, Leland was somewhat indifferent to the
gospel. Undistinguished at West Point, a mere cadet sergeant
who didn't bother to polish his shoes and joined formations with
an occasional ballet leap, he had the insouciance of an heir. I
knew little about him then, even in the manner that underlings
know things, and nothing at all of his fiancée until the frantic
June afternoon he graduated and left. On the floor of the basement, unintentionally abandoned, were strewn the intimate love
letters she had written, now being read by everyone, passed from
hand to hand.

He went into the Air Force, was assigned to attack bombers,
A-20s, and was shot down somewhere over Europe and made a
prisoner of war. By the time I saw him again he was a staff officer
in a headquarters at Hickam Field, had a set of quarters, a son
who had been born while he was in prison camp, and a beautiful
wife. I had been at Hickam a few short months when I ran into Leland. Did I play golf? he wanted to know. I began to with him. He
was a wonderful companion on the golf course, graceful and good-
natured. Instead of a kind of reunion it was as if we were meeting
for the first time and taking immediately to each other. I understood only later that he had more or less been looking for me, a
friend to divert him from difficulties that beneath the surface existed at home.

Their house was just behind the headquarters where he
worked—small, company grade, a bit of lawn, the bedrooms upstairs. I entered for the first time one Saturday morning and there
she was, young, greenish gaze, slightly mocking air. There was a
vague mention of breakfast. I asked if there were any eggs.

"Eggs?" she said as if the word were completely novel.

"Poached eggs?" I asked. Which was what they served at the club. From the first moment we were nipping at each other. She gave me a look almost of unexpected admiration. There were no eggs, she said. We ate cold cereal. Paula didn't like to cook, Leland explained to me later. Nor did she like air bases—she loathed them. Going to the commissary was a horror. She looked down on military life, made fun of the army wives who didn't have her so-phistication or style—"they," she called one in particular—and was too clever for bridge. In short, dangerous.

I loved her looks. I liked to talk to her, be in her presence. The situation was perfect. I didn't have to be nervous about it—she was there. And from the beginning I felt she was attracted to me. I began to see them all the time. I don't remember the first physi-cal contact. It was probably at a dance. When we stood up she floated immediately into my arms and her body touched mine with complete familiarity. I finally screwed up my courage enough to tell her, at least discreetly, of my real feelings. If I had met her first I would have married her, I said.

"Funny," she said, "because I'm a little in love with you, too. I was going to tell you tonight."

Before long we were leaving movies early and going off to the warrant officers' club, where no one knew us, to drink and talk. Leland was on duty in the headquarters. When we came out she stopped just past the door and said, "Will you do me a favor?"

"Yes. What?"

She raised her face. "Will you kiss me?"

Leland was too prosaic for her. I knew it and she told it to me. Suddenly I was painfully aware of the meaning of possession. The unseen privileges of the marriage bed, the intimacies of dressing and undressing, clothes in the same closet, a woman brushing her hair, putting on stockings—these were performances I tried not to think of. I had felt this once before but not so strongly. There had been one married couple among us in Salt Lake City when we lived for a month in a hotel there. She was blonde and unhurried and you could smell her perfume. After dinner in the hotel or a nearby restaurant she and her husband would go up to their room and in the morning, sometimes, come down for breakfast.

There was a poem of Scott Fitzgerald's that we wallowed in:

> *In the fall of sixteen*
> *In the cool of the afternoon*
> *I met Helena*
> *Under a white moon—*

It was our poem, Paula's and mine. We shared a taste for books and sentimental lines. Leland shrugged at it. He didn't have that particular weakness. He was rather like an English aristocrat, a man of decency, little sensitivity, and certain prejudices. The things he knew he knew very well, and they were social things: on which side the guest of honor sat at dinner, how to carve a roast, tie a dress tie, which shoes were best, which clubs. When Paula and I fell in love he overlooked it, for her happiness and to keep her, I suppose, and probably because he was sure of me. He himself was not the sort of man to be unfaithful or to find distraction in affairs, and besides there was little opportunity—he didn't have a job in which he traveled much, and post life was intimate; anything seen was quickly known, especially if repeated. He was completely uxorious—his marriage was his life just as his uniform was, his golf shoes, his good name. The overwhelming attraction between his wife and friend would eventually die down, he had to believe that. Meanwhile we lived as three, or nearly, the house charged with a force I did my best to appear unaware of, and more than once he carried her upstairs as she waved wistfully to me over his shoulder.

We had dinner, we went to places in town, to the club. It had to be obvious. At a party in Kahala she sat by me, talked to me, and smiled so tellingly at me I was sure that everyone knew what was happening. She pressed against me and, as if no one could see it, squeezed my hand.

"I dreamed of you last night," she said to me. "Wildly. I feel particularly close. Oddly enough," she added, "I dream of you all the time."

Meanwhile at bingo games Leland sat sulkily throwing beans at her across the table.

"You're getting into my dress, Leland."

He, doggedly: "Isn't that where I'm supposed to be?"

And she and I would dance and whisper our deepest confessions. She hadn't slept with him for three months, she told me, it was a crisis anyhow. "I dread nightfall," she said.

"Paula is in love with you," a mutual friend told me. I didn't know what to do. I loved her passionately and I knew I would never find a woman like her again.

She could divorce him, but it would not be that easy. Divorce was a rarity in the society in which we lived. Besides, we were trusted. Afterwards, where would we go? A general's wife told her a story about a well-known officer. He was stationed on the same post with a married woman named Eleanor Farrow. Her husband had to leave on a trip for two months and asked him as a friend to drop by and cheer his wife up while he was gone. The upshot was that when the husband returned, his wife asked him for a divorce. Farrow finally agreed, but with a condition: that she never see her little daughter again. She gave in and married the other officer. Of course, the general's wife continued pointedly, they weren't accepted in Hawaii after that and had to leave. After some years the wife died. Their son, who became a famous officer himself, used to say that his mother had died of a broken heart because she could never see her first child.

That was another thing, Paula's son. He was well over a year old and they were having difficulties with him—something was wrong. He would not learn to talk or behave. It turned out that he was deaf—he had lost his hearing before birth as a result of Paula having German measles early in her pregnancy. There was also a heart defect. He would need more and more care, although we hardly thought of that—we were dealing only with today and to-morrow. I was not yet twenty-two. I had spent four years in a prep school, three more in military school. In the words of the epigram, I was magnificently unprepared for life.

"You know, you're really stupid," another officer's wife said to me.

We were driving back from a party. I had been her escort—her husband, a classmate of Leland's, was away. She'd been drinking. She was tall, in her lustrous twenties, the neck of her evening dress cut low.

"You don't understand anything, do you?" she said.

"Some things," I said warily.

"No, you don't."

Her hand was on my leg. Paula and Leland were in the back seat. This woman was the wife of their friend, and I didn't know what she would say, I was afraid it was going to be some terrible, drunken truth. I could feel her looking at me as I drove.

"How is it you're so stupid? I thought you were supposed to be smart." I realized Paula was watching, amused. I caught a glimpse of her in the rearview mirror. The woman had moved closer. Her head was in my lap. "You're not very smart. You don't even know what I'm saying," she mumbled.

"Yes, I do."

"Well, then?"

It wasn't the right time, I said. The time? The right time, I said. She gave a moan of impatience. "Have it your own way," she said, "I don't care. Have it any way you want to"—she raised her head partway—"but for God's sake, have it!"

I felt like a fool. I was made fun of afterwards but I didn't mind.

It was the same thing later with a navy nurse from Pearl Harbor—
she was a lieutenant commander; I went with her to prove how
mature I was, and then with the daughter of a coast artillery
colonel to show some sense of propriety. The colonel's daughter
was blonde and lively. *The Treasure of the Sierra Madre* had just
come out, and she liked to call herself "Fred C. Dobbs." One night
we went to Trader Vic's and then for a midnight swim at one of the
little beaches past Waikiki. We lay down in innocence for a few
minutes in the darkness beneath the palms, and suddenly someone was shaking me and shining a light in my eyes—it was the
morning sun.

I drove her home just before going to work. Half an hour later
the telephone rang; her father wanted to see me. I went over at the
end of the day. She met me outside and told me what had happened—they had taken her to a doctor for an examination.

"And?"

"Of course, I'm all right," she said with relief.

A doctor. I couldn't believe it. She shrugged. She had long
blonde hair and pretty shoulders. We hadn't even been swimming
in the nude.

All these things I told to Paula. I was going out partly to enter-
tain her and also I didn't want to seem too tame. I was in a troop
carrier squadron and I had another, in fact a primary, life. We flew
to Hilo every day and Kauai twice a week, and there were irregular
trips to Australia, Japan, or one of the dots of islands in the south,
usually with double crews. Distances were greater then. Setting
off for Sydney or New Caledonia meant being gone for a week.
Flying hours were what was sought, either on routine flights or the
long ones, when it came in large, sedentary servings. There were
very few crashes. With native boys we walked at night in the knee-
high surf of distant islands, the sea warm and pulling, hunting for
lobsters, reaching down to grab them with gloved hands. That is
what one remembers, the rain, the solitude, the dampness, and of

course the longing, stepping outside the ramshackle buildings late at night wondering what they were doing elsewhere, in Honolulu or at home.

———

As the tide receded there had come back from the farthest reaches the last of the men who had gone out in wartime, some of whom landed in Hawaii.

From Shanghai, with a small "v" in his front teeth and a defiant jaw, came a nonrated major whom I first met playing cards. His name was something like O'Mara. He was in his mid-thirties and had the jaunty style of a bootlegger, gray already streaking his wavy black hair. He became the figure one finds in European books, my tutor. He flicked his cards across the table with a snap and smoked a cigar in the center of his mouth, holding it with two fingers above and a thumb below. In these as in other things, I imitated him. I was a choirboy to him, someone from a privileged neighborhood, and he set about showing me, without formal instruction, the way to act and talk.

How little one knows or cares about the background of idols. He knew military matters much better than I did, regulations and articles of war—he had been an adjutant and his expertise was irrefutable. In Shanghai he had won a large amount of money, twenty-five thousand dollars they said, then worth ten times what it is now. He did not dispute the figure. He had brand-new golf clubs, a camel's-hair coat, and a Cadillac convertible. What I admired more than all this, however, was the impression he gave of a man who could face any odds.

We went often to town. He was going with the young wife of a navy pilot who was away in Kwajalein on extended duty. She was going to divorce him. She and O'Mara were going to have children, lots of them. "Five or six," he agreed, moving his hand upwards in stages to show their height. Off they would drive in the soft, tropical night. She lived in quarters somewhere, Kaneohe probably, with the unfamiliar cream-colored car parked outside until first light of day.

Things run in cycles, and I did not know, and perhaps neither did he, that he had already gone through the best of his luck. In the nipa huts behind the officers' club he drew losing hands and would disdainfully scoop up his cards and flip them over, face down. He had a wife in Philadelphia from whom he was estranged, someone he had mistakenly married in youth, before the great days. I heard occasional vague remarks; I don't think I ever knew her name or saw a photograph. We were smoking Bankers and Brokers, skipping the club dances, and meeting every evening after work, sometimes not emerging from the huts before morning, having played all night.

The joy of meeting him, of seeing him walk unconcerned down the path—he was like the owner of a racing stable, in precarious shape, as it turned out, who had come up from nothing, and for a time I more or less wore his silks. Not officially, of course—I had a future. I was a lieutenant and he a major but my rank had weight. I was a regular. I had become a general's aide. Through me he touched inner circles and legitimacy. He liked to hear stories about West Point, the visit of the president of Brazil, the saber accidentally left stuck in the ground after the parade had passed.

When not with him I would hurry to the quarters where Leland and Paula lived. Off we would go to the Hale Kalani, the Ala Wai Club, Gibson's, or Elmer Lee's. Leland knew Elmer Lee from before the war, he used to surf with him. Elmer Lee would come to the table.

"How's your *umalima*, Elmer?" Leland asked.

"What's that?"

"You know." Leland put his elbow on the table and pretended to arm-wrestle.

"Oh, no. I got to learn the language all over. I thought it was something else."

The nightclubs and restaurants, The Willows, and La Hula Rumba. Chun Hoon's. More than once Leland was passed out in the car.

The current was pulling faster and faster. Nothing is as intense as unconsummated love. She was married to the wrong man. He was decent, loyal, understanding, though he would never really understand her. He was also finally jealous. When he returned quivering like a bull, she supposed, from one particular trip, she would have to calm him by being "very wifely and submissive." The words made me tremble.

She had been so young when she married. It had been a kind of accident. She was then and would become an independent woman who drank, liked people with money, was scornful, and could charm anyone she chose to. You are the one, she said, why hadn't she met me? Why hadn't I met her? *It would have been so easy,* I wrote,

> *Could have been,*
> *For every place you were*
> *He came to later,*
> *You could trace his footsteps*
> *To the same*
> *Hop, hotel, or football game . . .*

"Read it again," she said to me.

When we didn't see each other we spoke for hours over the phone. Across the hall in the rickety bachelors' quarters a friend of mine had a phone I could use. It would have been impossible to use the common one downstairs and carry on the low-voiced, endless conversations.

I flew my first fighter, a P-47—big engine throbbing slowly as I taxied, hard tires jolting on the concrete—out over the base softball game and all of Honolulu, and when I landed, proud of myself and my sweat-darkened flying suit, went right to their house. "My God," Paula said, "I've never seen you look so pale."

I would die in a crash, I knew, without ever having made love to her. There is that certainty of a woman who was made for you just as Eve was for Adam. On my dresser was a photograph taken at their engagement party, laughing, joyous, filled with life, the best one of her I had ever seen. She had made Leland bring it over to me one day. She was ready to give anything, do anything, and we were held apart by all that was drawing us together: honor, conscience, ideals. There was no way out.

We used to take our planes, the four-engine transports, back to the States for major inspections and modifications. On one of the trips I went to Los Angeles for the first time and in the late afternoon, driving along Sunset Boulevard, was passed by a convertible with the top down. There were three or four people in it and one of them—she turned and I saw her clearly—was a girl I had been infatuated with in high school. I was in uniform and called out and waved. I saw her wave back but then whoever was driving the car sped up and cut through the traffic. I couldn't catch them. I watched her disappear down the silky road and vanish around a curve, it was near Bel Air. The world of schooldays and youthful dreams from which I had never really separated myself had suddenly passed me by and gone. I was in a new world, a more serious world, in which love was even stronger and more consuming.

II

It didn't end as I expected. The fever never broke as Leland had hoped, but Paula, sensing something perhaps, the impossibility of our situation, the hopelessness of pretending, put her mark on me in another way, a very feminine way, I came to see later, subtle, lasting, sure. She chose for me the girl I ought to marry, whom I

had met one afternoon in the courtyard of the Moana, Ann Alte-
mus, good-looking, unspoiled, very much of her class, which was
minor society, she was from the horse country in Virginia. Her
father owned a big farm near Warrenton. She was perfect for me,
Paula said, exactly the kind of girl I needed. I believed her. Who
else loved me as much or knew me as well? What she did not say
was that she saw someone she knew she could be friendly with
and who would not be a threat to her.

We were all stationed in Washington together for a year and a
half, and not long afterwards I stood at the altar in the chapel at
Fort Meyer with my wife-to-be. We had more or less strolled into
marriage. Our parents—her father and my mother—disapproved.
They did not understand that the rest of the world was pleased
with the idea. We, too. I knew, as one does, that she saw life as I
did but felt misgivings at the solemnity of the vows. To myself I
said, "Five years." Paula and Leland were there—he was my best
man. The reception was in their little house in Georgetown. Paula
held her new baby in her arms, a little girl, and my wife and I drove
off in a dashing yellow MG, stopping for the first, uneasy night in
some nameless motel on the road to Florida.

———

After I left Honolulu I saw O'Mara only once. It was in Valdosta,
Georgia. He was driving through and came to dinner. We were stationed there, living in an apartment above the two spinsters who
were our landladies and watched all comings and goings from the
parlor below. I had been promoted but I could see I had fallen in
O'Mara's estimation, settled into predictable life with a woman
who obviously did not take to him and was not stimulated by the
things we were remembering. It was not that I had lost promise
but rather, he must have felt, that I had been bridled. It was a
friendly evening, but uninspired.

Later I heard he had gotten into trouble. Through cards he had lost his car and the beautiful golf clubs. He'd been at Kelly Field in an administrative job, feared and disliked, a martinet and, what seemed to say everything, an inconstant one, polished and immaculate one day, unshaven and inexplicably rumpled the next. So he passed from sight.

———

When our first child came she was named for Leland and he was her godfather. As couples we were living far apart by then. Leland was an attaché in South Africa. It was a great bore, Paula thought, but they traveled and had a certain status. *We adored Rome. After a brief tour I am feeling extremely cultured and so annoyed with Nero.*

I was assigned to a headquarters in Germany. Paula's letters had beautiful stamps with animals on them. *Everybody is a lieutenant colonel,* she wrote, *I love you.* We saw them once or twice in Europe—once they drove up from Paris to visit. He was the same, cordial, more moody perhaps, the lines deeper in his face, a glass more often in his hand. They were giving each other false little smiles. They had come to a rocky part of marriage, but we knew they would continue together. They were bound by children, friends, career—everything that had once stood between Paula and me. It was the long journey that held them together. It was good sense, plus all they had lived through.

———

They were divorced in 1959, two years after our second child was born. It was Paula who insisted on the divorce—she must have been young and happy once but she couldn't remember, she said. Leland was shattered by it. He married again soon after. She did not, and we once more drew close. By then I was out of the Air Force. She came up from Washington frequently and we went there. *A sudden burst of missing you unbearably,* she wrote. There

were three of us again, and it was still she and I who were inti-
mates, excluding the other. When she was visiting I would come
back in the evening and find two women, both amiable, smiling,
sitting on cushions on the floor and waiting for me. We would
drink and have dinner at a low table in front of the fire. She would
tell stories of dates with other men, or the lack of them, just as I
had once done with her. Someone had a man they wanted her to
meet. Unrewarding adventure—he brought his sister along, they
were obviously in love with each other, and it looked like a long affair, she added. She worked for a while on Capitol Hill, then for a
foundation, then a boutique, and wrote for *The Washington Star.*
For years she had an off-and-on relationship with the alcoholic
son of an old family she and Leland had been fond of, but she was
too intelligent to marry him. Finally she met the man she was
looking for, a journalist, divorced, urbane. He and I seemed to
have limited interest in one another, or perhaps he felt her interest should end. In any event, the curtain descended.

I saw Leland once more. It was in 1961 during the Berlin crisis.
As a reserve, I'd been sent to France. Leland was stationed at
Fontainebleau and one weekend I drove up there. He, his wife,
and I had dinner. It was as always—at the last minute there wasn't
enough food in the house and he and I went out in the evening
dark for some hasty shopping, a bottle of wine, meat, some cheese.
He was in fine spirits and on good terms with the shopkeepers. I
was impressed that he knew the French word for "wedge," as in
"wedge of Camembert." He spoke good French. He called his wife
darling. Somehow I didn't believe it.

He retired as a colonel and they went to live in the south of
Spain. I had news of him only rarely. I imagined him as he had always been: a perfect companion on the links, drinker in the bar afterwards, the heels on his loafers a bit worn down. Like an
unimaginative British officer in some remote town, but knowing
exactly who was who and what their business was.

Then I heard he was dead. It was completely unexpected. He hadn't been ill. The night before they had gone out to dinner and played bridge with friends. In the morning he couldn't be wakened.

I called Paula. I hadn't spoken to her for a long time—she was living near Palm Beach. Yes, it was true, she said. She seemed undisturbed by it. There was some Spanish law that a body had to be buried within twenty-four hours, and because arrangements to fly him home couldn't be made in time, he was buried there, in Spain. A memorial service was being held in Washington but she wasn't going up for it; she would not look back.

A SINGLE DARING ACT

Late in the summer of 1951 I entered at last the realm long sought and was sent to Presque Isle, Maine, to the 75th Fighter Squadron.

The operations officer, distinguished by having had his photograph, while fighting in Korea, on the cover of *Life*, had been killed in an accident a few days before I arrived. What the history of the squadron was I did not know and was not told. Its tradition was embodied for me by the new operations officer, a plump Southerner, lying on the floor of a bar in town, too drunk to stand but still animatedly talking to and later borne from the place by his admiring pilots. It was he who gave me my first jet rides. His equipment always looked as if it had been borrowed—helmet oddly perched on his head, flying suit too small and deeply pinched by parachute harness—but he was an experienced pilot, the stick held daintily in his stubby hand. It was September. The heat had never died. Flies were trying to come indoors for the winter and a pennant race that turned out to be the most famous ever was going on. In a car parked out near the runway my wife waved congratulations as I taxied in alone in the trainer for the first time.

I felt I was born for it. One of the initial things I did when I went up without a chase plane in an F-86 was climb to altitude and shut the engine off. The sky was suddenly flooded with silence, the metal deadweight. Calmly, though my fingers were tingling, I went through the steps to restart it, air start, it was called. Afterwards I did it again. I wanted to be confident of the procedure in case of a flame-out, and following that I never thought of them with dread.

The true hierarchy was based on who was the best pilot and who flew the most. There might be an obvious leader or two or three near equals. One quickly sensed who they were. In addition there were those who had flown in combat. Their stories were listened to more attentively. There was a big, overconfident pilot in another squadron who starred in one of the first I heard. He had flown F-80s, the earliest jet, in Korea. He was coming back from a mission one day, leading his flight home, at thirty thousand feet on top of an overcast. He called radar for a vector, "Milkman, this is Maple Lead." Milkman answered, identified the flight on the radar screen, and gave them heading and distance to their field, which was K-2: One hundred and seventy degrees and a hundred and twenty miles.

The flight was low on fuel and the weather deteriorating. They would have to make an instrument approach, the leader knew. He called his element leader for a fuel check, "What state, Three?"

The fuel gauge on the F-80 had a small window where the pilot set in the number of gallons he had at takeoff, and thereafter, like an odometer in reverse, they clicked off during the flight. "Sixty gallons, Lead," the element leader replied.

"No sweat."

The clouds were solid. They could see nothing. After a while the radar station gave them another steer, still one hundred and seventy degrees, ninety-five miles.

"How are you doing, Three?"

"Forty-two gallons."

"Roger."

The ships, not far apart, could do nothing to affect one another though they shared a common fate. There was no need to speak. Silent minutes passed. The gallons fell away.

"Milkman, Maple Lead. Where do you have us now?"

"Stand by one, Maple Lead. We have you . . . steer one eight zero to home plate, sixty-six nautical miles."

"Roger. Sixty-six out. Will you inform K-2 that we're in the soup, low on fuel? We'll be declaring an emergency." Then, to the element leader, "What do you have, Three?"

"Twenty-four gallons."

That was six or seven minutes of flying at altitude, throttled back to minimum cruise, but they also had to let down, make an approach, line up with the runway if they could find it. The heads in the cockpits were motionless, as if nothing of interest were going on, but they were facing the unalterable. The wingmen might have even less fuel than the element leader. After a while the flight leader called again, "Milkman, Maple. How far are we out?"

"We have you thirty-four miles out, Maple flight."

"Roger." He looked over at the element leader, who was perhaps fifty feet away. "What do you have now, Brax?"

"I've got nine hundred ninety-eight gallons, buddy," the reply came calmly.

Not long afterwards, one by one, they ran out of fuel. The entire flight dead-sticked onto the runway at K-2.

It was among the knowledgeable others that one hoped to be talked about and admired. It was not impossible—the world of squadrons is small. The years would bow to you; you would be remembered, your name like a thoroughbred's, a horse that ran and won.

———

In November, in northern Maine, you might see two of them from far off, at the end of the runway set amid the fields. They are barely identifiable, early F-86s with thin, swept wings. Nearer there is the sound, wavering but full, like a distant cataract. Then, close, it becomes a roar with the smoke billowing up behind. They are being run up, engines full open, brakes on, needles trembling at their utmost.

The pilot of the first airplane has his head bent forward over the instruments as if examining them closely. Red-haired, gaunt, he had so far said almost nothing to me. His name was Stewart. I knew little about him. He was a Korean veteran and a maintenance officer. Lined up beside him, I waited. Why do you remember some things above all others and men who have hardly spoken a word to you? I was new in the group and nervous. I was determined to fly good formation, to be a shadow, almost touching him. We were taking off just before sunset. No one else would be flying.

His head rose then and turned towards me. His hand came up and hesitated. I nodded. The hand dropped.

Wreathed in thunder we started down the runway. Gathering speed I saw his arm suddenly swinging wildly in a circle. I had no idea what it meant, was I to go on, was he aborting? In a moment I saw it was neither, only exhilaration; he was waving us onward as if whipping a bandana around in the air. The noses came up; we were at liftoff speed. I saw the ground fall away and from that moment for him I ceased to be.

There was a low overcast through which we shot, and above it brilliant reddening sky. I was barely twenty feet from him but he never so much as glanced at me. He sat in the cockpit like a prophet, alone and in thought, head turning unhurriedly from side to side. We had reached thirty thousand feet when the tower called. Weather was moving in, our mission had been canceled. "Operations advises you return to base," they said.

"Roger," I heard him say matter-of-factly. "We'll be in after a few minutes. We're going to burn out some petrol."

With that he rolled over and, power on, headed straight down. I didn't know what he intended or was even doing. I fell into close trail, hanging there grimly as if he were watching. The airspeed went to the red line; thousands of feet were spinning off the altimeter. The controls grew stiff, the stick could be moved only with great effort as we went through rolls and steep turns at speeds so great I could feel my heart being forced down from my chest.

We burst through the overcast and into the narrow strip of sky beneath. I'd moved to his wing again. We were well over five hundred knots at about fifteen hundred feet. It was almost impossible to stay in position in the turns. I had both hands on the stick. All the time we were dropping lower. We were not moving, it seemed. We were fixed, quivering, fatally close.

Five hundred feet, three hundred, still lower, in what seemed deathly silence except for an incandescent, steady roar, in solitude, slamming every moment against invisible waves of air. He was leading us into the unknown. My flying suit was soaked, the sweat ran down my face. A pure pale halo formed in back of his canopy and remained there, streaming like smoke. I began to realize what it was about. Never looking at me, absorbed by the instruments in front of him and by something in his thoughts, sometimes watching the world of dark forest that swept beneath us, hills and frozen lakes, he was gauging my desire to belong. It was a baptism. This silent angel was to bring me to the place where, wet and subdued, I would be made one with the rest. If, like a scrap of paper held out the window of a speeding train, my airplane were to instantly come apart, torn bits tumbling and fluttering behind, he would only have begun a large, unhasty turn to see what had happened, his expression unchanged.

I had surrendered myself to all of it and to whatever might come when unexpectedly he turned towards the field. We had already crossed it two or three times. This time we entered on initial approach and dropped dive brakes, slowing as we turned. I had a feeling of absolute control of the airplane. It was tamed, obedient. I could have gently tapped his wing with mine, I felt, and not left a dent. I could have followed him anywhere, through anything.

I remember that moment and the smoothness of landing in the fading light. Now that the sound of our passing violently overhead had disappeared, on the field all was still. There was unbroken calm. Our idling engines had a high-pitched, lonely whine.

Afterwards he said not a word to me. The emissary does not stoop to banter. He performs his duty, gathers his things, and is gone. But the snowy fields pouring past beneath us, the terror, the feeling of being for a moment a true pilot—these things remained.

————

My closest friend in the squadron, a classmate, had hair flecked with gray and a wry way of talking that I liked. William Wood was his name. He was older—he'd been perhaps twenty when we became cadets, and afterwards had gone right into fighters; he'd been in them since the beginning. He was relaxed and could be very droll.

Early that winter, he and I went to Korea. We had eagerly read—it passed from hand to hand—the first definitive report, a sort of letter about the enemy airplanes that had suddenly appeared in the war, Russian planes, MIG-15s, and when the chance came, like men running to a claims office, we had raced to volunteer. There were two openings that month and we got them. It was not only the report, the war itself was whispering an invitation: Meet me. Whatever we were, we felt inauthentic. You were not anything unless you had fought.

Come now, and let us go and risk our lives unnecessarily. For if they have got any value at all it is this that they have got none. We arrived in Korea, as it happened, on a gloomy day. It was February, the dead of winter, planes parked among sandbag revetments and bitter cold lying over the field adding to the pall. The ranking

American ace—mythic word, ineffaceable—a squadron commander named Davis, had just been shot down. With the terrible mark of newness on us, we stood in the officers' club and listened to what was or was not fact. We were too fresh to make distinctions. We had come, it turned out, to join a sort of crude colonial life lived in stucco buildings in plain, square rooms, unadorned, with common showers and a latrine that even the wing commander shared.

We were there together for six months, cold winter mornings with the weak sunlight on the hills, the silvery airplanes gliding forth like mechanical serpents not quite perfected in their movement and then forming on the runway amid rising sound. In the spring the ice melted in the rivers and the willows became green. The blood from a bloody nose poured down over your mouth and chin inside the rubber oxygen mask. In summer the locust trees were green and all the fields. It comes hauntingly back: silent, unknown lands; distant brown river, the Yalu, the line between two worlds.

That first night they were talking about the MIGs, how good they were, how superior at altitude. Whatever anyone said we accepted as truth. I stayed close to Wood, as if to suggest we were equals. The group commander, an older, admired figure—Preston was his name—was there. He had been leading the fatal mission on which Davis, with only a wingman, had attacked a large formation of MIGs. He'd gotten the leader and then slowed down to try for one more. He was successful but it killed him. He was hit just behind the cockpit by cannon fire from still another airplane. The last victory was his twelfth.

Fighters don't fight, as St.-Exupéry said, they murder. He did not fly one himself—he spoke as their possible victim, which in the end he became. He was flying a reconnaissance plane when it happened, unarmed and relying only on speed, though they are never quite that fast. He was too old for the war and too civilized.

The fighter aces had names like Adolph and Sailor, Ginger and Don. They had five or more kills and appeared suddenly and unseen, in the first terrifying seconds letting loose a stream of fire. A kind of blood poured from the plane being hit—black smoke really, but it foretold everything. Pieces of metal were flying off, the whole carefully constructed machinery was coming apart miles above the earth, shedding wings, hurtling out of control.

At Pointe de la Baumette on the southern coast of France there is a lighthouse with a tablet recording the end of St.-Exupéry. He disappeared in July 1944, his aircraft one of the many simply lost without trace in the great sweep of the war. Blue sea of glittering beauty, the sea on which Cervantes fought and where history was born—somewhere within it lie the bones of this secular saint.

We were replacements, new wingmen—fighters fly always in pairs—and it would not be long before we too were sleek for murder, crammed with gear into the cockpit, like overcoated gangsters in limousines, high above North Korea in the late afternoon, the sun low, the ground lost in reflection and haze. Farther and farther north we go. "Dentist" is the call sign of the ground radar. Nothing is being reported by them yet. Cautious voices in the dusk in a sky that is ominously empty.

———

Just as, they say, in North Africa during the war the thing to have immediately to hide your innocence was desert boots, so the first requirement of a pilot in Korea was a folding plastic-covered map of the long peninsula that projected down from China into the Yellow Sea, the muddy Yalu its northern border, the spattering of numerous islands, and midway, the enemy capital, Pyongyang. Over the area of North Korea we drew a fan of lines, all converging on our base. This gave headings, especially to home. Arcs of distance crossed these vectors to show at a glance how far you had gone or had to go.

From the front lines, which crossed the country at the waist, it was about two hundred miles, twenty-five minutes or so, to the river and only a few more to the enemy fields in China, where we were forbidden to go. There was no struggle for possession of the air. Like a backroom deal, that had already been decided. The MIGs entered the sky over North Korea at will, fought if they chose to, and went back to their fields. We were trying to exterminate the enemy, but even the boy who mows the lawn knows that you do not kill wasps one by one, you destroy the nest. The nests, however, were not to be touched. Everything in between was contested.

We sought to keep them from attacking our fighter-bombers that were heading north, laden and often low-flying, to cut railroads and bomb bridges. We did not escort but patrolled instead. The noses of the MIGs were sometimes yellow, afterwards red, then purple, then black.

It turned out that this was because their ideas were the opposite of ours. We had only two wings of air-to-air fighters in Korea and they remained there, replenished constantly with pilots to keep them up to strength. Thus there were always veterans with eighty or ninety missions and brave boys ready to scatter who had none, plus the in-betweens. The Russians—they were mainly Russians—whom we fought moved entire air regiments through, probably to initiate as many of them as possible. They would arrive with very little experience and leave three or four months later, battle-hardened. But it meant they were all bathed in innocence at the same time and learned together, and this proved costly.

What occurred in the rest of the war meant little to us. There remains with me not the name of a single battle of the time or even general other than Van Fleet, who had an honest face and the history of having risen, like Grant, belatedly, a colonel in Normandy when his classmates were commanding corps—Van Fleet and of course Ridgway.

In the sky were weather and widely separated operations conducted by the Navy, Marines, and Air Force. We had little to do with one another. It was only in the headquarters, approached on rutted roads and the dusty, tree-shaded avenues of Seoul, in the theatrical evening briefings with the commander sitting silverhaired, stars on his collar, smoking a cigar and in a woman's voice saying thank you after each presentation, that orchestration took place. Here were all the strikes, targets, losses—everything a general might need to know.

War is so many things. It is an opportunity to see the upper world, great houses that have become hospitals or barracks, precious objects sold for nothing, families with ancient names at the mercy of quartermaster sergeants. In the familiar footage the guns jump backwards as they fire, the tanks roll past and forgotten men wave. It is all this and also the furnace of the individual in a way that a life of labor is not. Its demands are unending, its pleasures cruel. Goya knew them, and Thucydides, and Isaac Babel. One morning there is the wonderful smell of breakfast, and on the next the sudden arrest and hasty sentencing. The fate that seemed impossible, the justice Lorca knew. He could not cry out, I am a poet! They know he is an intellectual, or worse. They put him in a truck and he rides, with others and without a shred of hope, to an outlying district, where he is handed a shovel and told to dig. It is his grave he is digging, and in silence, the silence he will soon be part of, he begins, who was raised in this country, who became its very voice. *Death laid eggs in the wound,* he once wrote, *at five in the afternoon. From far off the gangrene is coming, at five in the afternoon. His wounds were burning like suns, at five in the afternoon, and the crowd was breaking the windows* . . . In his grip is the smooth wooden handle, and the first shovelful of earth is one of the most precious moments of his life, if only it could last. But in war nothing lasts and the poets are killed together with the farm boys, the flies feast on their faces.

For us it was simple and always the same: Who was scheduled, what was the weather, what had the earlier missions seen?

———

The first morning light over the top of the wing. The first, easy missions. Out of the dust of memory, with a faint coating of dust himself, childlike, shrewd, comes Amell, the squadron commander.

A name is a destiny. It is the first of all poems. Even after death it keeps its power; even half-buried in newsprint or dirt, something catches the eye. Paavo Nurmi had such a name. So did Jean Genet; a stunt pilot named Lamont Pry; the Swedish Match King; a small-time fascist, Adrian Arcaud—I am beginning to portray an era—and in the huge graveyard my toe kicks up another: Zane Amell.

I don't remember how I first saw him. He remains fixed, in any event, as in a photograph, with a fur hat like a cossack and a navy revolver in a holster under his arm. He had a husky, somewhat thespian voice. As an actor his speeches tended to be slightly long, although he could be succinct on occasion. One morning on leave, arriving back in Tokyo in a staff car, in a wrinkled uniform and reeking of alcohol, he was awakened by the Japanese driver and asked if there was some particular place he would like to be dropped. "Yes," Amell answered hoarsely.

"Where?"

"Anywhere," he muttered and fell back asleep.

His first words to me that I recall were at a briefing. I was flying as his wingman on my second combat mission. The task of a wingman can be easily described: it is to stay with the leader and to look, especially behind—almost all danger comes from there. I knew I was being tried out. I was ready for advice or words of warning. As the aircraft numbers were written next to our names, he commented genially, "Great. You have old No Go, and I've got the Guzzler." They were two of the oldest and slowest airplanes, but he didn't have them changed.

I was fearful as we climbed in the cold air, the planes bobbing slightly. Perhaps it was the day I saw my first MIG, silver, passing above us, complete in every strange detail, silent as a shark. There were many in the air that day. They were coming from the north in flight after flight, above us. I remember how helpless and alone I felt. My throat was burning as I breathed.

His eyes were bad. They used to say that if anyone had the chances Amell had, they would have shot down ten airplanes—he ended up with three victories and a wingman drenched in flame who went down one day near Sinuiju. As I think now of his eyes, they seem to me small but like those of traders or old policemen, wise. In the air you heard his grating voice and assurance, like a man stepping blithely into traffic looking the wrong way. He liked to drink and was given to extravagant gestures.

Perhaps there is a price for insouciance, but I did not see him pay it. A few years later, in Michigan, he swerved off the runway while landing to avoid planes coming the other way. The ground was soft, however, and he flipped over and was killed.

———

Speed was everything. If you had speed you could climb or overtake them and, more important, not be easily surprised. You could rid yourself of speed quickly in a number of ways, but to obtain it, especially in the instant it was needed, was impossible.

By subsequent standards these were uncomplicated airplanes, but they could fly above forty-five thousand feet and, going straight down, flirt with the speed of sound. There was a second red needle on the airspeed indicator that moved to mark the limit beyond which you were not supposed to fly though we often did, the needles crossed by thirty or forty knots, usually at low altitude or in a dive, the ship bucking and trying to roll. "On the Mach"—the absolute limit and a favorite phrase.

The difference between our planes and theirs was in most ways insignificant, but in one, crucial. They had cannon—the maw of a MIG seemed swollen and menacing. We had machine guns, which were almost feminine in comparison; the skin of the ship had faint gouges, like the imprint of a spoon, near the nose where the guns poked through. There were six of them. The cannon shells were as big around as a drinking glass and the damage they could do was severe. Machine-gun bullets, on the other hand, were the size of a finger or wine cork. It was the sledgehammer versus the hose. The hose was more flexible and could be adjusted quickly. The slower-firing cannon could not; you could almost say, Oh, God, between the heavy, glowing shots. Once machine guns had their teeth in something, they chewed rapidly.

We test-fired on the way north, a brief squeeze with the switches on. The trigger was on the stick and the safety pin for it, with a red streamer attached, in one of your pockets. Now it was all real; it had only been a picture before, the familiar one of a formation hung in vacant sky. There were only eleven seconds' worth of ammunition altogether. A burst in a fight might last two or three. The secret was simple: get in close, as close as possible, within fifty feet if you could, so close you could not miss.

Often at dawn, drifting across to us was a great, swelling sound, the running up of engines. It reached a climax and stayed there, this roar that devoured our lives. Then slowly it would diminish, down unseen runway, fading as the flight became airborne. After a moment it began again: first-light reccey, off to the Yalu.

The names that appeared on the mission board three or four times a day were not a list of the most able. They included laggards and incompetents as well as men whose only failing was prudence. The war had swept up and reclaimed former pilots who had returned to ordinary life and become stockbrokers or schoolteachers, and there was one veteran captain—I'll call him Miles—who had been badly burned in a crash and never recovered his nerve. He was a man for whom things went wrong. Dishonor was always staring him in the face, or worse, another crash. On a mission his engine was always running rough, it seemed, and he would call that he was turning back. I flew with him several times, once in early March, in my first real fight.

The sky that day was clear and deep. Heading north at forty thousand feet, there were smooth, straight contrails streaming out for miles behind us which could be seen from far off. The spares, unneeded, had already turned back and were somewhere near Pyongyang. They were talking calmly. "There are bogies at twelve o'clock," the wingman observed routinely.

"Roger."

After a few moments the wingman added, "They look like MIGs."

"They *are*," the other said. He began calling us. "Lots of them. They're turning north," he advised.

There were twelve of us. We began a slow turn to the south while the conversation went on; we were trying to find out more, how many of them there were. The sky was empty but my hands were tingling. Then we saw contrails, faint and distant. "Drop tanks, everybody," I heard.

We carried external fuel tanks, large as bathtubs but more gracefully shaped, beneath the wings. At a touch of a button they could be jettisoned. The plane jumped slightly, became lighter, as the tanks fell away. The hostile contrails turned slowly towards us.

For an interminable time nothing changed, we drew no closer. Then there were specks that were making the contrails. Suddenly we were almost in range. "Everybody pick one of them," I heard.

It was almost impossible to hold the gunsight on something so small but we fired as they shot past. It was at a slight angle and we were on the side closest to their course when, instead of turning after them, Miles rolled over and started down. Fifteen thousand feet lower, in some haze, he pulled out. His aileron boost had gone out, he called. Was I still there, he asked brusquely? "Do you have me in sight, Four?"

I was at three o'clock, I told him. There was a pause, "My boost seems OK now," he announced. Then, for the benefit of anyone who might be listening, "Let's climb up and get back into the fight."

Far above, like the surface after a deep dive, were scrawled and broken contrails. We could hear the calls: the squadron leader that day had gotten one, the pilot of the MIG had just bailed out at thirty-two thousand feet.

At debriefing I heard Miles explain that he thought he might have hit jet-wash and been thrown out of control. He had a tight, embarrassed expression on his face. The skin of his neck was unnaturally smooth from the ancient scars. His back and arms were burned too, I knew. I couldn't bring myself to look at him.

At the same time, however, there were acts of aplomb. Most were things of the moment and lost in the huge tapestry of war. In a day or so they were forgotten, but a few were passed down. "Lead, they're shooting at us!" "That's OK, they're allowed to do that."

———

Colman's arrival in the wing—in fact, there were two arrivals, the first having gone unnoticed—made him famous. He often told the story himself, in an awkward sort of way, laughing and revealing cigar-stained teeth.

He had been in a National Guard wing at a base in northern Japan—Misawa, I think. I have never been there but I know the drabness, the cold of the mornings. They were flying dangerous, repeated raids on enemy supply lines. One day he caught a ride to Korea, to our base, and made his way to wing headquarters, which was not far from the flight line. There he asked to see the wing commander. For what reason, they said, and who was he? It was about a transfer. He was Captain Philip Colman.

The wing commander looked like a fading jockey and had the uncommon name of Thyng. He had piercing blue eyes and wore eagles that because of his smallness seemed doubly large. I can hear his voice as his plane suddenly whips over on its back. "MIGs below us, fellows," he cries. Down we go.

Colman stood before him with a respectfulness untinged by the least subservience. He was, after all, only tossing the dice. He was that dauntless figure, a free man. Soldier, yes, but only occasional soldier; it was all somehow implicit in the crispness of his salute, his effort to be unsmiling, his stained flying suit. He was an experienced fighter pilot and had been an ace in China only seven years earlier. At the moment, he explained, he was in fighter-bombers, which was a waste of his talent; he would like to come to the Fourth.

Thyng was always on the lookout for able men. Did he have any time in the F-86? he asked Colman. Yes, sir, Colman said, about two hundred hours. He actually had none and had merely picked a figure that seemed probable. Thyng, interested, told him to leave his name and other details with the adjutant and he would see what could be done.

A few weeks later orders for the transfer came through and Colman left for Korea carrying, he said, at his own suggestion, his flight records with him. These records, sometimes sent separately, are a pilot's full credentials and are sacred. They list everything— every flight, date, weather, type of aircraft. En route to Korea, Colman slid open the window of the transport plane and casually dropped this dossier into the sea. The pages, torn apart, slid under.

Fishes nosed at the Japanese planes shot down, night flights in Georgia and Florida, rail-cuts near Sinanju, the entirety.

In the new squadron, the one I was soon afterwards to join, he was asked for his records. They were being mailed, he said blandly. In the meantime, for convenience, he offered a rough breakdown of his time, very close to the fact but including several hundred hours in the F-86. Like the bill in a fine restaurant it was an impressive sum.

Airplanes are the same in the way that ships and automobiles are the same; they are similar, but there are also specifics. On his first flight Colman climbed into the cockpit and after a few minutes beckoned the crew chief to him. It had been a while since he'd flown this model and he didn't want to make a mistake; why didn't the crew chief show him the correct way to start the engine? he asked. The rest was easy—radio, controls, instruments, all these were the usual. He taxied out behind his leader and off they went on a local flight. They were carrying drop tanks but Colman hadn't found out how to turn them on. As they were flying along about forty minutes later, he saw every needle suddenly wilt. His engine had stopped.

He had a flame-out, he reported.

"Roger," the leader said. "Try an air start."

This was another gap in his knowledge. "Just so I do it right," Colman said, "read it to me off the checklist, will you?"

Item by item they went through the procedure. Nothing happened. The engine was all right and there was plenty of fuel, but it was all in the drop tanks. They tried a second time and then declared an emergency. Colman would have to try and make a dead-stick landing.

He might have done it easily except he was a little short of altitude. Nothing can amend that. At the last, seeing he was not going to make it, he picked out the best alternative he could, railroad tracks, and landed on them wheels-up, which was the right way.

He went skating down the rails as if they were a wet street, finally coming to a stop just inside a wire-mesh gate which happened to be the entrance to the salvage yard. The plane, damaged beyond repair, would have ended up there anyway. Eventually the fire trucks came, and an ambulance, and Colman, who had injured his back slightly, was taken to the hospital.

One of the first things noticed in the wreckage was that the drop-tank switches had not been turned on. Amell was in a very unfriendly mood when he arrived at the hospital. As soon as he entered the room, Colman held up his hands defensively. "Major, you don't have to say it," he began, "I fucked up. I know I fucked up. But you have to admit one thing. *After* I fucked up, nobody could have done a better job."

Impudence saved him. He was in disgrace but at the same time admired. You could not help liking his nerve.

He was, in many ways, incomparable. I was a member of his flight and we flew together many times. In place of a hard plastic helmet, he wore an old leather one he had brought with him, probably from China days. His head, as a result, looked very small in the cockpit. Like rivulets feeding a stream the planes would join the main body as it moved towards the runway. The mission was forming. One of the ships seemed to have a mere child piloting it. Who was that? the colonels asked. "Colman."

He also, for a time, carried binoculars. Someone had suggested they might be a help for distant sightings and he rounded up a pair. We were encumbered in the airplanes—heavy clothing, life vest, pistol, flares—and on top of all this and his knotted, white scarf, the binoculars hung. They were not very practical—their field was small and the sky they jerked across immense. He pretended they were useful. He was like Nelson holding a telescope up to his blind eye. In any situation, he was ready to engage. In this he was like Quixote, with whom he shared certain characteristics though he was not, like the knight, a deeply serious man.

In the air he was imperturbable and, rarer, magnanimous. We were in many fights together, often uneven fights, but his mere presence, he felt, made any odds equal. He was not methodical. He fought the way a man does who has a few drinks and sits down to play poker, the cards may be running right. Calm, congenial, he enjoys the game and if he finds himself over his head can still smile and say good night or, as a famous black champion once addressed reporters, having lost the bout of his life, "Gentlemen, I have had a most entertaining evening and I hope that you have, too."

One day I watched him turn, in a huge tilting circle, with the leader of a flight of two MIGs. He had hit him earlier, but at long range, and was trying to finish him off. The wingman had disappeared. Into and out of an enormous sun that seemed to burn black in the sky, we flew. In crossing from side to side to stay in position I had moved slightly ahead and called to Colman that it was me passing in front of and beneath him—there had been cases of mistaken identity. "I'm between you and the MIG."

"Go ahead," he replied. "You take him."

It was a lavish gesture, though no more than I expected of him. It would have been a victory we shared. I had already damaged a MIG a week or so earlier and seen they were not untouchable. I knew, with the confidence that assures it, I would have many, entirely my own. "No, you've got him," I said.

I was looking behind. It seemed very leisurely. After a while I heard, "Do you still have him, Two?"

I looked to the front. Nothing.

"I seem to have lost him," Colman remarked idly.

The sickening losses of more than forty years ago. The leaders have died of old age, the fights along the river in the dusk are forgotten. Still I see it clearly, the silvery fleck that is his plane, the string of smoke that trails from it as he fires, the serenity of it all, the burning fever. The invitation to join at the feast.

We traveled far together, sometimes to forbidden places, deeper and deeper into Manchuria, almost to Mukden, looking for them in the sanctuary, so high that the earth seemed neuter. It was a great, barren country, brown, without features. The Yalu was behind us, no longer even in sight. Farther and farther north. Every minute was ten miles. No one would know what had happened to us, no one would ever hear. My eye returned to the fuel gauge again and again. The needle never moved but then it would be lower. How much do you have? he asks. Nine hundred pounds, I reply. Two brief clicks of the mike; he understood. Finally, giving up, we turned.

It was not duty, it was desire. Duty would not search with such avidity in the waning light, coming down the river one last time, the earth already in darkness that was rising slowly, like a tide, the heavens being the last to go. A strange high sound begins in the earphones: gun-laying radar. Along the river a final time. Near its mouth the darkened earth begins to light up, first in one place and then another, like a city come to life. Soon the entire ground is flashing. They are firing at us far below. Black shellbursts, silent, appear around us, some showing an unexpected red core.

It was victory we longed for and imagined. You could not steal or be given it. No man on earth was rich enough to buy it and it was worth nothing. In the end it was worth nothing at all.

———

Now as I shake the box there falls onto the desk not dust but a kind of particulate from old things, along with matchbooks, paper clips, stamps without glue, and a talisman that I carried and for a long time could not bring myself to throw away. I switch on the lamp. Memories of the past. In the early evening, the hour when civilization is at its most comforting, the talisman gleams in an almost forgotten way. It is made not of anything material but of something less lasting: words spoken once, late at night, in the coldness of that winter, after a day of flying. I was with Woody in the quiet of some room. We were like figures out of Beckett, bundled up, dirty as ranch hands. We had about fifteen missions apiece. The months, with whatever was to come, stretched out ahead.

His face ran in an arc, the chin jutting out to one side. His hair was like brushed silver. "You're going to get a lot of them here," he predicted.

I felt my heart race. He was unbrash by nature. We had been drinking but he was not drunk.

"You think so?" I said casually.

It was not only you against them but you against obscurity. There were men who had made a name for themselves and stood above the rest, older men, some of them in their thirties, with the broad hands and deliberateness of carpenters, men who kept their own counsel and knew in the thick of it what to do. Most, though, were younger. I was twenty-six and could have used a few things, gunnery practice for one. No matter.

"You're going to hit the glory road here," he said.

He was far more experienced. His words to me meant more than I could say. I carried them around as if they were written on a slip of paper. No one else had heard them, no one knew about them. I alone.

————

We had many aces: Thyng himself, Asla, later shot down, Baker, Lilley, Blesse. In our squadron alone there were Love, Latshaw, Low, and Jolley, as well as latent others with four victories, ready on any day to climb down from their plane in triumph, grinning, genuine at last. For me, though, for reasons I cannot fully explain, Kasler was the nonpareil.

He was in our flight, together with Low. I cannot remember exactly how he looked, and yet in a way I can. The image is like a dream just at the moment it begins to be lost in the light of day. He had a round head, thin lips, cold uninquisitive gaze. He was laconic, the words barely slipped from his mouth. He had dignity, from what I don't know. It had been given to him, I believe, just in case. Skill, of course, great natural as well as acquired skill together with nerve, and a furied patience like that of a lion lying flattened in the tall grass. Crowning it all was the unsentimentality of a champion. He had served a long apprenticeship, first as a B-29 tail gunner and older than the others when he got his wings. He was an obscure lieutenant when he came. He left renowned.

There are certain indestructible people, stalwarts—leaders of squadrons and their best followers; mechanics numb-fingered in the cold; bleak colonels with eyes reddened by late hours—all having one thing in common: They are the dikes that stand against aimlessness and indifference, that hold back the sullen waters that would otherwise mingle and flood. Kasler was one of these. I flew on Colman's wing and Kasler, in turn, flew on mine.

Darkness, silence, the dawn mission getting up and appearing, dull with sleep, in the lighted mess hall, gloomily looking into the empty steel pitchers. "Where's the bunja juice?" I hear Kasler ask coldly. The Koreans call the canned orange juice "punch." "Havano," they say helplessly. We eat in silence, looking at the tray, and ride in silence down to the flight line.

Two hours later we are over the river. There is the reservoir, the ice of its wide surface crazed with dark lines. It looks like death invading the tissue—all is disorder, all has failed. You can gaze at it for only a few seconds—the sky seems dead, too, abandoned, but can come alive at any moment with fateful glints.

Then it is late in the day again and there has been action. We are looking for them desperately—radar is continuing to report enemy flights—the sun is sinking, the earth beginning to be awash. We fly and see nothing. "They're up by the mouth of the river!" someone calls. Heading there, the sky remains maddeningly empty and then, in an instant, there are planes everywhere. The impatience, the frenzy—every one we come close to is friendly. A minute or two later we have somehow passed from among them and into emptiness again.

Suddenly a plane flashes by beneath: huge tail, red stars, incredibly close. I turn after it, glance quickly behind, my heart pounding. It's clear, but Kasler cries, "Check your right! Look right!"

Not two hundred feet away, plain, foreign-looking, is the wingman. I turn hard towards him and then partway back. He seems fixed, frozen there, like a hare in the headlights. I'm nearly behind him. It will be point-blank. Before I can fire there are four of them almost on top of us, coming in from the other side. "Break left!" Kasler is calling. They turn with us, like cars on a speedway, and we are going down, I can't see if they are firing. Then we are alone; they've broken off when we didn't see it. It's over. Above us the contrails are already fading.

———

The members of a flight, five or six pilots, lived together in one room. It was a makeshift life amid spare furnishing. There was a large table at which we sat or played cards and a houseboy who pulled the blankets taut on the cots, swept, and did errands. During the day you might often be alone in the room when not flying or at other tasks. At night, never, but there was the officers' club and the bar. There you could talk to strangers but rarely did.

Someone, the houseboy perhaps, had found a couple of photographs and put them on the table in the middle of the room. They were the size of postcards. Picking them up idly, you saw the faces of two former members of the flight who, missions completed, had long since gone home. These photos, in a border of black, found their way onto the wall within a large, painted frame in which there was room, as in a cemetery, for others. A simple date was beneath them—the date, in fact, they had left, so far as could be recalled. It appeared to be something more final.

Glancing at his wristwatch, someone would quietly announce the time, "Nine o'clock."

Colman stood up. "The wall," he said.

Everyone rose to his feet. A bundled-up figure—Smith, who liked to go to bed early with a white scarf wound around his eyes like a bandage—jumped up and, standing on the bed, unwrapped his head. His right hand, like everyone's, covered his heart.

It was a solemn performance. All eyes, including the bewildered visitor's, were turned to the photographs outlined in black; there were eventually three or four of them. The cast remained motionless for a full minute, a long time to hold so fixed a pose, and then abruptly and without a word, relaxed. Smith, puffy-eyed, rewound his soiled turban. The card game started up again.

Occasionally there were even toasts: The boys on the wall! The rarest moment was the first evening of someone new in the flight. Whoever it was dared not openly disbelieve, even if every instinct said to, and the least hint of reverence delighted the liars who were posing. It led to absolute refusal, on the part of the duped, to stir whenever someone rose and announced, "The wall!"

———

Every six weeks or so we were given a few days in Japan.

In Tokyo it was different. We came in from what amounted to the front, unsophisticated, raw, and found the city in the possession of those who were stationed there and had everything: cars, comfortable billets, telephone numbers. It was the life of conquerors, brothels and floorshows, sensual nights. The taxis were ancient and took you wherever you liked, down ill-lit boulevards and nameless streets.

The Imperial Hotel, the eastern palace Lloyd Wright designed that had survived the great earthquake and the war, was standing then. Horizontal, deep-eaved, with green-tiled tubs and the feeling of a ship, its very bricks had been specially made. In its rooms and lounges were civilians, dignitaries, Red Cross girls. They were indifferent to the war in Korea, at least to its unconfirmed heroes. Their interests lay in the capital and the life they were arranging. Looking at them, talking to them, seeking information from them, you saw that they had everything. But there was one thing they did not have, as believers say: They did not have the truth—that was in the *Stars and Stripes* one morning in early April. I read it sitting in the lobby of a hotel, hotel without a name and day without a date, though they had them then. Kasler had gotten his first. It was strange how, in a single moment I lacked all interest in anything; envy can do that. Coming back from Tokyo it was as if I had never been away, but there was a void, three days during which the war had gone on and which were irreversible.

Something begins and you have your run, like a player at the table or a batter. Kasler's second I actually saw, by chance, hit the ground in a bright splash during a big fight. I was with Colman at the time; we were chasing two but never got close. In the debriefing afterwards I recognized a new contender, one hand bending abruptly behind the other to show how he had done it, the sooty marks of an oxygen mask still on his face. We had been among the uncounted, he and I, and I watched as if from afar.

At the beginning of May, Colman and Kasler each got their third. I saw them landing afterwards, the planes sleek and bare.

The fourth and the fifth I will tell about later.

There were so many things that could happen, a large part was chance. Perhaps it has rained for days—the planes sit out in the weather and dampness affects them, the radios become unreliable. *Break!* they are crying in a fight and you hear nothing. The silence is uncanny. *Break right!* they are shouting, *break right!* For some reason you look back and there, behind you, is an intake the size of a locomotive. In fright you pull too hard and the plane shudders, snaps, begins to spin. The earth is revolving, dirt from the cockpit floor is floating up, and they are following you down; when you pull out at low speed they'll be waiting.

There were days one felt a dread, when something was wrong, something impalpable. Like a beast lying in a field sensing danger, you could not run from it, you did not even know what it was. It was an eclipse, not total, of courage. People were getting hit, Woody, Bambrick, Straub. Carey was lost, Honecker. Sharp, with his savoir-faire and black moustache, was shot down—the MIG dropping out of the clouds behind him—and rescued. While turning final one day I had the controls freeze—something had gone wrong with the hydraulics, I could not move the stick—and barely missed being killed. Still you went to the briefing, carried your gear to the plane.

Late in April we heard that more Russian squadrons were coming in. They were crowded onto their fields, wingtip to wingtip. The sky was filling with the bright cumulus that comes with fair weather.

I was with Colman, just the two of us. We had been four but had become separated—it was the alert flight and we'd been scrambled. The radar was directing us; enemy flights were in the air. We might never find them, wandering as we were among monumental clouds and talking occasionally to the absent pair with the vague idea of rejoining.

That was when I saw them for the first time.

"Two bogies back at eight o'clock high," I called.

"Roger. I've got them," Colman said lazily. He was like a veteran fielder watching a high fly ball. We continued on.

"They're closing, Lead," I said a few moments later. "They're turning in on us."

"Roger," he said.

They were at seven o'clock then, only a few thousand feet back. "They're MIGs," I said.

"I've got them," he said again, confidently; it hardly occurred to me then that he hadn't. I couldn't imagine what he was thinking.

"They're going to six o'clock. They're firing! Break left!" At last Colman saw them and was turning. I was with him, outside and trailing. We had waited too long. We were in a stream of fire that was moving with and ahead of us. I was not aware of it, but Colman was being hit.

Behind us they had the scent of the kill, they could see the strikes; nothing would dislodge them. I was in panic but also calm, as if observing from some higher, safer place. We were turning as hard as we could and they were turning with us. The altimeter was unwinding. Straining to look back, I could see them, steady and unmoving, like the pods behind you on an amusement park ride that rise when you rise and go down when you go down, mechanical and effortless. There were fights, I knew, that went down to the deck and swept across the hills just above the trees, roaring, relentless.

Somehow we had pulled ahead a little. We were flying too desperately for them to lead us. The other element was calling—they could hear us—to ask where we were and whether they could help us, but neither Colman nor I could answer. It was pitiless. It was like being held by a python—the least relinquished space, it constricts to hold. We were being crushed in boundless air. We were below twenty thousand feet when Colman tightened his turn even more and pulled the nose up. He was going to dance with them this way, at low speed, having gained nothing at high.

They didn't stay. They broke away; I saw them beneath us heading for home. I called to him to reverse his turn and follow, but for some reason he didn't and they became specks. We picked up speed and began to climb. He said something about almost having been unconscious—his oxygen hose becoming unplugged—and then asked me to close in and take a look at his plane.

"What's wrong?"

"I think I may have been hit," he decided.

From a distance I could see the holes in his tail and, when I drew closer, the wing.

Almost out of fuel but full of exuberance I landed too long that day, amateurishly long, and ended by collapsing one of the landing gear. I have made that landing a hundred times and never failed to put the plane down as gently as a glass figurine on a cabinet shelf, the wheels seem to touch with a feline softness, but the single time it was not in my imagination, I failed. The group commander was forgiving. I would make up for it, he declared. He'd had a serious accident himself, in England, colliding with a friendly bomber and killing all on board. This was Mahurin and a greater trial awaited him; he became a prisoner in North Korea and made statements for the benefit of the enemy. I could never, despite it, bring myself to dislike him.

When the weather was bad, as it was that spring, we did not fly. In the long days of rain there was restlessness and a kind of melancholy. The hours passed slowly; the hand-wound phonograph playing "China Night," singsong and shrill. Remembering the girls at Miyoshi's (officers only, pilots and artillerymen from every part of the war), the firecrackers bursting at the feet of hostesses in vast neon nightclubs, the special houses outside the gate at Fuchu, the bowing Japanese, Amell in his rain-soaked uniform getting out of a car, he had no idea where, it looked like the main railroad station . . . Thinking of it all and waiting for the weather to change, to pull onto the runway again and, in the rush of noise with its chilling central shriek, tremble to go.

One day down at the flight line, in the latrine, I came across a

broad-faced pilot named Braswell who had been first captain a
year or two after I graduated. He was flying fighter-bombers and
had landed, low on fuel, on the way home from a mission. The
ground crew was attending to his airplane, an F-84, exotic to
them, with straight wings and heronlike landing gear. We stood for
a while and talked. What was it like, fighting MIGs? he asked.

I described it. I remember the pride I had in telling him, a pride
I was careful to conceal. He was listening intently. I knew he felt I
was giving testimony that he could trust. There are really only two
kinds of officer, those with virtue and those without. Not that either is preferable—there are times when virtue is a terrible defect—but I felt myself to be one of the former. Braswell was an
exemplar, of course. I was handing over to him something he may
have recognized—though incomplete and not in correct order, it
was everything I had learned. There passed before me all the ranks
of cadet lieutenants and captains, football players, bloods, as the
English might call them. I say passed before me, but it was I who
passed before them, walking up to the privileged figure who stood
alone, if only for a brief moment, at the head of them all and
speaking to him, not as a subordinate but like two men in a field.
We were both captains now, of another sort. If I were to meet him
years later he would not remember this—neither landing there,
nor me, nor anything I said—but I had given it nevertheless, and
to someone who might matter. I felt shriven.

———

It was May when Colman flew what no one except he knew would
be his last mission.

He had four victories by then, and that day, in a fight near the
Yalu, Kasler, leading an element, got his fourth as well and then
got behind another MIG and followed it down to the deck. They
roared across the mud flats wide open, needles crossed, the MIG
like a beast of legend fleeing ahead. Kasler strove to get closer. The

controls were unyielding. The ground rushed beneath them. Destiny itself, unrehearsed, shimmered before his eyes.

They were coming to the open water, the delta where the river widened, and suddenly the MIG pulled straight up, climbing, and continuing around. Colman was above with his wingman, watching it all. In his pocket, figuratively speaking, was a telegram he had received that morning—his father was gravely ill, he must come home—when the MIG rose in front of him, the long-sought fifth, entire and slow. It was his final chance.

"May I?" he asked politely.

Kasler, blood pulled from his face, did not answer. He passed by himself, up, up, and brilliantly over, fierce with lust, heading down again. At the bottom the MIG, going too fast, misjudged and hit near the water. Kasler barely pulled out.

I had landed half an hour earlier from a mission which encountered nothing, and was standing by the barracks watching when they came back. The first thing I saw was that they were without drop tanks. They turned off the runway at the near end, close to the road. I could recognize Colman's head, small, like a bird's, in the first ship. His gun ports were clean. So were his wingman's. The other two planes had just reached the end of their landing roll. Theirs were black—they had been firing.

Kasler had gotten two and his wingman one. The single daring act—it was hard to imagine the enormous distance that it placed between us. The fifth was more than just another; it was beatification, the step across the gulf. On the tail of another plane at top speed, determined, closer than one dared, not knowing the other pilot or what he would do, down to the treetops, to the fatal earth—I had flown this very flight myself, it had been my initiation, though I hardly imagined repeating it in war. Kasler had his fifth, but more than that, he had reordered the state of things; he had begun like me, as a gunbearer, and now was where boldness had placed him, on the other side.

Colman left that day. In the wake of his leaving I realized that I knew very little about him. He was married and I think had children. He was lighthearted and self-promoting. Day-to-day truth was probably not in him, but a higher kind of integrity was, a kind not wasted on trivial matters. He had an infectious spirit. We were unalike. I adored him.

The farewells were the briefest. He merely picked up and left as if the game had meant little to him; he walked out without a backward glance. Finis.

I have forgotten when Kasler left, sometime later and after another victory. The MIGs had come down south of Anju on the early mission. He saw them low, but couldn't catch them and then it developed there was an unknowing one behind him. His sixth.

I went to find him as he was getting ready to leave. I had a flight of my own by then and other loyalties, but part of me had stayed behind. We said goodbye. He was somewhat taciturn, as usual. I wondered if he was as yet aware of what he had won and would have for a long time thereafter, the luster of those hunting days when his name became storied.

Later he came by to say a few words—to console me, I think. There would be other chances. Of course, I said. We would see each other sometime, we agreed. It was heartbreaking to see him go, not for the slender friendship we had, but for the achievement he was carrying off with him. I saw his name one other time, in an article all down a column of the *Times* during the Vietnam War. He was flying there. He was known, it said, by name in the war room of the White House itself. He had the bad luck later to be shot down and made a prisoner, but even then he was invincible. He was held for seven years. Torture did not break him. Nothing could.

I know how they appeared to me, and I try to step aside for a moment to observe myself, how I seemed to them. Even now I cannot be sure—a marked figure, certainly, convivial and aloof at

the same time, not uncourageous, driven, impetuous, a bit un-
wise. They may sometimes have wondered what happened to me
in the aftermath. Word grew infrequent. Did I go on, did I rise?

———

The first good weather in a week. The fighter-bombers are going
north again in strength, to someplace up near the border. The
briefing room is crowded and electric. It's maximum effort—everything that can fly. Six hundred enemy aircraft have been counted
on their fields. We are sending up forty.

Far beneath us the silver formations were moving slowly, it
seemed, across barren hills. Enemy flights were being announced,
one after another, and then someone saw them along the river at
thirty thousand feet. Blood jumping after the idle days, we
dropped tanks and began to climb. We broke through a thin layer
of clouds and into emptiness.

Moments later, coming from nowhere, they are on us, four of
them at eight o'clock. We turn into them, they pass behind and
disappear.

The flight has split up, we're in two's. By this time MIGs are
being called out everywhere. The radio is brimming with voices,
among them someone calling out MIGs south of the river at
twenty-four thousand feet. How many? someone asks.

"Many many!"

We head that way and see two, far out, sail past us on the left.
We turn to follow, and they climb and begin to turn also. The sky
is a burning blue, a sky things seem black in. I am on my back, Im-
melmanning up to get between them and the river, rolling out
slightly beneath the leader, who is turning hard to the right and
cannot see me. I duck my head and try to find the gunsight, which
is an image projected onto a thick, slanted piece of glass that
serves as the windshield. There's nothing there—turning has
pulled it all the way off the glass. The MIG begins to level out and

the sight drifts into view. About a thousand feet back I press the trigger. The tracers fall behind him. He begins to climb again and I am cutting him off, closing, glancing quickly back to see if my wingman is still there, firing again. A few hits in the right wing, then tremendous joy, at closer range a solid burst in the fuselage. The flashes are intense, brilliant, as of something vital shattering. He abruptly rolls over and I follow, as if we are leaping from a wall. He begins to pull it through. I am still shooting and something flies off the plane—the canopy. A moment later a kind of bundle, the pilot, comes out.

"Cope! Did you see that?"

"Roger," my wingman says. He may have been talking to me all along, telling me I was clear, but this single word is the only one that remains.

The MIG, now a funeral craft that bore nothing, was falling from thirty thousand feet, spinning leisurely in its descent until its shadow unexpectedly appeared on the hills and slowly moved to join it in a burst of flame.

Six enemy planes were claimed on this mission and two of our own were lost, an ace and his wingman. The leader was rescued but the wingman drowned.

Here then, faintly discolored and liable to come apart if you touch it, is the corsage that I kept from the dance.

———

In the end there is a kind of illness. A feeling of inconsequence, even lightness, takes hold. It is, in a way, like the earliest days, the sense of being an outsider. Others are taking one's place, nameless others who can never know how it was. It is being given to them, the war with all its fading, romantic detail, its disasters and lucky chances. They will be coming home through the intense skies of autumn, settling gracefully in over the boundary of the field. The smooth black runway floats up to meet them. The ships are empty,

feather-light, the fuel tanks almost drained, the belts of ammunition vanished; they are bringing back nothing except that thing we
prized above all.

North for the last time, north again on a *razzia*. The radios are
silent, only an occasional brief word crosses the air. We are hoping
to surprise them, but it is a vain hope, already we are greenish
marks on some radar. They are speaking a dark language, it flickers
back and forth, deciding where we are going and what they will do.

As I fly this time I remember missions over endless sky beaches
formed by clouds, the solitude and clear, ionized taste of pure oxygen, looking hard at nothing with no chance, it seemed, of other
than nothing, searching along the empty horizon, then a little
higher, or back where the enemy sometimes materialized in the
rearmost corner of one's eye—lackluster missions when out of
nowhere, suddenly, here they come.

I finished with one destroyed and one damaged, which I would
sometimes, among the unknowing, elevate to a probable, never
more; to do that would be soiling the very thing fought for.

When I returned to domestic life I kept something to myself, a
deep attachment—deeper than anything I had known—to all that
had happened. I had come very close to achieving the self that is
based on the risking of everything, going where others would not
go, giving what they would not give. Later I felt I had not done
enough, had been too reliant, too unskilled. I had not done what I
set out to do and might have done. I felt contempt for myself, not
at first but as time passed, and I ceased talking about those days,
as if I had never known them. But it had been a great voyage, the
voyage, probably, of my life.

I would have given anything, I remember that. The moments of
terror—alone, separated from the leader, and seeing, like a knell,
drop tanks with their foreign shape and thin, vaporous trails
falling silent to both right and left—the sometimes ominous briefings and preparation, the dark early mornings which for me were

the worst—none of it mattered. A few years afterwards I won a gunnery championship in North Africa and led an acrobatic team—I had, in short, learned equitation. We dropped from the sky into distant countries and once in a while in a locker room or bar I would hear a remark that someone, a name from those days, had been killed in a flying accident, but like Conrad's shipmates on the *Narcissus*, I never saw any of them again.

BURNING THE DAYS

I FLEW IN THE 75th, the 335th in Korea, the 22nd in Germany, and at the end with the 119th Squadron in New Jersey, years of it, like cavalry years, the waiting by empty runways, the barren operations rooms, the apocalyptic sound of engines tremendous and uneven, the idleness and cynicism, the myth.

In those days there was nothing in the world but us. The rarity was fine. There were other squadrons, of course. Some you knew quite well. Ships from all three squadrons in the group and also from other fields came in past the little shack on wheels by the side of the runway. Many times it is you yourself who are returning, coming back beneath the clouds, seeing the long straight runway, or the hangars alongside it blurring in the rain—an incomparable happiness, the joy of coming home.

———

We had pilots named Homer and Ulysses, country boys unfrivolous by nature who took good care of their cars. Farm boys, for some reason, always seemed the truest men. They were even-tempered and unhurried in the way of someone who will watch a man doing something foolish and not make any comment—the joke will come at the end. They became flyers instead of going to the city though of course it was not the same thing, and they saw the world from a distance—the Grand Canal like a gray thread winding among the barely distinguishable piazzas far below, the unmistakable narrowing spire of Paris rising above the haze. Beneath them passed all the miracles of Europe, few of great interest—their wonders were more elemental, in a room, standing naked with a member like a grazing horse's, in front of a full-length mirror with a German whore. Some married waitresses.

You knew them, that is to say their ability and to an extent their character, but much was hidden. After two or three years you knew little more than at the start, but still you were attached to their silence, the honesty of their thoughts. One night one of them, on a motorcycle, sped into the concrete pillar of a bridge and was in the hospital for weeks, legs broken, jaw bound together with silver wire. Nevertheless when I came into the room he managed to smile. He had a willing nature and the name of an ace, strange and abrupt: Uden. Broad and capable hands, fearless eyes, yet somehow it all came to nothing. Face-to-face for the last time at the noisy farewell party, the blue, farm-country eyes suddenly filled with tears. "I know I've disappointed you."

"That's true."

"I just wanted you to know one thing—I won't do it the next time."

That was true also. There was no next time. A year later someone was describing an accident at Myrtle Beach, a night takeoff with full fuel load, 450-gallon drop tanks, the planes wallowing, the overcast seamlessly black. The join-up was in sky undivided between the darkness of air and water, a sky without top or bottom; in fact there was no sky, only total blackness in which, banking steeply to try and catch up with the lights of the fleeing leader, the number-three man, low in the roaring nightmare, determined to do well, went into the sea. Uden.

The leader of that flight was one of the great war aces; highly visible and bulletproof; there were a number still around. Combat had never really ended for them. The sign on the desk of one read, *The mission of the Air Force is to fly and fight, and don't you ever forget it.* Blakeslee, another, an untamable fighter whose reputation was one of temper and violence, I met only once, in my final year of flying. It was at a dinner dance in Germany and he walked into the bar of the club not in uniform with two or three significant ribbons but dressed like the owner of a 1930s nightclub in an out-of-fashion tuxedo with a stiff shirt. He stood down at the end, a little apart; I would not have known who he was had the bartender not greeted him by name.

A couple of young officers, transients like myself, approached him as he stood waiting for his order. They were F-104 pilots from England. In war it is not like other things, where youth is arrogance. War is terra incognita. The young are usually eager to have the curtain lifted, even slightly, by one of the greats.

"Evening, Colonel," they said.

He looked at them without expression. His power was such that he could destroy the ego of all but the most aggressive.

"Sir," one of them said, "I just wanted to ask you a question. It's something I've never been able to get an answer to. It's about German aces."

Blakeslee, who had been a colonel and then reduced in rank, possibly for cause, so he was now a lieutenant colonel, stood there. He listened without showing the least sign of interest.

"Is it true," the young captain went on, "that the Germans counted their kills by the number of engines and would get four victories for, say, shooting down a B-17?"

Perhaps Blakeslee knew the answer. Perhaps he was weighing the real intent of the question. His face was heavier than it once had been, his body thicker. The electric skies over the Reich with their decks of clouds, shouts on the radio, confusion and vertical descents, those legend skies were gone. Finally he spoke.

"I don't know," he said slowly. He was picking up three or four glasses. "I only know one thing: it's all phoney," he said.

They like to say you cannot understand unless you've been there, unless you've lived it. You could not argue with his scorn.

———

How well one remembers that world, the whiff of jet exhaust, oily and dark, in the morning air as you walk to where the planes are parked out in the mist.

Soon you are up near the sun where the air is burning cold, amid all that is familiar, the scratches on the canopy, the chipped black of the instrument panel, the worn red cloth of the safety streamers stuffed in a pocket down near your shoe. From the tailpipe of the leader's plane comes an occasional dash of smoke, the only sign of motion as it streaks rearwards.

Below, the earth has shed its darkness. There is the silver of countless lakes and streams. The greatest things to be seen, the ancients wrote, are sun, stars, water, and clouds. Here among them, of what is one thinking? I cannot remember but probably of nothing, of flying itself, the imperishability of it, the brilliance. You do not think about the fish in the great, winding river, thin as string, miles below, or the frogs in the glinting ponds, nor they of you; they know little of you, though once, just after takeoff, I saw the shadow of my plane skimming the dry grass like the wings of god and passing over, frozen by the noise, a hare two hundred feet below. That lone hare, I, the morning sun, and all that lay beyond it were for an instant joined, like an eclipse.

One night in early spring there were two of us—I was wingman. No one else was flying at the time. We were landing in formation after an instrument approach. It was very dark, it had been raining, and the leader misread the threshold lights. We crossed the end of the runway high and touched down long. In exact imitation I held the nose high, as he did, to slow down, wheels skipping along the concrete like flat stones on a lake. Halfway down we lowered the noses and started to brake. Incredibly we began to go faster. The runway, invisible and black, was covered with the thinnest sheet of ice. Light rain had frozen sometime after sundown and the tower did not know it. We might, at the last moment, have gone around—put on full power and tried to get off again—but it was too close. We were braking in desperation. I stop-cocked my engine—shut it off to provide greater air resistance—and a moment later he called that he was doing the same. We were standing on the brakes and then releasing, hard on and off. The end of the runway was near. The planes were slithering, skidding sideways. I knew we were going off and that we might collide. I had full right rudder in, trying to stay to the side.

We slid off the end of the runway together and went about two hundred feet on the broken earth before we finally stopped. Just ahead of us was the perimeter road and beyond it, lower, some railroad tracks.

When I climbed out of the cockpit I wasn't shaking. I felt almost elated. It could have been so much worse. The duty officer came driving up. He looked at the massive, dark shapes of the planes, awkwardly placed near each other, the long empty highway behind them, the embankment ahead. "Close one, eh?" he said.

This was at Fürstenfeldbruck, the most lavish of the prewar German airfields, near Munich. We came there from our own field, Bitburg, in the north, the Rhineland, to stand alert or fire gunnery close by. Zulu alert, two ships on five-minute, two on fifteen. The long, well-built barracks, the red tile roofs and marble corridors. The stands of pine on the way to the pilots' dining room, where you could eat breakfast in your flying suit and the waitresses knew what you preferred.

We were not far from Dachau, the ash-pit. One of them. I had seen its flat ruins. That Otto Frank, Anne Frank's father, had served as an officer in the German army in the First World War, I may not have known, but I was aware that patriotism and devotion had not saved him or others. They might not save me, though I swore to myself they would. I knew I was different, if nothing else marked by my name. I acted always from two necessities; the first was to be like everyone, and the second—was it foolish?—was to be better than other men. If I was to be despised I wanted it to be by inferiors.

Munich was our city, its great night presence, the bars and clubs, the Isar green and pouring like a faucet through its banks, the Regina Hotel, dancing on Sunday afternoons, faces damp with the heat, the Film Casino Bar, Bei Heinz. All the women, Panas's girlfriend in the low-cut dress, Van Bockel's, who was a secretary and had such an exceptional figure, Cortada's, who smelled like a florist's on a warm day. Munich in the snow, coming back to the field alone on the streetcar.

I flew back to Bitburg with White, one of the two men in the squadron to become famous—Aldrin was the other—on a winter day. It was late in the afternoon, everything blue as metal, the sky, the towns and forests, even the snow. The other ship, silent, constant on your wing. With the happiness of being with someone you like, through it we went together, at thirty-five thousand, the thin froth of contrails fading behind.

White had been the first person I met when I came to the squadron and I knew him well. In the housing area he and his wife lived on our stairway. He had a fair, almost milky, complexion and reddish hair. An athlete, a hurdler; you see his face on many campuses, idealistic, aglow. He was an excellent pilot, acknowledged as such by those implacable judges, the ground crews. They did not revere him as they did the ruffians who might drink with them, discuss the merits of the squadron commander or sexual exploits, but they respected him and his proper, almost studious, ways. God and country—these were the things he had been bred for.

In Paris, a lifetime later, in a hotel room I watched as on screens everywhere he walked dreamily in space, the first American to do so. I was nervous and depressed. My chest ached. My hair had patches of gray. White was turning slowly, upside down, tethered to the spacecraft by a lazy cord. I was sick with envy—he was destroying hope. Whatever I might do, it would not be as overwhelming as this. I felt a kind of loneliness and terror. I wanted to be home, to see my children again before the end, and I was certain it was near the end; I felt suicidal, ready to burst into tears. He did this to me unknowingly, as a beautiful woman crossing the street crushes hearts beneath her heel.

White burned to ashes in the terrible accident on the launching pad at Cape Canaveral in 1967. He died with Virgil Grissom, with whom I had also flown. His funeral was solemn. I attended, feeling out of place. To be killed flying had always been a possibility, but the two of them had somehow moved beyond that. They were already visible in that great photograph of our time, the one called celebrity. Still youthful and, so far as I knew, unspoiled, they were like jockeys moving to the post for an event that would mark the century, the race to the moon. The absolutely unforeseen destroyed them. Aldrin went instead.

White is buried in the same cemetery as my father, not far away. I visit both graves when I am there. White's, though amid others, seems visible from some distance off, just as he himself was if you looked intently at the ranks.

———

You remember the airfields, the first sight of some, the deep familiarity of others.

Apart from those that finally appeared when you were coming in, nose high, in fog or heavy rain, the most beautiful field I ever saw was in Morocco, down towards the south. It was called Boulhaut, a long, flawless black runway built for strategic bombers and never used, the numbers at each end huge and clear—no tire had ever marked them. You could not but marvel at its extraordinary newness.

I liked fields near the sea, Westhampton Beach on Long Island, Myrtle Beach, Langley, Eglin, Alameda, where we landed in the fall, ferrying planes to be shipped to the fighting in Korea, and went on to Vanessi's with the navy pilots' wives. I liked Sidi Slimane for its openness and the German fields, Hahn and Wiesbaden, Fürstenfeldbruck.

There are fields I would like to forget, Polk, where one night, as a rank amateur, I nearly went into the trees, trying clumsily to go around with my flaps down. Later, in the wooden barracks, came another lesson. Two men in flying suits, drab in appearance, paused at the open door of the room where I sat on a bed. "Are you the one flying the P-51? Where are you from?" one asked.

"Andrews," I said. I felt a kind of glamour, being connected with the silvery plane and its slim, aggressive shape, parked by itself on the ramp. It was not hard to deduce that they were lesser figures, transport pilots probably. I told them I was in the Fourth Group rather than going into the less interesting facts—I was actually a graduate student at Georgetown. They did not seem very impressed. "Ever hear of Don Garland?" I said, naming a noted pilot in the Fourth.

"Who's that?"

"One of the best pilots in the Air Force."

"Oh, yeah?"

I offered a few exaggerations I had overheard at one time or another in the Andrews Club. Garland flew the slot position on the acrobatic team, hanging there with his bare teeth, so to speak, the proof of it being the blackened rudder of his ship, stained by the leader's exhaust and as a mark of pride always left that way— no mechanic would dare to rub it clean. He was a wild man, Garland—I could tell them any number of stories.

"What does he look like?"

I gave a vague answer. Was he a decent guy? they wanted to know.

I had almost been in a fight one evening at Andrews, not with Garland but with another member of the team. "Not particularly," I said.

Suddenly one of them began laughing. The other glanced at him. "Shut up," he said.

"Oh, for Christ's sake," the first one said. Then to me, "This is Garland," he said, gesturing.

I was speechless.

"What the hell's your name?" they wanted to know.

I left early in the morning, before they were up.

Later, when I actually joined the Fourth, they were luckily gone by then. There were other Garlands. At Bitburg one of the wing lieutenant colonels used to sit in my office, aimless as a country lawyer, looking at the board on which there were photographs of our pilots—I was squadron operations officer then—and ask, if war broke out, which of them would become aces? We sat examining the faces together. "Emigholz," I said.

"Who else?"

A pause. "Cass, probably. It's hard to say. Minish."

There was no real way of judging. It was their skill but also their personalities, their remorselessness. "Maybe Whitlow," I added. I was trying to match them to the memory of aces or near-aces in Korea. Emigholz was like Billy Dobbs, Cass was like Matson. "And Cortada," I finally said. He was from Puerto Rico, small, excitable, and supremely confident. Not everyone shared his opinion of his ability—his flight commander was certain he would kill himself.

With the instinct that dogs have, you knew where in the order anyone ranked. Experience counted, and day-to-day performance. Pilots with few flying hours, in the early years of their career, were the most dangerous. They were young, in the well-being of ignorance, like flies on a sunny table, unaware of the fate of countless others. As regards flying, they had only a limited idea of the many ways to fail, most of them deadly.

With a lanky, indecisive lieutenant named Kelly, I left Bitburg late one day bound for Marseille. Destination weather was forecast to be scattered clouds and eight miles' visibility. I had put him in the lead. It was important to give pilots the chance to make decisions, gain confidence. The ships in a flight, for whatever reason, might become separated, setting every man on his own, or a leader's radio could go out and force a wingman to take over. In an instant the responsibility for everything could shift.

Over Marseille at thirty-five thousand feet we had just under eighteen hundred pounds of fuel remaining. The field, Marignane, was not visible. It was hidden by a deck of clouds that had moved in unexpectedly from the sea. In addition, neither Marignane nor Marseille Control would answer our calls.

The sun had already set and the earth was dimming. Kelly signaled for speed brakes and we dove towards a corner of the great lagoon that lay east of the field. We leveled out at three hundred feet. Ahead, like a dark reef, were the clouds. Squeezed as we were into a narrow layer of vanishing light and haze—the bottom of the overcast was perhaps a hundred feet above us—we missed the field. Suddenly the ground began to rise; it disappeared in the clouds just ahead, and we pulled up, breaking out on top at two thousand feet. It had grown darker. I looked at the fuel gauge: a thousand pounds. Kelly seemed hesitant and we were at the threshold of real difficulty.

"I've got it," I said. "Get on my wing." I could hear something he could not, the finality of the silence in which we found ourselves, in which the sole sound was that of the Marignane radio beacon— I rechecked the call letters against my let-down book, FNM.

I turned immediately towards the beacon and examined the let-down diagram. The light was dim. The details were complex—I noted only the heading to the field from the beacon, and the distance and time to fly. At 175 knots this was a minute and twenty-seven seconds.

When things do not go as planned and the fuel gauge is slowly going down, there is a feeling of unreality, of hostile earth and sky. There comes a point when the single fuel needle is all you think about, the focus of all concern. The thought of bailing out of two airplanes over Marseille because we could not find the field in low clouds and darkness was making me even more precise. It was the scenario for many accidents. Did I have the right frequency and beacon? I checked again. It was right. A moment later, for the first time, the tower came on the air. I suspected they had been waiting for someone to arrive who could speak English. Talking to them, although they were hard to understand, gave some relief: the field was open; there were lights.

We passed over the beacon at two thousand feet, turned to the reciprocal of the field heading and flew for thirty seconds. It seemed minutes. The world was thundering and pouring out. I was determined to do everything exactly, to make a perfect approach. We began a procedure turn—forty-five degrees to the left, hold for one minute, turn back in. The direction-finding needle was rigid. It began to quiver and then swung completely around as we hit the beacon.

We started to descend. The minimum altitude for the field was eight hundred feet, minimum visibility a mile and a half. At five hundred feet we were still in the clouds. Four hundred. Suddenly the ground was just beneath us. The visibility was poor, less than a mile. I glanced at the fuel gauge: six hundred pounds.

A minute had passed. The second hand of the clock was barely moving. A minute and five seconds. A minute ten. Then ahead, like distant stars, faint lines of them, the lights of the field. Speed brakes out, I signaled. Gear and flaps down. We landed smoothly together in the dark.

A taxi drove us into town. We talked about what had happened, what might have. It was not an incident; it was nothing; routine. One flight among innumerable. We could find no place to eat. We slept in a small hotel on a tree-lined street and left early in the morning.

Once in a great while there was a letter from Horner. He had re-signed his commission and was in his father-in-law's business, land-scaping. *Dear Fly-boy,* he would write, with a touch of wistfulness it seemed, *I hope you're having a good time in Europe. I used to.*

At one reunion, years later, the rumor spread that he had just been seen driving through the main gate with two chorus girls. It turned out to be untrue. The days of chorus girls were past though we had once gone with two from the Versailles when we were in pursuit of everything except wisdom. *Susie and I were there the other night,* he wrote of another place, *and the violinist came up to our table and asked us where the gentleman was who had been so fond of "Granada." I assumed he was speaking of you, so I told him that you had returned to the front . . .*

There are things that seem insignificant at the time and that turn out to be so. There are others that are like a gun in a bedside drawer, not only serious but unexpectedly fatal.

For Colonel Brischetto, it was not a single detail but a series of them, none of great importance and spread over months. He was the new wing commander at Bitburg who had arrived in August, filled with ambition but having very little jet time. Tom Whitehouse, the old commander, diminutive and gallant, turned over to him a veteran fighter wing. It was like turning over a spirited horse to a new, inexperienced owner who would, of course, attempt to ride.

All wing and group flying officers were attached to one of the squadrons. The wing commander flew with ours, not very fre-

quently, as it happened, and not very well, though there was
nothing alarmingly wrong. You could feel his weakness on the
radio where he was like an actor fumbling for his lines, and in following instructions in the air there was often a slight, telltale
delay.

We went, each year, to North Africa to gunnery camp. The
weather was always good there. At Wheelus, a large airfield in
Tripoli, we lived in tents for four or five weeks and flew every day.
It was essential for all pilots to qualify during that time though
there were occasional opportunities for a few planes to go and fire
elsewhere. There were fighter wings from all over Europe scheduled into Tripoli throughout the year, nose to tail. Not so much as
an extra day there could be begged.

That year we were booked for Wheelus in the very beginning of
January. All preparations had been made but we did not go—the
weather at Bitburg prevented it. Throughout the holidays there
had been freezing rain and low ceilings; the runway was covered
with heavy ice. In North Africa the sun was shining and irreplaceable days were passing. At last the rain stopped and the forecast
seemed encouraging. All through the final night there were airplanes taxiing slowly up and down the runway, trying to melt the
ice with the heat of their exhaust.

At noon the next day the ceiling lifted sufficiently. We were
ready. It was six days after our intended departure.

An outwardly calm but impatient Colonel Brischetto was to go
in the first flight. He was on the wing of an experienced pilot, a
lieutenant, his favorite instructor, in fact, Cass. They were already
on the runway when he called that his tailpipe temperature, a crit-
ical instrument, was fluctuating wildly, and asked Cass for advice—he had already had some minor difficulties with the ship.
Airplanes had their own personalities. They were not mere mechanical objects but possessed temperaments and traits. Some
were good in gunnery, others hopeless. Some were always ready to

fly, others rarely. Some planes, if not creaking like ships, nevertheless made strange noises. Without minds or hearts, they were
somehow not wholly inanimate. An airplane did not belong to one
pilot, like a horse, but to all communally. There were no secrets—
pilots talked freely about the behavior of planes and in time flew
most of them.

When Brischetto asked Cass whether or not he should take off
with an erratic indication, he was told that such a decision was up
to the pilot. Despite his great anxiety, Brischetto made a prudent
choice and aborted. He taxied back to the ramp, was assigned another airplane, and became part of another flight.

Now it was early afternoon. The first planes, Cass and his flight,
were well on their way to Rome, where they would refuel before
continuing. The clouds at Bitburg were holding at six hundred
feet. The bases were ragged, the top of the overcast layered and
uncertain; the visibility, threatened by rain, stood at five miles.
Brischetto had just forty minutes of actual weather experience in
the airplane. He felt, probably correctly, that he would have more
difficulty flying on the wing of another plane in these conditions
than having another plane flying on his, and he indicated he
would like to lead the flight.

The four ships, in elements of two, the colonel leading, taxied
out to the runway. The takeoff interval between elements was to
be five seconds, and they were to join up, if possible, beneath the
clouds so that all four could penetrate together with a single
leader and a single voice.

Brischetto read his clearance back to the tower incorrectly. He
was obliged to repeat it three times before permission was given to
take the runway. He had a very steady pilot, Tracy, who had never
flown with him previously, however, on his wing. So, after many
delays, some unavoidable, they were ready to depart.

The planes lined up on the runway together. The noise of their
engines swelled. With an almost dainty slowness, the first two

ships began to roll. Five seconds later, the next two. I was watching with no particular interest, sitting in the cockpit in the squadron area, a flight leader, waiting to start. Very quickly the four planes disappeared into the clouds. They had not—I attached no meaning to it—come together as a flight.

In the air the colonel, as it happened, had responded with a distracted "Roger" to the request to reduce power slightly to allow the second element to catch up after takeoff. He then gave the command to change channels, from tower to departure control. Changing radio channels meant reaching down and back. The indicator was hard to see. It was best done by counting the clicks between numbers—perhaps Brischetto did this, though he was never heard on departure control.

On the ground time passed slowly, slipping by in the small, hesitant movement of the second hand on the instrument panel clock. Though it is hard to imagine, it was passing at different rates, not to be calculated in ordinary seconds, for the colonel and his wingman when they went into the clouds. For Tracy on the left wing it was like the regular, slow beat of a pulse, but for the colonel, in an abstract world of utter whiteness and noise, it had begun to accelerate. He had started a slight turn to the left towards the departure beacon, which became tighter, nearly vertical, his wingman at full power pulling hard to stay in position. Then, suddenly correcting, he began to roll the other way, to the right, going past straight and level, banking steeper and steeper, past the point where Tracy could stay with him, becoming inverted, heading down.

"Cousin Echo," Tracy called, "I've lost you."

Rolling out, on his own instruments then, Tracy managed to stop his descent. He found himself going over five hundred miles an hour. He called his leader a number of times on both channels, tower and departure control, but there was no reply.

The last few seconds, beneath the clouds, must have been a collapse of all reality for the colonel as he burst into the visible world in a nearly vertical dive. Everything he knew and had known was suddenly of no avail. If, even for a moment, he thought of bailing out, it was already too late. As if in a nightmare, in the final second his eyes smashed through surfaces, he entered a new dimension.

The first awareness for us that anything was wrong was the announcement by the tower that the field was closed to all traffic, an emergency was in progress. There was nothing more, no voices on the air, no instructions or calls. Only silence and a few dark birds flying low, near the wintry clouds.

Brischetto was forty-one years old. He had a family, children. In the housing area the telephone must have eventually rung in his apartment. "Colonel Brischetto's quarters," one of them would say.

The aircraft was completely demolished, the accident report read. Cause of death: *injuries multiple extreme.* The body, it was stated, was destroyed beyond recognition. More than that can hardly occur. It was impossible to know with certainty why it all had happened. Most likely the colonel had looked away from his instruments for several seconds, absorbed in trying to read the number on the channel selector, down by his left elbow. That had caused the first unintentional, steep turn. He had corrected that. Perhaps he could not understand why he heard no one on the radio and looked down again. Perhaps when he returned to his instruments he saw chaos beyond his power to decipher.

Subdued, we nevertheless flew to Rome that afternoon and on to Africa where we fired gunnery for weeks over the green, unoccupied sea.

———

North Africa had its spell. Silent, forgotten cities along the coast, joined by a single empty road. The marble columns from Roman days pillaged over the centuries for European palaces and estates.

On windless mornings we took off early and headed out to sea. The tow plane was already on course, at twenty thousand feet, the slender white target moving serenely some distance behind it.

The first mission of the day. The air has a full, damp quality. Long, holy streamers curve through it, marking our passes. There is a rhythm, like section hands dreamily pounding spikes. In the gunsight the target grows larger, slowly at first and then with a rush, in range for only a second or two. The bullets leave thin traces of smoke as they vanish into the cloth—each plane's have been dipped in a different color paint so they can afterwards be counted. To the south, invisible, on the one great road of the kingdom, paralleling the sea, there are arches of palms and thousands upon thousands of stiff, laundered flags to mark the route of the wedding party traveling west from Benghazi. The king had taken a second wife, who was Egyptian.

That night in Tripoli, amid the rancid smell of smoke, a torchlight parade passed along the street through the crowds. I stood outside a tailor shop and watched. The owner, Salvatore Perrucio, stood beside me. "What is it, is the king coming?" I asked.

"Oh, no," Perrucio said. "He wouldn't dare."

"Why not?"

"They kill him," he said.

I laughed at the joke.

"Don't," he warned. "Never laugh. If they see you doing that, they kill you, too. Never laugh at them. Call them anything you want, but never laugh."

It was difficult to know who he was talking about, the mobs in the street, the short dark men in double-breasted suits in the Uaddan Hotel, the wraithlike figures drifting without apparent purpose along the beach, the bare-legged men working in the salt flats near our planes? We knew none of them. They were part of something impenetrable. Together with the buildings and statuary of an ancient colonial world, they went back at least two thousand years, to the days of Leptis Magna and Sabratha. Surviving within them all this time was a seething and unalterable code.

Perrucio made suits, bespoke, for thirty or forty dollars, as I recall. When he was twelve, he told me modestly, he could make a complete suit all by himself. He'd been a prisoner of the English during the war and had made uniforms for them. The time he spent in prison camp was the happiest of his life, he said. "A lovely country. Such beautiful women—and so easy to get. Of course, I was different-looking then. I wasn't like this"—he clasped his wide waist with his hands. He had the full, pleasant face of a man in touch with life. Inside the shop, half concealed by a curtain, a boy sat, two thin legs in shorts and a plum-shaped body, cutting and basting patterns, the very age Perrucio had been.

I flew south one day, a hundred or two hundred miles into the desert, the earth changing from ruggedness to orange dust. There was no life, no roads, no trace of anything. Turning, I began to descend in long, uninquisitive arcs until finally, at fifty or a hundred feet, I was heading back north.

At that height one can see only a few miles ahead. Unexpectedly, things began to appear, occasional lonely shepherds, grazing camels, a low, dark group of tents. Suddenly there were animals scattering before me, children throwing themselves to the ground, the momentary glimpse of women who had hurried to tent doors. In twenty minutes I would be on the ground at Wheelus but I would remain aloft much longer in the minds of these unknown people, crossing their world with furious sound and then gone.

Beyond them, past shale mountains and stretches of sand, came the first faint tincture of civilization: telegraph wires, cultivation, roads. Farther still, hard and gleaming, the sea.

It was from the other side of this sea that Perrucio had come, from the long, rugged peninsula that had been the center of the world. It was easy to see the long throw of his life, Italy, North Africa, the war, and finally North Africa again in unmarked exile, a life begun perhaps ten years earlier than mine and meant from the beginning to be more conventional and unesteemed. I envied its simplicity, the fineness of the suits he so carefully made. The days of pale English roses, probably less well scrubbed than I imagined and coarser voiced, were far behind. He lived among a less exotic species now, his wife, daughter, mother-in-law.

At the Bath Club, dreary and English, there were desiccated copies of *London Illustrated News* spread on the tables and a drink of scotch cost a dime. One night, when her escort had gone off for a few minutes, we invited a watery blonde, the only woman in the club, to come to the base on Saturday night. All right, she said. She wanted to bring along a friend, someone named Emma.

"Who is Emma?"

"You'll like her," she said.

I seem to recall Emma now as being older. Saturday night was always crowded and boisterous. Half-drunk and suddenly remembering the invitation, three of us went to the main gate to meet the women and guide their car to the club. "We're waiting for a couple of visitors," I told the guards.

The road leading to the base was empty. There were no headlights, only alien darkness. Minutes passed.

"What time is it?"

"Eight-thirty."

"What time did we say?"

"I forget."

After a while one of the guards turned his head. He heard someone approaching. "Might be your visitors," he said.

"Couldn't be," I said with assurance. "They'll be in a car," I explained as the shadowy figures of the two demoiselles materialized down the road. They were walking in high heels. It was miles to town. Such was the allure of our pay and wrinkled khaki.

These European women, few as they were, now seem faint pencil marks on the North African page. It was more or less clear why they had come and also that they would find little here. The bargains that could be struck were meager. Perhaps it was exactly this, the injudiciousness, their need for luck, that made one remember them at all.

———

In Morocco, where we went for good weather in which to fly the new airplanes, F-100s—more powerful and less forgiving—with which we were to be equipped, the air was different. Morocco had been a French colony and bordered another sea. From its coast one could reach England or even the New World. There were boulevards, apartment houses, the elegy of French names.

Fedala was to the south with wide beaches and surf breaking close to shore. It was for off-duty hours, inexplicable blue bulbs in the ceiling of the hotel and a waiter awkwardly pouring the wine. We would sit on the terrace in the evening, the faces around the table slowly becoming indistinct. In the distance the sea, which defined everything, fell endlessly upon itself. Our glory was endless, too. We were great captains all. We sat at ease. The beeves had been slaughtered; the cooks, all in white, stood ready to prepare the meal. The idle hours are passed in drinking, talking, desiring. There are weeks left in the campaign; another follows.

Later there is the Sphinx, named probably for its predecessor in Paris on Boulevard Edgar Quinet. You could see it from the air, iron gates and a gravel driveway. Inside it was tiled, a nightclub: downstairs, blue films and books; upstairs, women. The rooms on the second floor faced the sea. "As many times as you like," she said, speaking French at the bar. At the far end of the room a band was playing. She was from Marseille, skin pale and shining like fruitwood. Her dress was cut low, her breasts smooth and perfectly separated. We danced like a couple, as if we had come there together. She was pressed against me. The black tile pillars slid before my eyes, the mirrors, the trio at the floorside table, two men and a girl with short black hair, the gold of a wedding band on her finger. They were the *haut monde,* come for titillation.

Canadian pilots are entering. The band is playing something I would like to remember. Far away it seems, unmourned, are all the other nights, the unattainable women, nurses, admirals' daughters, the colonel's wife that time unsteadily playing blackjack. "Just give me a little bitty one," she pleaded, "don't give it to me unless it's little." It was dealt. A jack. She stared at it, looked at her hole card, stared again. Her handsome, slurred face. "All right," she announced, "twenty-one." But it was not. The dealer took the money.

The morning light of Africa is brilliant and flat. The empty street, the silence. How was it? they want to know. That, one can embroider, one can tell, but there is a foolish thing one cannot— she came to the gate to say goodbye. She asked if you would write, a postcard from Port Lyautey, addressed simply to Dené, Sphinx, Fedala.

In Tangier the peddlers and guides were outside at all hours, some displaying letters of recommendation. In 1956 you could buy a palace—baths, servants' quarters, patios—for twelve thousand dollars. Like other exotic cities, Tangier reeked of dust, of the endless cycle of living and dying. The market was teeming, hundreds of stalls, chickens with their feet tied lying docilely on the ground, mounds of tomatoes, many misshapen, goats, women nursing babies, bags of grain. It seemed merciless. In the garden of the sultan's palace legions of ants were streaming around a dead sparrow.

I wake from a nap. The city is at its most frightening, most implacable. Day is past and night is falling. Across the avenue two girls at the beach club are hanging up their bathing suits to dry. To be alone here, I think . . . to be improvident or penniless, to feel the darkness on every side.

I am not sure where the terror of North Africa comes from—

from its emptiness, I suppose, from all that is unknowable. Life is cheap there, it is only a husk. Perhaps it is the cruelty, the mutilation, the followers of El Glaoui drenched with gasoline and set afire, although, as someone said, it had thoughtfully not been done in front of their children and wives; the British sergeants found with their genitals sewn in their mouths; the man who was in "that square" in Marrakech and turned to bargain with someone—when he turned back, his wife was gone, never seen again. Perhaps it was the trade in sex, the White Horse, where beneath bright lights, as calmly as if undressing backstage, a young Spanish girl, flawless as a statue, steps from her clothes. A heavier girl produces a threatening device and straps it on . . .

We crossed Gibraltar, like a pebble far below, and then brown, hard Spain. We were going home with new airplanes, the first of those that could routinely fly faster than the speed of sound. They landed at high speed, touching down at a hundred and eighty miles an hour. On the luxurious runways and in the smooth air of North Africa this was not a challenge, but our own field was much smaller. We were at thirty-seven thousand feet, and letting down, I felt a nervousness I couldn't get rid of. We entered traffic, dropped gear on the downwind leg, turned onto final. Everything looked all right. Two hundred and twenty on approach, then across the end of the runway, power off, waiting to touch. A faint jolt. The ground is streaming by. As we park, the group and wing commanders hand up cold beer.

In the end I missed North Africa. I missed its desolation and the brilliance of the light. We, too, were nomads there. We traveled and lived in tents; we had our time-worn code, our duties, and nothing more: to fly, to sit in the shade of the canvas and eat a white-bread sandwich with grimy hands, to fly again.

We were equals there, all ranks. "Hit me," the colonel says. "I can't, I'll get court-martialed," Geraghty, who is dealing, squeals. They are drunkenly comparing Rolexes. "What's wrong with yours? It has no calendar, must be experimental," Geraghty says. All these faces, so well known. All these lives, so momentarily intimate.

In formation with Minish one day, coming back from a mission, I on his wing—without a word he pulled up and did an Immelmann, I as close as you can get, then another and another, then some loops and rolls, two or three away from me, all in hot silence, I had not budged a foot, the two of us together, not a word exchanged, like secret lovers in some apartment on a burning afternoon.

———

We went in the autumn, a squadron at a time, to the Gironde, in the southwest of France, for more gunnery. The field there, Cazaux, girlishly white, was beside a lake. A squadron from another wing, one I had for a time flown with, was already there. They were sitting outside the barracks when we arrived, like ranch hands, sucking blades of grass. It often seemed not so much a profession as a way of wasting time, waiting for something to happen, your name to come up on the scheduling board, the scramble phone to ring, the last flights to land. The faces of these others had not changed in the year or two since last seen: Vandenburg, Paul Ingram, Christman, who married a countess, Vandevander, Leach. They greeted us casually. It was as if we had come to graze and they were another clan, peaceful if not friendly, now obliged to share.

We laze through the days. They become the sacred past. The days that Faulkner said were the most exciting of his life. He said that to Sylvester, a major who'd been an information officer stationed in Greenville, Mississippi, not far from Faulkner's home, during the Korean War. A librarian Sylvester knew had offered to introduce him to Faulkner as a favor. At the agreed-upon time, Faulkner appeared. He was drunk. He was wearing a wrinkled planter's suit in the coat pocket of which was a bottle, Sylvester took it to be gin. They talked about flying and the days, Faulkner said, when he had been a flyer in France. He had never been that. He had told it many times, to women, to men. Perhaps he had come to believe it.

There is a feeling Faulkner probably had—I have had it myself—that somewhere the true life is being lived, though not where you are. He may have heard the sound of it in Greenville, the rich, destructive roar not of planes such as he had known but ones far more potent. Something in him responded to that, the same thing most likely that had made him pose as an officer in the Royal Flying Corps, invent combat missions, crashes, a silver plate in his head. He was a small man. He could sit in a chair and his feet sometimes might not touch the floor. His world was small, an illiterate county seat, a backward state, though from it he fashioned something greater, far greater perhaps than even he knew. A writer cannot really grasp what he has written. It is not like a building or a sculpture; it cannot be seen whole. It is only a kind of smoke seized and printed on a page.

One thing about Faulkner I like, apart from the simplicity, on the whole, of his life, was that he wrote on the bedroom walls. That seems to me the true mark of a writer. It is like a pianist practicing in the middle of the night when the whole household is asleep or trying to sleep—the music is greater than any of their lives.

That day in Greenville, Faulkner, ten years from his death, offered to write a story about the Air Force if in exchange he might have a ride in a jet. Sylvester promptly called the base commander, a colonel, who listened to the proposal. At the end his reply was only "Who's Faulkner?"

———

One Monday, just after the pilots' meeting, the phone rang. It was a clerk in combat operations. Did I know that one of my pilots had bailed out over Chaumont? Chaumont? In France? It must be a mistake—we had nobody flying yet, I said.

Then I remembered the two planes being ferried.

The preceding Friday night, in the camaraderie at the club, someone had suggested that the planes being sent to the depot at Châteauroux for overhaul, since they still had some hours remaining on them before inspection, be released to fly over the weekend. Why not? I thought. Pilots always wanted flying time. I did not check where they had gone. It was of no importance. They were heading for Châteauroux by a roundabout route.

We waited uneasily to hear something more. After a while it came. One pilot, it was reported, had bailed out on the approach. The second had landed; it was Carney. Of DeShazer, nothing further was known.

It developed that they had gone to Munich, where the ground crew had signed off the planes as fully serviced but failed to check the oil. After the weekend they had left early in the morning for Châteauroux. At thirty-five thousand feet DeShazer had a loss of power. It was the oil-operated main fuel regulator failing. He went over to his emergency fuel system and headed for the nearest field: Chaumont.

They made a long, straight-in final to Chaumont. Carney, flying on DeShazer's wing, saw a burst of flame, brilliant and terrifying, come out of the tailpipe. The bearings had failed. The engine was devouring itself. "Get out, Bill!" he called, but DeShazer anticipated him. The canopy shot away. The seat followed, up and over, tumbling behind the airplane, DeShazer's arms fluttering wildly. All our planes were equipped with a device that opened the safety belt automatically and allowed the pilot and seat to come quickly apart—all planes, it turned out, except one. The seat fell and fell, Carney trying to keep it in sight. Finally the seat and pilot separated. A long white writhing shape streamed out and reached full length but never completely bloomed before going into the trees. The sum of trivialities had reached a certain number—the result was the disappearance of a man.

They looked for him all day. At last, in midafternoon, they found him. He was dead.

Unmarried, homely, balding, with widely spaced teeth like pickets, he was good-natured. Someone had asked to borrow money and DeShazer said there was some in the bureau in his room. It was Kelley, I think, who went there and found five or six hundred dollars lying loose and uncounted among the clothes.

After it was over and the reports had been sent in, I stopped at the club for a drink on the way home. An accident occurring in another squadron seemed a consequence of some kind; in one's own squadron it was fate, heavy and humbling. The days became divided, those before and those to come. DeShazer's name would be taken from the board on which pilots were listed, the loss probably of his chief distinction. His personal effects would be packed and shipped home. The squadron commander, Norman Phillips, would compose a letter to his parents. In the year to come, four or five new pilots would arrive in the squadron to begin their tours, none of them having heard of DeShazer or prepared to believe in the sudden amazing flare, like the gust before a magician's act, announcing the unfathomable.

Yet he would not be forgotten. Like others he would reappear, like the fair-haired, imaginary aces Faulkner wrote poems about. DeShazer, far more unassuming, with his wide, cracked-lip smile, would remain in one's life. Arms flapping, he would tumble endlessly, his parachute, long and useless, trailing behind.

Not at first, and not until you accept that you are mortal, do you begin to realize that life and death are the same thing. DeShazer had gone elsewhere. Into the stars.

———

Munich for the last time, glittering in the darkness, immense—the shops, the avenues, the fine cars. The wingman's ship is out to one side near a crescent moon. The Arend-Roland comet is visible, its milky tail flying southwards for thousands of miles, an inch in the sky. I lean back and gaze at it, my helmet against the padding. I will never see it again or, just this way, all that is below. Some joys exist in retrospect but not this, the serenity, the cities shining in detailed splendor. From the deeps of the sky we look down as if upon our flocks.

The farewell party a few weeks later seems like any other though it is the last; drinking, singing, the end of the tour and an occasion that fixes everything but that is also something else, not quite animate, an episode in the life of a squadron that will go on without you, without everyone. All will be superseded, all forgotten.

Uden and Tucker have come with German girls. The father of Uden's had been a pilot, a Luftwaffe pilot, she said. He had never returned from his third raid over England. They never had any further news. She had been five or six years old when it happened, a child of the war, handsome now and composed.

For me it is particularly poignant, not her lost father but the evening. At the appropriate time, rising to my feet, I try to say something of what I feel, the allowable portion. I cannot simply say I've liked being in the squadron, I tell them—my life has *been* the squadron, a life, I do not explain, that I am abandoning. A few months earlier, Spry, who had graduated a few classes after me and was in group operations, had told me he was resigning. Almost at that instant—he had somehow given me the freedom, hurled the first stone—I made the decision. It was far from decisive. I discussed it with my wife who, with only a partial understanding of what was involved, did not attempt to change my mind. I had perhaps waited too long, but there was still part of me that existed when I was a schoolboy and had never really died—it was in me like a pathogen—the idea of being a writer and from the great heap of days making something lasting.

The Air Force—I ate and drank it, went in whatever weather on whatever day, talked its endless talk, climbed onto the wing to fuel the ship myself, fell into the wet sand of its beaches with sweaty others and was bitten by its flies, ignored wavering instruments, slept in dreary places, rendered it my heart. I had given up the life into which I had been born and taken up another and was about to leave that, too, only with far greater difficulty.

To those that night, among whom there were some that fate would beckon, I said I would see them again. Good luck.

———

I was on leave at Langley and drove up to Washington to resign. It was June, the tenth, the day on which I'd been born. It seemed fitting.

All the way, in anguish, I weighed the choices. I had published a book that year, the first, written at night and on weekends, page by unsuspected page. *The Hunters* appeared under a nom de plume. Salter was as distant as possible from my own name. It was essential not to be identified and jeopardize a career—I had heard the sarcastic references to "God Is My Copilot" Scott. I wanted to be admired but not known. I was thirty-two years old and had been in uniform since I was seventeen. I had a wife and child with another coming soon. As I walked into the Pentagon I felt I was walking to my death.

On various floors I stopped and looked at the directories, brigadiers and major generals one had never heard of, hard at work in their bureaus: Plans, where I used to drop in and talk to Beukema about fighters. Would it be difficult, he wanted to know, for him to make the transition to them? He'd been trained in B-29s.

He had been in my company, a class ahead of me at West Point, outstanding in studies and captain of the hockey team. Superior in every way, charming, unsuperficial, an exceedingly rare type, he had grown up at West Point in an idyllic boyhood, the son of a professor there. He had married General Bradley's daughter and was marked—though not by that—everyone agreed, for greatness. I knew the room in barracks he had lived in, the exact color of his blond hair. I could easily see him as a fighter pilot—it seemed natural.

He was ultimately assigned to Langley and F-84s, a plane with a fine appearance but underpowered and with a long takeoff roll. At thirty thousand feet one day, as squadron commander–designate, he told his flight leader he wanted to try something. He began a shallow dive. It continued and began to steepen, more and more. It was a characteristic of the airplane, which may have come into effect here, that when maximum speed, the red line, was exceeded there was a control reversal, and pulling back on the stick made the nose go further down rather than come up.

He crashed in the water off Langley at high speed. He perished, not from having flown too near the sun—he was the sun's angel—but from taunting the demon of speed.

I sat at a desk in Separations and typed out my letter; then, like the survivor of some wreck, I roamed, carrying it, through the corridors for more than an hour. Finally I saw a colonel I knew, Berg, coming out of a doorway. He worked in Personnel, in charge of promotion boards. Needing the confidence of someone, I told him what I was about to do. He made no effort to dissuade me. He merely nodded. He mentioned several other officers who had recently resigned. I found it of little comfort. Late in the afternoon, feeling almost ill, I handed in the letter. It was the most difficult act of my life.

In thick heat I drove up Connecticut Avenue to an apartment we had the use of. Alone, I began to weep—the emptiness, the long years, all the men, the places. My former wing commander from Bitburg who had come back to Washington some months earlier was in Arlington, in the suburbs. I still felt close to him, one of his own. I called him on the telephone and, in unhappiness, managed to tell him what I had done. "You idiot," he said.

I went there for dinner. Why had I done it? he wanted to know. I had intended to tell the truth but broke off at the last moment knowing it would sound foolish to him and instead, as an apology, brought forth something from the schoolroom. I had done it, I said, because the future looked unpromising to me. As Napoleon had remarked at his coronation, if he had been born under Louis XIV, the most he could have hoped to be was a marshal, like Turenne. I cannot imagine what he thought.

Over and over during the days that followed, with nothing to do, I watched the cars going down the avenue in the morning or looked at the lighted Capitol and the city spread brilliantly around it at night. A baby, my daughter, was crying in the next room. Never another city, over it for the first time, in the lead, the field that you have never landed on far below, dropping down towards it, banking steeply one way, then the other, calling the tower, telling them who you are. Never another sunburned face in Tripoli looking up at you as you taxi to a stop, the expression asking, ship OK? A thumb raised, OK. And the dying whine, like a great sigh, of the engine shutting down, the needles on the gauges collapsing. It is over.

We went back to Langley. A strange, bottomless reaction had set in. With Paula and Leland, in whose house we were staying, I could hardly talk and found it impossible to laugh. Paula said she admired my courage, though what I'd had felt gone. We spent that evening talking about God. They were firm believers. It all seemed unimportant and beside the point.

———

Dreams remained. For years afterwards in nightmares stark as archive footage, I was what I had been. We were in Asia some-where. Disaster was in the air. We were surrendering and there had been a warning from the enemy, a written warning, that because of the many atrocities we had committed there could be no guarantee of safety. I was standing in a hospital near three or four pilots, one of whom I knew. They were going to try to cross to where their planes were parked, take off, and continue fighting. They started for the field. There was firing, heavy and relentless. Someone came to ask if I would take the fourth plane. An F-100. I hadn't been in one for years . . .

I did fly, however. On weekends I flew with the National Guard and went with them to summer camp in Cape Cod or Virginia. In the fall of 1961 we were placed on active duty—it was the so-called Berlin crisis—and went to France for nearly a year, to Chaumont, where DeShazer had crashed and where my agent, Kenneth Littauer, had flown during the First World War. They had lit bonfires at the corners of the field, he said, to guide planes home after dark.

It was September. We landed in a light rain, the first ones, having flown the planes across the Atlantic, stopping in the Azores and Seville. I asked the crew chief who met me what the town was like. He answered without hesitation, "Looks all right."

That year, I understood quite well, was the close of things. We were reserves—I had looked down upon such as we were now. I wore the uniform still, the colored ribbons, but the genuineness was gone, even when Norstad, the glamorous theater commander, came on a visit and lay sideways in an easy chair in his flying suit, chatting about the outbreak of war and what it would bring as he saw it, or even the brusque appearance of LeMay himself, with a retinue that filled an entire plane. We were able to conduct ourselves well enough if called upon and convincingly say "Sir," but it was only for a time.

This transparency set me free. All that before had been insignificant, unmartial, caught my eye, buildings, countryside, towns, hotels. As a lieutenant colonel I had a room of my own at the head of the stairs. There, late at night, back from a restaurant, back from the bar, I sat writing. I had three lives, one during the day, one at night, and the last in a drawer in my room in a small book of notes.

There were wonderful things in that book, things that I am unable to write or even imagine again. That they were wonderful was not my doing—I merely took the trouble to put them down. They were like the secret notebook of the *chasseur* at Maxim's, without ego or discretion, and the novel woven around them (*A Sport and a Pastime*) owed them everything. The leather-seated car I drove is gone; the house of Lazan and his wife, where we went for Thanksgiving and Christmas dinner, I know is off towards Langres somewhere but I doubt I would be able to find it again; the elegant couple in Paris have divorced; the young girl, the essential element—of course, she cannot change; that is the whole point—went to America and became what you might expect. Ironically, the portrait I made of her she never read.

Much has faded but not the incomparable taste of France, given then so I would always remember it. I know that taste, the yellow headlights flowing along the road at night, the towns by a river, the misty mornings, the thoughts of everything that happened there, the notes that confirmed it and made it imperishable.

———

In the blue twilight, lightning descends to the dim Texas plains. I can hear it crackling on the radio. The sky is filled with storms, a huge line of them. I am barely on top at forty-two thousand feet; they boil beneath me, shot with lightning like a kind of X ray, heaving the airplane around. Down there is Frederick, Oklahoma, where we were stationed for a while just after the war. There were shining new planes in rows but no one to maintain them. The bare wooden barracks in which we sat idle grew cold as autumn advanced.

By now it is dark. The radio compass is erratic. I believe I have

Tyler but can't be sure. A bit later I try Baton Rouge—nothing. The fuel is just at fifteen hundred pounds. I call for New Orleans destination weather: scattered and ten miles' visibility, they reply, but beneath me it is overcast despite the report. Then, not more than five minutes out, the clouds begin to break, there are lights.

Years when I crossed the country alone, like some replica Philip Nolan, in thousand-mile legs. Taking off from Wright-Patterson in a tremendous rainstorm, unable to even see the end of the runway or the trees. Taking off from McGuire in another downpour— Ritchings with an umbrella walking me out to the ship—taking off at Mobile, taking off at March and Forbes. Taking off at Tyndall, the earth like dust on a mirror, a long, unmoving line of smoke— from the paper mill, was it?—running south as far as eye could see. Going out early in the morning, hands still numb, the magical silence of the runways, the whole pale scene. Heading for the Gulf under its blue haze, counties and parishes intent and unaware though I know their lives in vast detail, Brookley shining like a coin in the light off Mobile Bay.

Sometimes, because of the light, in the visor there is the moist dark of one's own eye, bigger than a movie poster. Sometimes there is the sun directly ahead making it impossible to read the instruments. The earth below is shadowed. There are mythic serpents of water, lakes, rivers smooth as marble. Empty sky, the rumbling aircraft, the radio overflowing with voices and sounds. Above the yellow horizon, near the vanishing sun, suddenly, a dot. Behind it a faint line, a contrail. By some forgotten reflex I am stunned awake, as in days past when we watched intently, when the body filled with excitement to see it: the enemy!

There were airfields everywhere, left over from the war, relic fields the names of which I knew from stories, Wendover, Pocatello. Leaving them and climbing out, over the alkali, the thin trace of roads, railroad tracks, dust. Not a city, not even a house.

Snow on the distant hills, which are slowly sinking as I rise, all else brown. The West. From here it is endless, land that goes on forever. Down there it is the sky that has no end.

One night as I was calling for a letdown near St. Louis, the city jewel-like and clear, a voice in the darkness asked, "Flatfoot Red, is that you?" Flatfoot, our call sign from Bitburg, and Red, the color of the lead flight.

"Yes," I said. "Who's that?"

En route you seldom saw other fighters and almost never recognized a voice.

"Ed White."

The pleasure, the thrill, in fact, the sort that comes from a lingering glance across a room, a knowing nod, or a pair of fingers touched briefly to the brow. We were able to exchange only a few words—How are you? Where are you headed? I looked for him in the blackness, the moving star that would be his plane, but the heavens were littered with stars, the earth strewn with lights. He was on his way to somewhere, the heights, I was sure. I was going in to land.

"See you," he said.

Who could know it would be otherwise and he was one whom I would never see again? We had flown on the acrobatic team together, he the right wing, Whitlow the left, Tracy in the slot.

After his death his widow remarried. Not many years later, she herself died, apparently a suicide. The waters had closed over them both.

I often thought of White and that hail across the darkness I took as a last meeting. I thought of him as I watched a parade in the city one day. It was November, Armistice Day, but there was the heat and fullness of late summer. The dirt was blowing in the streets. I was part of New York myself by then, returned to it. They came along Fifth Avenue, the ranks of the American Legion, the police and high-school bands, teenage girls dressed in blazers, ten-year-old colonels wearing sunglasses, fat men, limpers. The drums went by. The sidewalks were crowded with people. Rows of silver trumpets passed. Then the flags. The crowd watched. Not a hat was lifted, not a hand stirred.

———

Once at a dinner party I was asked by a woman what on earth I had ever seen in military life. I couldn't answer her, of course. I couldn't summon it all, the distant places, the comradeship, the idealism, the youth. I couldn't tell about flying over the islands long ago, seeing them rise in the blue distance wreathed in legend, the ring of white surf around them. Or the cities, Shanghai and Tokyo, Amsterdam and Venice, gunnery camps in North Africa and forgotten colonies of Rome along the shore.

I couldn't describe that, or what it was like waiting to take off on missions in Korea, armed, nervous, singing songs to yourself, or the electric jolt that went through you when the MIGs came up. I couldn't tell about Mahurin being shot down and not a soul seeing him go, or George Davis, or deArmont, who used to jump up on a table in the club and recite "Gunga Din"—the drunken pilots thought he was making it up.

I couldn't tell her about brilliant group commanders or flying with men who later became famous, the days and days of boredom and moments of pure ecstasy, of walking out to the parked planes in the early morning or coming in at dusk when the wind had died to make the last landing of the day and the mobile control officer giving two quick clicks of the mike to confirm: grease job. To fly with the thirty-year-old veterans and finally earn the right to lead yourself, flights, squadrons, a few times the entire group. The great days of youth when you are mispronouncing foreign words and trading dreams.

We came in from the flight line at Giebelstadt or Cazaux, weary, faces marked, unknown, and went into town to drink. Money meant nothing and in a way neither did fame. I couldn't tell any of that or of the roads along the sea in Honolulu, the dances, the last drinks at the bar, or who Harry Thyng was, or Kasler, or the captain's wife.

II

FORGOTTEN KINGS

IN MY HAND is a blue square of paper, the blue of Gauloises, and slowly I unfold it once more. I feel the excitement still. The creases have acquired a memory, opening, they reveal the invitation:

> *Can you meet me for a drink Relais*
> *bar Hotel Plaza Athénée Saturday*
> *evening seven P.M ?*

It is signed simply, *Shaw.*

November, the darkness coming on early, or perhaps December, late in the fall and the year, 1961. The city, as I thought of it, was like a splendid photograph, every wide avenue, every street. I had never met a writer of distinction. My agent, who was Irwin Shaw's agent also, had given him my name, and I was driving to Paris to meet him, coming in from the chill provinces by way of the thrilling diagonal that ran on the map from Chaumont, up through Troyes, to the very heart.

I had a large, elegant secondhand car, blue also, the shade of uniforms of the fleet, steering wheel on the wrong side, four speeds forward and four in reverse as well, small ignition key like those to a safe-deposit box or clock. The engine purred, the boulevards blazed with light. I drank the very air, I was entering Paris.

Crossing a vast intersection crowded with traffic I suddenly jammed on the brakes and managed to stop in the act of barely kissing—there was no sensation attached—the gleaming rear fender of the car ahead, a brand-new, as it happened, Citroën. The owner kept on shouting in a French more rapid than any I had ever heard, cars were blowing their horns and inching around us, we were trying to find an invisible dent in the shining black finish. At length police arrived and finally dismissed the case. Half an hour had passed. I arrived at the Plaza Athénée sick with despair. It was nearer to 8 than 7. I had missed the appointment. The doorman—the car was frequently saluted by them in those days—allowed me to park in front, and empty-hearted I went into the Relais. The first thing I saw was a solidly built man standing at the bar in an open trench coat, a copy of *Le Monde* stuffed in one pocket. I recognized him instantly. "That's all right," he said as I stumbled through an apology, "what are you drinking?" It was quintessentially him.

Time with its broad thumb has blurred nothing. He was forty-eight that year and already late for a dinner he was going to on Avenue Foch. He gave me the address—come afterwards for coffee, he said. A few minutes later, paying the bill, he left. Thus I discovered that Paris. There were worlds above, I learned, but there are also worlds below. I found Avenue Foch—the name itself has only a faint resonance now, the century is ending and into its crypt all such things will vanish, marshals of France as well as unknown *poilus*—and I also found the Île St.-Louis, rue de Grenelle, Place St.-Sulpice, and apartments and restaurants as well as other towns and regions, not always in France, because of him. He was my unknowing Virgil, brief in his descriptions, irrefutable, fond of drink. Years later I heard him give some advice: never be in awe of anyone. He was not in awe of Europe. He tossed his coat on her couch.

That first night was for me like the ball that Emma Bovary never forgot. There were fourteen in the dinner party including a young Peruvian actress in a black silk dress cut astonishingly low. An older man took her aside to say, "I don't know who you came with but you're not going home with him. That's definite." They were telling stories of theater, films, the maharajah of producers who refused to allow the woman he was escorting to use the ladies' room in a fashionable hotel. He rented a suite instead. She went in, came out, and he paid the bill, fifty pounds.

"The new Trubetskoy," someone observed.

We drove down the Champs. The air was filled with the bite of autumn, it was tingling. The sea, endless and black, was falling against the coasts. I had met screenwriters, owners of restaurants, *joueurs*.

———

I had been to Paris a number of times. On my first trip to Europe we drove there, three of us: Farris, me, and the club officer from Wiesbaden whose car it was. We started early in the morning, the roads empty, and sometime after noon entered the outlying neighborhoods, gray and unknown. We went straight to the Littré Hotel, which the military had appropriated and from the windows of which there was nothing to be seen but the bleakness of buildings forty feet away across the street. It was a winter day. Later we drove up to Montmartre to change some money on the black market.

I had a poor impression of Paris which not even the Champs-Elysées, wide as a carrier deck and with only occasional cars, was able to improve. Paris seemed a dark, somewhat dishonored city that had managed to survive the war. The monuments and stone façades were black, but it was grime, not the smoke of disaster, that had stained them. The French had collapsed in the first round and given up the capital intact, an act which was practical if unheroic.

I spoke some French, the residuum of schooldays. The discipline of studying things you did not want to learn had not fallen out of favor, and my own education was stamped by this. We read episodes of *Wind, Sand, and Stars* with the index finger of illiterates. The notion of a person, place, or thing being masculine or feminine seemed to have no purpose, and the possibility that one would ever use French, unlikely. It was merely another hurdle.

I don't know where we went that night or what we drank, but the real Paris appeared near dawn, in the faint light, with an image like Mahomet's paradise: driving through the streets with six girls and the top down, some of them sitting on it or beside us, two on our laps. It was like riding banked in flowers. Montmartre was grainy in the early light in which everything, every deformity and cheap enterprise, every grubby restaurant and shop, was pure.

There is the Paris of Catherine de Médicis at the Tuileries, as Hugo wrote; of Henry I at the Hôtel-de-Ville, of Louis XIV at Invalides, Louis XVI at the Panthéon, and Napoleon I at the Place Vendôme, but there is also the Paris of those who did not rule, the poets and vagabonds, and it was the Paris of Henry Miller we were in; I had not read him but I had presupposed him, carnal, crazed, at odds with everything and the next moment embracing it, in worn-out corduroy, tieless, walking home through the streets. This Paris where you woke bruised after tremendous nights—indelible nights, your pockets empty, the last bills scattered on the floor, the memories scattered too. We went upstairs with three girls apiece and the club officer napped in the car.

Paris. Early morning. Its cool breath astonishingly fresh. Its elegance and ancient streets, its always staggering price. The sound of early traffic. The sky blemishless and wide. Somewhere in the gallery of love where the pictures stir one beyond speaking—the light, the divinity, the absolute poise, where in rumpled beds at morning, in hushed voices, life is presented to you—somewhere in here for me there is a frame of Farris, an utterly intimate glimpse, his naked arm fallen from the side of the bed like Marat's. He was like a god, or, if not, with a grace God sometimes bestows, the gift to every stag and hare but not to many humans. Then it begins to quiver, this image and indistinct place, the happiness is unquenchable and worth anything, someone whispers, coaxing, someone is laughing, there are cars in the street, the sound of water running in the room. It was all a game, the one I had been seeking. An hour later the streets reclaimed us, the night was past.

Near the Gare St.-Lazare, Babel had once seen, late at night, a tall, beautiful woman in a faded evening dress waiting for clients. She was just like Hélène Bezukhov, wasn't she? he said to his companion. She might easily have been cast as the refined figure in *War and Peace* though her price was the same as all the rest. The first night, Paris was like that to me; it reminded me of something finer. In 1950 it was not weary of us. We were still handsome and admired; they smiled and turned on the street. The rooms were chill but they had proportion and there was more than a hint of another life, free of familiar inhibitions, a sacred life, this great museum and pleasure garden evolved for you alone.

———

In the empty morning a decade later I was lying in bed in my hotel, inexpensive and drab, behind the Place Vendôme. Startling me, the telephone rang with a jarring sound. It was Irwin Shaw. What was I doing, he asked, did I have any plans? "Come for lunch," he said.

I was overwhelmed. It was so natural, unimagined and longed for. They were living on Place Lamartine. The building number, like the number that pours chips into your hands on a winning night, I of course remember still, 2 *bis*.

There were just three of us, he, his wife, Marian, and me. The lunch was served by a uniformed maid in a latticed dining room which seems, as I think of it, to be pale green. We sat amid the silence of the 16th, the conservative, wealthy arrondissement of Paris, and leisurely had an omelette, salad, and for dessert, *ananas givré*—fresh pineapple ices in a hollowed-out half of the fruit. There was the ease and implication of French life, unseen gatherings all about us, flirtations, gossip about money. It was the end of the fifties, the years of the Sulzbergers, Matthiessens, Plimpton, Teddy White. A family lunch, and I was already seeing him as a kind of father—my own was gone—a father like Dumas or an ex–boxing champion, something in him extravagant, never to be taken away.

———

Max Wilkinson, the agent we shared, was a remarkable man also, though his name will not be found among those of the era. A Southerner, a born storyteller and dandy, just a country boy, as he was fond of saying, and his recitation included a number of obscure places: Tupelo, Mississippi; Jackson; perhaps a murmured New Orleans. The old Southern townsman was in him, unhurried and conspiratorial. His voice was easy and hinted of the unreliable. He remembered wearing his father's straw hat when Dempsey fought the Frenchman—Carpentier—and the summary of rounds came up one by one in the telegraph-office window in Courthouse Square.

"The first time I met Irwin," he said, "he came into the Collier's office with a story on some yellow paper, the kind that newspapermen wrote on, a lovely story about a wife who wanted to go back to Kansas City. He had—he never changed much—a sweet face. We didn't take the story," he added, "which was a shame."

It *was* a sweet face. It was often reddened, but it had no malice in it. It was a man's face, established, well-shaven, with a nose that was too large. Behind it, you understood at once, was no one devious. Even years later, when the veins in his cheeks began to burst, there was something boyish about him. Candor, even bluntness, was his style. Of self-pity he had almost none. If he ever cried, and I doubt it, he cried by himself. In public his lip never trembled, even when honors which he might have deserved passed him by.

There are men who seem to have seized the trunk of life, and he was one of them. It might not be for everyone, the great, scarring thing you could not get your arms around, but it was there for him. You ate well with him and, of course, drank. In a restaurant he would order first, to set the pace, so to speak, and immediately order wine. His method was simple: he worked nearly every day and avoided angst in the evenings. I knew him in Paris, Neuilly, at Fouquet's, the Hôtel des Bergues in Geneva on the quay, in Cap d'Antibes, Southampton, and Klosters. He was always absolutely the same. I can see him at the Delmonico in a room that had the expensive feeling of a stateroom, good clothes and things of every kind strewn about which the steward would see to, the phone ringing with invitations for the evening. "Call me back at about five-thirty," he would say, "and I'll have a better idea." By then he would know all the possibilities.

The thing I admired most in him was his behavior. It came from a way of living that seemed his alone, and was as irreproachable in itself as the stationery of a bank or the presentation of a menu by a headwaiter. In the world I had grown up in it seemed they did not know how to behave, and this was what he showed you. It was not manners—he dispensed with those—it was the confidence of the leader. When you were with him it was as if a cabinet minister was shuffling around in his slippers and a loosened robe, saying, "There's a bottle by the bookcase there. Help yourself."

Even his stupidities did not disgrace him. In a fury he once hit a much smaller man who was wearing glasses and had been tormenting him with a persistent insult, "You're a good writer, why are you such a whore?" In the bathroom afterwards with a cold washcloth on his forehead he was overcome with regret. The victim had been a journalist, it would be all over the papers. "Don't worry, Irwin," someone consoled him, "I don't think *Variety* has a sports page." They had to take him out the back door.

Through more than twenty years of friendship I never knew to which group of friends I belonged—he'd had at least eight sets of them, he once said. In any case I was a latecomer, after success, after the war, and not in a class with, for example, *the* friend of his life, as he thought of Robert Capa. In the south of France Capa had lived with them, brought women back to the house late at night, burned holes in the furniture, and sat lazily with cigarette ashes drifting onto his clothes until in the end Marian insisted that he leave, "He had decided he was running the house." It was Irwin who told him he had to go, an act for which he never forgave himself.

His was a friendship which lasted, though. He had gotten the Styrons married and the Taleses. You might not see him for years but it was instantly the same. I named a son for him: Shaw.

One afternoon long after, a writer at last, I sat reading a letter I had received. *I am so attracted to you and your ways . . .* Something drifted up from the sentence, a perfume, and in that moment for some reason I thought of him. This was what he knew, people attracted to him and his ways.

———

The truth was that, in the beginning, he saw in me the arrogance of failure. I had written two books, but the power I had was that I had accomplished nothing. My strength, like the evil-tempered dwarf's, was that my name was unknown. He, on the other hand, was a writer of magnitude. On the coffee table was a smooth silver cigarette box inscribed to him from his publishers at Random House, who were proud of both him and of *The Young Lions.* His fame seemed unshakable. There were the early plays, *Bury the Dead* and *Sons and Soldiers,* which was directed by Max Reinhardt, and the first, virile stories in *The New Yorker* that had created such excitement. He was brimming with energy and power. He wrote "The Girls in Their Summer Dresses" and "Sailor Off the Bremen" in the same week, the first of them in a single morning.

John O'Hara, the other blazing *New Yorker* writer of the time, was a difficult and unpredictable figure. His publisher referred to him as the master of the fancied slight. A fellow guest at a wedding in Rhode Island once came into the room where O'Hara was resting and asked, "Why is it you went to Fordham but you always write about Yale?" O'Hara got up and drove back to New York.

Irwin could be prickly too, but for the most part he was forbearing. Some early hurts were never forgotten. Until the end of his life he could run his fingers over nearly vanished scars, but he had known glory. He was paid just two hundred dollars for "Girls in Their Summer Dresses," a figure he liked to recall in inflated times, but with it came renown.

He was not a theorist. He had known the anguish of trying to find the right path, working on things for months and nearly throwing them away, then in amazement seeing them win prizes. He had no formal ideas about writing; he sat down and did it. There are stories one must tell, and years when one must tell them. He used to get up at four in the morning to write—that was in Cairo during the war. As an enlisted man in a special photography unit he was largely removed from danger, though you could have no doubt about his courage. His entire character was defined by it.

The night of nights when his son was born—not in Paris, as imagination for a moment might conceive, but far uptown in New York—he'd gone into "21" and encountered Hemingway, who had taken to calling him the Brooklyn Tolstoy. It was an unambiguous remark, a slur. Brooklyn meant Jewish. Hemingway had other, festering reasons for disliking Shaw, who'd had an affair with Hemingway's fourth wife before their marriage and in fact had introduced them. A man whose habit, both in writing and life, was not to pass up an insult, Hemingway had reportedly been telling people that he was going to punch Shaw in the nose when he saw him. In "21" that night he was at a table with Harold Ross, the editor of *The New Yorker*. Shaw walked over. "I hear you'd like to punch me in the nose," he said, omitting a prologue, "I'll be waiting over at the bar." Hemingway, who under various conditions had been known to be violent, stayed at the table.

Shaw almost never mentioned Hemingway. In Southampton years later, in the winter of his life, the doctors had crippled him, the overreaching trees were letting their leaves fall, the large world he knew was closing. Was he going to write these things down? No, he said without hesitation. "Who cares?"

He wanted immortality, of course, "What else is there?" Life passes into pages if it passes into anything, and his had been written. He could give an overgenerous estimate of himself. They were comparing him, at the table, to Balzac. No, he wrote better than Balzac, he said. "In French, he's hasty—he writes very short sentences."

"I love being a writer's wife, don't you?" someone said to Marian.

"No," Marian said.

The writer's life was a different matter, like the night Styron finished writing *The Confessions of Nat Turner*. It had happened at three in the morning in Connecticut. He went around and woke up all the children—they were small then—and sat them on the mantelpiece and put on Mozart. Never to be forgotten night. Irwin liked the story. He couldn't write any more, himself. The fire had died, the ashes were cold. There he sat, worn, hollow, like the remains of an old oak.

In the end the self is left unfinished, it is abandoned because of the death of its owner. All the exceptional details, confessions, secrets, photographs of loved faces and sometimes more than faces, precious addresses, towns and hotels meant to be visited given the time, stories, sacred images, immortal lines, everything heaped up or gathered because it is intriguing or beautiful suddenly becomes superfluous, without value, the litter of decades swirls at one's feet. The memory of Ernest at Rambouillet outside Paris in 1944 when they were about to enter the city—the room, you remember, was filled with guns—he'd killed 183 men in his lifetime, Hemingway boasted, and there were people who said he'd participated in executions in Spain. None of that, nor of many other things, a *biblios* of things, an era of them. They had wanted Shaw to write his autobiography, he said, but he could not decide. Too difficult. "All the love affairs . . . ," he mumbled.

Somewhere the ancient clerks, amid stacks of faint interest to them, are sorting literary reputations. The work goes on eternally and without haste. There are names passed over and names revered, names of heroes and of those long thought to be, names of every sort and level of importance. Among them is Irwin Shaw's.

It was not really Shaw, any more than Neruda was Neruda or Henry Green Henry Green. Curiously enough, he did not change his name himself. His father's name was Shamforoff, and the decision to change to Shaw was made at a meeting when the family began a real estate business in 1923. He was ten years old then, didn't like the shortened version, and clung to the name he was born with through high school.

The writer defines the world, however, and his name grows to be part of it. His legend, also. The book and the man who wrote it become confounded, just as real incidents and people become part of a truth that has been revised and clarified. At a certain point all stories are true, the question never arises. The characters in Dreiser, Cervantes, and Margaret Mitchell are eminently real, the possibility that someone only imagined these figures as well as what they said and did is at first intriguing, but we cannot for a moment doubt the existence of Lady Ashley or even Ahab. They rank with historical personages, and it is to the glory of their creators that they achieved, if they did not in the ordinary sense possess, actual life. Krapp, Swann, Lady Dedlock, lived and died and have the chance of living always.

He knew this, of course, but spoke of it rarely, if at all. He talked about writers, books, public figures, football games. He talked about fame, humility, the French, about once meeting John Horne Burns and being told by him that he, Irwin, didn't know anything about Jews. He talked about his own work and that of others, and he was usually generous, though he could be tart. "Well, I've done it again," a writer who'd had a great early success remarked to him. "Don't say that," Irwin said, "you didn't do it the first time."

He could be equally tributary. At a party once he beckoned to a writer he saw who was nervously awaiting publication. "I read your book," he said. "It's a great book. A masterpiece."

One remembers such things. "Those were his words," the writer said long afterwards—it was Joseph Heller, the book was *Something Happened.* "He didn't say it's a good book. He said great. A masterpiece."

Discussing what had come from his own hand, he was uncritical. He gave the impression he was well satisfied with it all. He seemed not to prefer one thing he'd written over another, and never really permitted himself to be put on the defensive. One night a woman was shamelessly praising him to his face—he wrote marvelously about women, she said, no contemporary writer knew women so well. She loved *Lucy Crown,* it was almost her favorite book. That was a hard book to write, he recalled. His wife had begged him not to write it.

"That's right," Marian said.

He had the most difficult time of his life with that book. It had taken four years. He wrote it as a play first but it was no good. Then he wrote a hundred pages of the book and again gave up, but his editor at Random House, Saxe Commins, persuaded him to go on. It eventually sold more copies than anything he ever wrote. The idea for it had come from a story told to him by a Viennese man. "It was a true story. When he was a boy he caught his mother having an affair with the tutor. He told his father, and the mother never forgave him. She refused to live in the same house with him, and he had to go and live with his aunt. He only saw his mother once or twice more in his life. I heard the story in 1938. I put it in my notes and carried it around for more than ten years."

"Why didn't you want him to write it?" Marian was asked.

"I hated the woman," she said.

"She fought me tooth and nail every foot of the way," Irwin muttered. He got letters about the book all the time. It had been translated into every language.

———

They went to Europe in 1950. That summer, at the urging of an old friend, they had rented a house in Quogue, on Long Island, and then found that they couldn't play tennis or go into any of the clubs—Jews weren't admitted. Although Marian was not Jewish she considered herself to be, so they went to Europe, where the ashes of some six million Jews lay, to escape anti-Semitism in Quogue, Irwin liked to say. And there, almost to the end, they remained. *The Young Lions* was a great triumph; they were in their thirties, the glowing decade that will never end, anything can be dared.

It was the Europe still very much of the 1930s, emerging from the ruins of a nightmarish war. There were yachts in the harbor at Cannes with names like *Feu Follet* and *Dadu,* the sea was blue again, the white sails beginning to flutter. One can be rich in France, you cannot imagine, travel the stunning countryside and sit at tables in graveled gardens.

Fame, soundness of body, a beautiful wife. He had met her in California. They had a passionate life. Young, tanned, unwed, driving across the country together with the top folded down. Her mother was scandalized; in those days to run off with a man you weren't married to was nearly unimaginable. They lived in New York on Forty-fourth Street. She was an actress, he was writing plays, and on this street of theaters their entire life was lived. For a while he was a drama critic but gave it up, he said, because as a critic he could no longer leave after the first act. He had to run six blocks to the theater. Marian would be late, the cab would be stuck in traffic, and he'd have to jump out and run. He arrived with sweat pouring down his face, even in midwinter.

The marriage was in 1939, the year the war started, as someone remarked. The difficulties he had with his wife! He would constantly talk about them, almost to himself, as if they were unexampled. One night in St.-Jean-de-Luz, during an argument in a restaurant, she took off her wedding ring and threw it away in a fury. The next morning she went back to look but couldn't find it; as she left, miraculously she saw it in the street.

Encouraged by a friend, Irwin, in late December 1951, drove down from Paris to a place in Switzerland called Klosters, then an unspoiled village with ancient farmhouses and the mountains piled with snow. The people were friendly. Eventually he and his wife moved there. It was perfect and they stayed. He took up skiing. A circle of interesting people began to appear regularly, people who would not have come there except for him. They were always in a crowd, it seemed. It was the best time of his life, and probably the most ruinous. Perhaps it would have been so anywhere, and this is only my idea of what he did and what he might have done. I never said it, but I felt it strongly, and of course what I blamed him for was the very thing I was afraid I was doing myself: living in a world that was not truly mine.

There could have been a number of children, but Marian had miscarriages, four in fact, and only once was she able to complete a pregnancy. That was with the help of a specialist in New York someone had told her about and to whom she had come from the south of France. He instructed her to go to bed and stay there. She was allowed up for only fifteen minutes a day. Six months later a child was born in Columbia Presbyterian and named for the first man on earth, Adam, who grew up to be, like his father, a writer.

Conjugal years, of *mutual and unexpressed understanding,* as he wrote, *private jokes, comfort in adversity, automatic support in times of trouble and hours spent in cordial silence in the long and tranquil evenings.* You never saw these evenings, of course. You saw them on the move, sheathed in glamour like movie stars. Irwin flew back to the States one time to attend a dinner Jackie Kennedy was giving for Malraux. John Cheever described him in a letter, blowing into Rome to pick up an Alfa Romeo and give a dinner party.

He never mentioned women, but it was impossible that so grand, so errant a nature should not be drawn to them, and there was also the theme of that first, central story, "Summer Dresses." The great engines of this world do not run on faithfulness. "Many?" I often wanted to ask him. I doubt he would have been revealing.

One night a faded blonde was going on about the luster of it, their wonderful life. "Have you ever," she asked him ingenuously, "I just wonder, have you ever really loved anyone besides Marian?"

He shifted his gaze to her, uncertain of her motive.

"Has he what?" someone said.

"I mean it," she insisted. "Have you ever—I don't mean while you were divorced—have you ever loved another woman?"

In the awkward silence, from across the table, Marian said, "I'll give you the list."

"No, I really mean it," the woman said.

"I'll have it alphabetized if you like," Marian offered.

Sometime around 1969 the marriage had begun to break up. Irwin, it was said, only had the nerve to leave a note on the pillow—he wanted a divorce. Not long afterwards she moved out, although in the end it was he who lost the house. It was eventually sold. Chalet Mia, it was called—Marian had built it, supervising the construction herself, one of the many beautiful houses she made for them. All the stories from this period I heard later, his living with another woman, a blonde who liked books; drinking even more than usual; sinking, friends told me, to the lowest point of his life. He came lurching into the small bar of his favorite hotel in Klosters, the Chesa Grishuna, cursing his wife, who was on the floor above having a peaceful dinner with other people. It was unlike him; he never used obscenities. He had supported her all his life, he roared. He had paid for this thing and that thing, even for her mother's burial, with these hands, he shouted. It was awful; he was slurring his words.

Everything dissolved, the palaces, the cloud-capped towers. He went unshaven. His shirttails were out, his pants hung loose on him like an invalid's.

The divorce, to me, was a surprise, it seemed an error of Providence. Whatever his transgressions or hers, there was something completely domestic about him. He was married and meant to be. In his world all the main figures save one, Capa, were married and family was the only untarnishable fact.

At the same time, remarkably, having lost house, wife, his utter foundations, he sat down and wrote, determined to be restored, *Rich Man, Poor Man*, a popular novel which was sold to television and resulted in a new fortune. What he had lost with one hand he retrieved with the other.

———

Now I must turn backwards for a missing thread that has not been woven in, the cause of a long unraveling between us.

Sometime around 1959 I had made a short film with a friend, Lane Slate, a man of taste who lived near me in Rockland County in a kind of indulgent squalor, an expert on painting, automobiles, and Joyce. It was called *Team Team Team* and was only twelve minutes long. It was about football, and one idle day, sitting in the country, we were dumbfounded to receive the news that it had won a first prize at Venice. Doors would open everywhere, we realized. They did not, but after I had gotten to know him I mentioned the film to Irwin, who later saw it and liked it. He was, at the time, more or less engaged in producing movies himself from his short stories—one, *In the French Style,* had been made—and he impulsively suggested that I write and direct the script for another. The story he had in mind, "Then We Were Three," was not outstanding but I felt I could make something of it nevertheless. I was laden, like a swollen-legged bee returning from the meadows, with knowledge, little of it practical, of films and the European directors, not far into their careers, who were the idols of the moment. I knew that John Huston had been a boxer and was said to have told his secretary when she was typing up the script for *The Maltese Falcon* to just take the dialogue out of the book. The miscellany gave confidence.

We eventually made the film, *Three,* which, though it had admirers among the critics, turned out to be of negligible interest to the public. Irwin did not like the movie. We had started out with optimism. Through expensive lunches with very good bottles of wine I had felt his confidence in me begin to slip, and also seen him, after I left the table and was near the door, mechanically pouring what remained in other glasses into his own. He was not involved in the actual production. The difficulty, he had told me at one point, was that I was a lyric and he a narrative writer. "Lyric" seemed a word he was uncomfortable with. It seemed to mean something like callow.

And so I missed the day in 1977 when, weary perhaps of the joys, and feeling the pull of phantom roots, he had lunch with his ex-wife. It was foolish after all these years to be angry with her. The meeting led to their being reunited. They prudently retained separate apartments, like Beckett and his wife or Sartre and Simone de Beauvoir, but finally, at Irwin's insistence, they remarried.

I had seen him only once or twice in a long time. One summer afternoon towards the end of the decade he had come across the lawn at a party to say hello, ask what I was working on, and add, "That was a lousy movie you made." I didn't bother to argue. It would not be long before he lay beneath the surgeon's unbrilliant knife.

He went into the hospital for an aging man's usual complaint and the operation had gone wrong—he very nearly died of an undetected hemorrhage. The patient, abdomen swollen with blood, and in great pain, lay for weeks in intensive care, longing to die. It was Marian who saved his life. She remembered something that had been done with her father, and kept after the doctors to do it. Finally they did; they injected a kind of gelatin, and some of it went to the spot and stopped the leaking.

He was never the same, even after he recovered. He had lost fifty pounds. There had been pneumonia, kidney failure, other unsuspected problems.

He opened the door in Southampton in the fall of 1981, thin, the shirt collar too big, his eyes unexpectedly large. It was a beautiful house, as always. Deep downy sofas, elegance, flowers. A young woman, his secretary, I assumed, was watching *Traviata* on television. "So, how've you been, Jim?" he greeted me cautiously. "What are you working on?"

He had an artificial hip, arthritis, and both knees were bad. It was September but he felt cold. In the restaurant—there were only a few people besides us—we talked about Europe. They were going back soon. He worked well there, he said, always had. He was only twelve years older than I was, but that evening it seemed much more. It felt like Europe—the trees, the tranquility, the wide street in front of the restaurant—I thought of Antibes, where we used to go.

I was longing to go to Europe myself, I said. It was beckoning me.

"Well, why don't you?" he asked.

"I don't know. Difficulties. I suppose I've created them. But I'd like to go to Sicily. Ever since reading *The Leopard*."

"That's a sad story," he said. "Terrific book. He wrote it when he was sixty-five and sent it to a publisher. They rejected it and he died before it was published by someone else. Very sad."

"You're assuming there's no afterlife," I said.

The waiter interrupted, a young waiter who wanted an autograph. He placed a blue paper napkin on the table, which Irwin signed.

He couldn't write any more, Irwin said, as if that had brought it to mind. He didn't have the mental energy, he said. He envied me.

The first of many evenings and days. We walked out through the large kitchen of the house on the way to restaurants, or there were dinners and many voices at the long, lacquered dining table. When I remember it I think of waiting for them at the bar somewhere, in the fall in the Hamptons. That was part of the pleasure, the lovely anticipation. The leaves have turned. The place is warm and soon to be lit by their presence, a few cars passing outside.

———

He had moved into the front lines. Friends were dying, enemies, critics who had once wounded him. His life was like a deck of cards nearly all out on the table and he musing on them, his eye returning to the same ones again and again. He remembered football games of long ago, playing in Lowell in the cold afternoon, the earth hard as cement, the ball on the two-yard line, final minutes and them with first and goal. On defense, he was safety. He remembers it with the skinny arms of age and a lessened frame.

He was also the quarterback; they stood waiting while he looked the other team over and then stepped into the huddle and told them what they would do. He guessed he was still that way.

"You *guess?*" Marian said.

"His trouble," the old cook said, "is that he drinks too much." She had a broad, handsome black face. She loved him, everyone did. "Drink and scratch, that's all he does."

He lay in bed thinking, like a blind sailor remembering the sea, of the happiest moments of his life, catching a pass, going out on the stage to cheers after the opening of *Bury the Dead*. They were not diamonds, they were sapphires perhaps or opals, but in them a shining star.

He was crumbling, he said. He was a fortress, but they were breaching the walls. "*I've* never breached them," Marian commented. He was hunched. His smile was like an old dog's, wry and faded. He was waiting for the end, for the angel of death. If necessary he was ready to do it himself, except that his mother was still alive, ninety-one, and he could not die before she did, the small woman filled with determination who had single-handedly kept the family alive during the hopeless 1930s. She was living in California. He seldom saw her but he was indissolubly attached. His father, he said, had been lucky—he had died suddenly, in a matter of seconds, while on a flight from Europe to New York. They were then going to make an emergency landing in London, but his mother said no, go on to America. She sat and held her husband the entire flight.

He did not complain, although he hated the fact that wealth had come to him at seventy, when he was in dissolution, rather than at forty, when he would have been able to enjoy it. This was not really true. In the second and third acts he had known all the material comforts of life and remained curiously undevoted to them. He seemed to pay so little attention to *things*. He lived both in and beyond luxury.

When I saw him for the first time after having been away for a few months, he reported that he'd been moderate, he'd gotten drunk only once during the summer. Only once did he have to be helped home. "Carried home," Marian corrected. There was something boyish about him, even as an old man, the clean pleasant face, the cordial manner.

There was a game he liked that he had once played all the time. It was who could get you to cry in the fewest words? There was a line in *The Three Sisters:* "You mean, I'm being left behind?" But Irwin always quoted the article by Gay Talese about Joe DiMaggio: On their honeymoon in Tokyo, Marilyn Monroe had gone off on a USO tour and come back and said, Joe, there were a hundred thousand people there and they were all cheering and clapping; you've never seen anything like it. Yes, I have, DiMaggio said.

Yes, I have! It was Irwin's favorite story. *Yes, I have.* Three words, and you cried.

––––––

And now it is April and the long campaign is ending. The winter was difficult, in and out of the hospital, his lungs filling with fluid and other problems no less grave. His son phoned from Europe— he was in the hospital again, heart trouble, lung trouble, kidney trouble. He was exhausted from the ordeal. His brother was there and some old friends, the Parrishes.

I set out to see Irwin for the last time. I landed in the morning. It was May. I had a bottle of Haut Brion with me that I was carrying on the off chance we could have a glass of it in the hospital room. They once wet the lips of newborn kings of France with such wine. I was thinking of that, and the journey he was soon to take.

On the train it began to grow dark. There was light only in the mountains to the west. The afternoon was moving towards America with the news, homeward, the yellow fields more bright as it went.

The hospital was in Davos, the same one in which Marian had lost a baby twenty-seven years earlier. The last connection I could make went no farther than a town about thirty miles from there. I called from the vestibule of a soiled-looking restaurant. At the apartment, a private nurse had no news. She suggested I call the hotel where the family was gathered. I did; Adam came to the phone. "Irwin died this afternoon, about an hour ago," he told me gently.

"Oh, God." I could think of nothing to say. "Well, I'll be there in the morning."

"There's no point in flying over now," he said.

"I'm already here. I'm in Landquart."

"Landquart? I'll be there in half an hour," he said.

He had died at about seven in the long, soft evening. Beneath the window of the room in which he lay was a stream, I could hear it there in the dark. There was a clean blue pillowcase on the pillow. His clothes were neatly folded, a blue sport shirt of silk or cashmere, corduroy pants.

I wanted to see him. We went to look for the head nurse. *Ein guter Freund* had come, Adam explained to her. They spoke for a few moments and she led the way to another floor.

He lay on a smooth-wheeled rolling cart, beneath a sheet, his head on a pillow, a white bandage around his forehead and jaw to keep it closed. He was shaved. His nostrils were large and empty. He looked papal. There was a red curtain behind him concealing the niche in which he must lie while the modern clocks of the hospital ticked through the night and patients slept.

I touched his hair, something I had never done in life. It was like my own, curly, gray. I wanted to remember everything and at the same time never to have seen it. *God bless us, a thing of naught*. That was something he had never been and, lying there, still was not. After a while I leaned down to kiss his brow in farewell. It was cold.

———

He died afar, surrounded by women like a biblical king. He had come a long way, like Dickens or d'Annunzio, from his beginnings. He died with the best of everything, a cook, Hungarian vodka, a fine apartment on the main street over the Patek Philippe store, a housekeeper, a secretary, a nurse. There were books everywhere. On the desk, a picture of his son. Above, a photograph of the football team at Brooklyn College, the grass brown, Irwin in the center, taller than you remember, lean, kneeling above the mythic ball.

There had been cancer. It had spread. He hated what he had become in the end, his useless body. He always imagined he would have a vigorous old age. It hadn't been that way. He had undergone a terrible beating at the last.

In the morning the phone was ringing with that strange European urgency, *ring ring, ring ring, ring ring*. The telegrams and calls were coming in from everywhere. *You must know the immense sorrow into which I was plunged upon learning this morning . . .* , cables in foreign languages. He was not a scholar or intellectual, though he was brighter than he looked. He was a kind of titleholder. He wrote a lot, among it much that people admired.

I wandered through the apartment, room by room, the kitchen into which he probably rarely ventured, the pharaonic bath in which he revealed himself to himself every day, two luxurious robes on the door. The presses of the city, of cities, had fallen silent. There was the murmur of foreign voices, the sound of women's heels. The household was speaking quietly in Italian and French. They had packed the clothes he was to be laid out in. The cook was older than the others; it meant something different to her. "We are all born and we must all die," a Swiss woman who knew him well told me. "I feel so sad. So many things . . ." The very things, of course, that in later years he wanted to gather and put in a book. "All these stories," he had said, "all these people . . . It's hopeless."

My thoughts went back—1957, autumn. I had a wife and two small children. We lived in a cold house on the Hudson. Thinking every day of the life I had left, unable to stop recalling it or to believe in myself apart from it, I sat down and tried to write. It's easy now to see how much I didn't know—the making of notes, structure, selection, the most elementary aspects were a mystery to me. I had written one book, out of my own life, the book everyone can write, and beyond that lay desert. After much wavering of nerve I set out to cross it. A few years later, succeeding, a second novel was completed. It was published. It disappeared without trace. That was about the time I met Irwin Shaw.

He was much to me, father, great force, friend. He lived a life superior to mine, a life I envied and could barely fathom, his courage, loves, embrace, were all so large. We lived, I felt, in their shadow and I think of him in Byron's lines about the sea:

> And I have loved thee, Ocean! And my joy
> Of youthful sports was on thy breast to be
> Borne, like thy bubbles, onward . . .
> For I was as it were a child of thee,
> And trusted to thy billows far and near,
> And laid my hand upon thy mane—as I do here.

Byron's poems, as it happened, were at his bedside at the end.

I see him sometimes in the city, stepping out of a restaurant in the cold, his coat open, ready without hesitation to talk for a moment or invite you to join him. The lighted apartments float above, the bars are crowded, the parked cars washed with rain. The sixth game of the Series is on or there's a play written by someone he's interested in or admires.

I have loved thee. I was as it were a child . . . The poets, writers, the sages and voices of their time, they are a chorus, the anthem they share is the same: the great and small are joined, the beautiful lives, the other dies, and all is foolish except honor, love, and what little is known by the heart.

EUROPA

THE PARTS OF Paris that were revealed to me first, before Irwin Shaw, were, as I say, the least welcoming: the Champs-Elysées, the Avenue de l'Opéra, the grimness of the 1st Arrondissement, department stores and stations. At the time I had in my pocket, for an initial guidebook, three or four filing cards written on by a tall, avuncular man with a seductive charm named Herschel Williams who was a fellow student in Washington where we were attending Georgetown together as officers. In his youth he had escorted debutantes, written a hit play, *Janie,* and probably been to Europe as part of an education, though he certainly went later on. Taking out a fountain pen one evening in 1950 in Billy Martin's, the leisurely act of a more polished world, he wrote down places and names for me as in years to come I would do for others.

More or less, I thus inherited Paris. The cards he jotted on are gone, but I still remember landmarks like a seaman who has seen, briefly and just once, a secret map. Curtained restaurants. Bourgeois streets. The nightclub he liked that has long since closed— it had violinists in dinner jackets and a bar of generous dimensions where after eleven-thirty girls who had failed to find a client for the evening would show up, girls like those on the train in Maupassant's story, of whom the old peasant woman says, "They are sluts who are off to that cursed place, Paris."

Also recommended was the Hôtel Vendôme, in the neck or perhaps the knee of the Place Vendôme. That time I passed it by, but the approach to it I later knew almost step by step. On the corner where rue de Rivoli and rue Castiglione meet, Sulka, an expensive men's shop. Past it, walking towards the Place, the sidewalk that is a mosaic of small tiles, cracked and sagging. Then the English Pharmacy and farther on, still beneath the shadowy arcade, at the corner, the tobacconist. The shop, though changed, is there still, dark marble around the display windows, in which there were pipes, lighters, and small gifts, perhaps a few guidebooks. Within, however, to one side in a tall case were books of the Olympia Press and the even more disreputable—with, as I remember, pastel instead of green covers—titles of the Obelisk Press and the Traveller's Companion.

Here, unhurried, one could browse for hours. Ordinary life drowned, went under. On the street outside, often cold and wet, it seemed, were passers-by in overcoats and expressions of care, but within the shop one leafed through pages in a kind of narcotic dream. I bought *Our Lady of the Flowers* here, *Tropic of Cancer,* of course, *The Ginger Man,* as well as Beckett, de Sade, Burroughs, and, later, Nabokov. The publisher of these distinguished books, Maurice Girodias, eventually closed up and was forced to go into exile.

He deserves more than a hasty footnote. He seems to have been a sort of lanky Falstaff, close to writers in their poverty and youth, probably not honest in his dealings, and cast aside by them later on. He may have had defects, but I was not able to see them on the one occasion I was at a dinner with him. His bitterness was unintense. We talked about the irony of it all and he was able to smile. For practical purposes he was still virtually in exile, he said, living in the 20th Arrondissement somewhere past Père-Lachaise, with Paris nearly out of sight.

In 1958 or so I came across Girodias's edition of Pauline Réage's famous apostasy, the first cool pages of which were like a forbidden door opening and the rest, as I read, unable to put it down, like the shimmering of a fever—not since reading Llewelyn Powys, paragraphs of whose *Love and Death* I could recite from memory at eighteen, had my legs given way like this. I am not sure it harmed me but it affected me deeply. Though I thought of it a good deal, I rarely spoke about it, and this preserved it for me until one night in the comfort of an editor's apartment in New York a young woman, when the subject somehow came up, told how she and her friends at camp one summer had read *The Story of O* and talked about it incessantly. I felt disappointed. If schoolgirls could stroll through it like a book group, what was there to safekeep?

———

There were the early places of Paris, in the beginning, at the bottom, rooms on an inner court with burned-out lights, when the city was unscalable with endless long errands in the rain, handed-down newspapers, and skipped meals. You were alone with little money and not much nerve and a name on a piece of paper— someone working for a steamship line or in the embassy who was never in the office or returned a call. Europe was still impoverished. The plaster was cracking, the drapes worn to threads. Only a year or two before it had been for sale for a carton of cigarettes. The desperation had been vast and the testimony stood before one's eyes: ancient telephones, outclassed cars, drab clothes.

Later came the Paris of hotels; they made up a kind of gazetteer, names like those of islands, each with its own aura and size. The Royal Monceau, where the plush exhaled an ancient fragrance and my wife and I—we were new to it—reigned in reduced-rate opulence. The France et Choiseul with its barren courtyard and poorly furnished suites; the Calais tucked in behind the Ritz; the hotel where the girl threw Farr's clothes out the third-floor window when he wouldn't pay her; the Récamier squeezed into the corner; the Esmeralda, Badoit outside on the windowsill in the cold; the St.-Regis with its dark, gleaming wood and luxury, the light from above; the Richepense just off the Place Madeleine one winter, incredible loneliness, Prunier down the street, where it was too expensive to go; the Palais d'Orsay, hotel of hotels, sentimentally speaking; the Trémoille.

On the glass top of one of the first night tables, in the Royal Monceau, I think, lay a mimeographed list of recommendations provided by the air attaché. There was Androuët, a restaurant judged unique because the meal was made up entirely of cheeses; and another place, where the menu had been inspired by Rabelais, with daring caricatures; also, the Lido ("sit at the bar"). The Mayol, it said, and we went there. It was dank and old with worn seats. Girls badly fed, stage bare, costumes that had lost their sheen, and one lovely pair of breasts as if, amid it all, France was showing what it could be capable of. I searched for them in the program The photograph there was a poor reminder, like looking at a passport photo. I could not admit what I was doing, of course. I was with my wife and the untrifling general who had brought me to Europe, Robert Lee, and his wife; we were in middle America.

There was the L'Aiglon, narrow and cream-colored, on the Boulevard Raspail, where I stayed when we were editing the film that Irwin Shaw judged weak. The lizard shoes of a famed director, Buñuel, were outside an adjoining door. Misty winter mornings, the cemetery endless beyond the window, the ivied walls. Simone de Beauvoir in her white nurse's shoes and stockings, her beauty gone, walking to the boulevard from the café on the corner where she often met Sartre for breakfast.

It was the elegance and attitude of Paris, aspects one saw from the first, which appealed to me, venerable things and luxurious new ones, the life of the streets and the life that survives upheaval and death. The old count who lived on Quai Voltaire in the same building with all his daughters and their husbands. There was an American woman who lived across the way and took pleasure in greeting him. One day she said she was going home on a trip, flying to America. The old count seemed interested. *"L'Amérique,"* he asked politely, *"est-ce que c'est loin?"* Is it far away?

The proper order of things is that they be seen first from a distance, then up close. Paris, however, could not be seen that way. It was a city of intimacy, by which I mean privacy, filled with the detail of life, moody, and above bowing to any individual. Kerouac went there once, for two or three days, and left saying, "Paris rejected me."

It was the skill of Paris to reject one, to make one desirous, just as the tradition of its functionaries at every level was to prevent the city from displaying a false smile. The sternness of the *concierges* and *gardiens* gave faith in the power of Paris to endure. The Paris of Atget. Of Brassaï—he was not French; he lived first, as a child, on rue Monge—photos of brothels on rue Monsieur-le-Prince or rue Grégoire-de-Tours; lights of bridges in the mist, not a sound, not even a cigarette dropped in the water, the river stone-still; old Matisse with a nude model, nipples cherry black; the luxurious squalor of the studios, Picasso's, Bonnard's; nights of Paris, and everywhere the grandeur, the parade; the game hanging in the butcher shops, the silk clothes in expensive windows, all part of a supplication: Grant unto me, bestow upon me . . .

On the rue des Belles-Feuilles a car with 77 on its plates—from the rich suburbs to the south—is stopped in the middle of the street, trunk open. Traffic, horns blowing, is backed up behind. Occasionally a man comes out of a building with a box to put in the trunk. Finally, not in any haste, a woman in a long fur coat comes out—the blocked cars are in a frenzy—says a last graceful something to someone, gets in, and drives off without a backward glance. Paris women, their eloquence, their scorn.

In the *épicerie* another, in jeans and a Levi's jacket, a turtleneck with a scarf wound insolently about, fine features, magnificent body—brilliant, uncirculated, as they say of certain coins—looking at you without curiosity or shame and then back to regarding the display window. A tall, fair-haired man in a leather jacket is with her. She hasn't bothered to get in line. She merely tosses back her hair, breathing self-esteem.

Or the blonde in the Closerie sitting in a booth opposite a man, smoking, making slight, continual nods of the head as he is speaking and looking right at him knowingly, as if to say, "Yes, all right, of course," and even more frankly, "Yes. You can."

They are not temptations so much as consolations, like the consolation of the proverbial, of things worthy to exist.

In days past you could be prepared for this by taking the boat to Europe, sailing on the *France*. One stepped into the perfection of the first hours on board, the excitement and sounds, corridors blue with fragrant cigarette smoke, the walls of the ship alive beneath your hand.

I think of the story of Styron and James Jones, who were sailing with their families—it was on the return crossing of the maiden voyage of the *France*. The Joneses were living in Paris then; they had a house on the Île St.-Louis and were traveling with a nanny, their young daughter, and a big dog. The Styrons had children with them.

The two men, invincible, were out all the preceding night in New York. Along the way they met a couple of girls at P. J. Clarke's and were buying them drinks. Warm feelings drifted back and forth. What are you doing afterwards, the girls wanted to know? Sailing to France, they said, want to come?

The ship sailed at noon. Jones had gotten home at seven that morning; perhaps he'd forgotten some of the events of the night before but as they passed the Statue of Liberty they heard, confirming all fears, shouts of "Yoo hoo!" and saw energetic waving from a lower deck. "Who's that?" Gloria Jones wanted to know.

The girls had stowed away. Styron and Jones had to sneak down to the purser and buy them tickets, not only for the crossing but, when Gloria found out, for an immediate return.

Gloria and James Jones reigned in Paris for perhaps a decade. They were not the Murphys. They did not have a salon; it could better be described as an open house. James Baldwin might be there, Styron of course, Romain Gary or Jean Seberg, his star-crossed wife. The atmosphere was carefree. There was money, there were friends. Jones never bothered to learn more than a few words of French; there was no need to. His wife had been a stand-in for Marilyn Monroe and had become a figure in her own right; good-looking, rowdy, possessive, she would say and to some extent do anything. In their living room one night an actress slowly rubbed my finger between the tips of hers. She was French. Was I going to make her spend the night alone? she asked, as if it would be thoughtless. I felt I was in the France of Ninon de Lanclos, one of her favorites, brought home to dine and be led into the bedroom—she was not as beautiful as her rivals but she had turned down the offer of a fortune from Richelieu to be his mistress. One of her rules had been never to be bored.

———

Slowly I rose to a view of it all, by rooms, apartments, and iron balconies—I passed from window to window and scene to scene. In the Hôtel du Quai Voltaire the river was very close with the long, gray curtain of the Louvre on the other side. Something overcame me there; I lay in bed trembling; my arms and legs ached. My skin was so painful I could not be touched. Unsteadily I descended in the elevator, by chance with a youthful Norman Mailer, dark-haired and silent, his health and fame unshakable, perhaps on his way to the Joneses'. I had flu, I thought, but it was more than that, I merely could not recognize the symptoms: it was hepatitis. I lay in the hospital for weeks, at first in a delirium and then through long days, sometimes reading in an Encyclopedia of Diseases and waiting for the report on the latest analysis of my blood. The starched white of nurses is a comforting thing and so is the daily paper. It had been winter when I was stricken—February—and shakily I emerged at last into the spring of 1962.

—

Europe gave me my manhood or at least the image of it. It was not a matter of pleasure, but something more enduring: a ranking of things, how to value them. What other men found in Africa or the East, I found there.

Europe was not only a great world but also a smaller one, populated by only a few of one's countrymen, sometimes in the form of mysterious exiles. The real inhabitants took up no space. Eventually you might come to know a few of them but often in an imperfect way. Their language was their own, and with it a definition of life.

But a part of one's never completed mosaic, in my case a crucial part, is found abroad. At the fingertips of my memory, so to speak, are the wide rivers with towns and sometimes cities along unruined banks; the ancient cathedrals; the silent courtyards of old hotels where the car is parked, an early waiter or two in the dining room. *Live for beauty,* Cyril Connolly's dream. Evening is falling in Paris and I sit on a green wooden bench on Avenue Franklin Roosevelt—it's 1975—opening the first letter in a week. It's about the book *Light Years,* not yet published. She has read it for the first time in its entirety. A stunning letter that flutters in my hand like a bird as I read it over and over. Cars are rushing homeward. *My darling, I must simply say* . . . Nothing is like that moment. Everything I had hoped for.

Kant had four questions that he believed philosophy should answer: What can I know? What may I hope? What ought I to do? What is man? All of these Europe helped to clarify. It was the home of a veteran civilization. Its strengths are vertical, which is to say they are deep.

The thing it finally gave was education, not the lessons of school but something more elevated, a view of existence: how to have leisure, love, food, and conversation, how to look at nakedness, architecture, streets, all new and seeking to be thought of in a different way. In Europe the shadow of history falls upon you, and knowing none of it, you realize suddenly how small you are. To know nothing is to have done nothing. To remember only yourself is like worshiping a dust mote. Europe is on the order of an immense, unfathomable class, beyond catalogue or description. The young students are exploring sex, the older ones dining, the faculty is being carried off to the morgue. You progress from row to row. The matriculation, as an English king once said of the navy, will teach you all you need to know.

———

Lunch near the Odéon. Paris day, a table by the window, handwritten menu, noon blue sky. The chef, who is probably the owner, is visible in the small kitchen in a white jacket and toque. Between orders he reads, with the calm of an historian, the racing page of the newspaper. I don't imagine him betting, not today, not at work. He's engaged in study.

I think back to repudiated years and a man I once saw in a dirty movie house near the Gare de Luxembourg. The lights had come on after the first film. Silence. There were ten or twelve men sitting there in the theater, waiting. He was much older than anyone else. A wonderful head of white hair, like that of a restaurant owner or horse trainer. He pulled out a newspaper and began to read it, leisurely turning the big pinkish pages. It was so quiet you could hear the sound of them turning. A man who ate solid dinners and had a dog; perhaps he was a widower. He had seen a lurid presentation of three young *bourgeoises* and what unexpected things befell them, an impure work less interesting than its title. When the lights went down again he folded his paper. You could see his fine, impressive head in the darkness. I thought then of a lot of people for no particular reason, people who would never be found here. I thought of Faulkner one year when he was trying to work as a scriptwriter, driving down Sunset Boulevard on the way to work, unshaven, his bare feet on the pedals and bottles rolling on the floor. I thought of the Polish doorman, very tall, who used to work at the entrance to my parents' apartment building in New York. He'd been a lawyer in Poland before he fled, but it was impossible here; it was all different and he was too old. He didn't have much to do with the other doormen—they scornfully called him the Count. I thought of Monte Carlo and the woman at the roulette table who had asked me for chips. Afterwards we had some drinks at the bar. She wanted to show me something in her room, the clippings of her before the war when she danced at the Sporting Club; I was able to pick her out in the chorus. The English were there then, she said, and she had gone with them; some were lords.

You were constantly—perhaps that was it—meeting people without money, people who amounted to something. Sometimes the more they didn't have, the more they amounted to.

Rising above the rest and very much of her class was a woman in London. She was a countess, though fallen from the heights. Her family name you would know instantly, that of Germany's greatest chancellor. Tall, with beautiful hair, she had once been a model for Chanel.

She'd been at a party one night where there was a film director, "this Joe Lozey," as she pronounced it. "I hate him," she said, "he's a bastard. He was saying what a great film was *Death in Venice*. I told him it was a beautiful painting but boring. He got very angry. 'Just who are you?' he said."

Yes, who? Only the real crop of Europe, she might have answered, the originals from families centuries old. She was already a barbiturate ruin, breasts thin and drooping, skin beginning to go. She ignored it. Her eyes were heavily made up, her mouth curved down. She had a low, commanding voice and liked to laugh. Her words were slurred but her eyes were still clear, the whites startling. She had been deflowered at fourteen by her uncle, and later, even after marriage, was the mistress of writers. She was imperious but very fine. She was also, in large measure, indifferent. She knew quite well what the world was, and in a sense, coming from a great family, she was responsible, but she could not be expected to control fate or the crowd. She was a woman who had loved deeply, and for years brought flowers to the grave of the writer, James Kennaway, whose photographs were in her marital bedroom. "He was buried standing up," she said. Her hands trembled as she talked and lit one cigarette from another. She was outspoken, impatient, and her wake stretched a long way back. Being with her was sometimes annoying but somehow it gave one enormous courage, the courage, really, to die.

———

I've left out the Kronenhalle and the hotels above the town in Zurich; Sicily; Haut de Cagnes; London in the evening and girls in Rolls-Royces, faces lit by the dash; the German dentist in Rome— the bombing of North Vietnam had just begun—"Good, bomb them," he said as he picked up instruments, "bomb them all." I've left out the place in Paris that for a long time was the essence of the city for me, oddly enough a household, that of the Abbotts. He was an old friend who had remarried, and his new wife, Sally, was young and like a sheaf of silver. Witty, taut, she was like a new child in school who had come from some unnamed but difficult elsewhere, someone who made friends and also enemies quickly and who cut a swath; Nate was her second husband. He had been a dashing Air Force colonel, a pilot in the war, and now was the European representative for a large company.

Their apartment, in the 16th, was majestic; the living room opened into a kind of dome. The sofas and chairs were comfortable, the doors everywhere eight feet high. Late one fall, the year of the Berlin crisis, we came up to Paris, four or five of us, from Chaumont, and that evening had drinks with them in the apartment. The city was black and gleaming, wonderfully cold. Nate drew me aside at about nine-thirty or ten. "Why don't you take them to the Sexy?" he said—it was a favorite of the president of his company.

I forget how we got there; there were photographs outside. I went in first to have a look. It seemed a place of style. "How is it?" they wanted to know when I came out. "Great," I said and we entered. "He comes here all the time," I explained.

There were a number of good-looking women. I think a band was playing; there was a bar. "Give me three hundred francs each," I said to them knowledgeably, "and I'll pay all the bills." Women were already introducing themselves. I could see Weiss and Duvall, neither of them inexperienced, exchange a brief glance as if to say, here goes. The money was gone after the second round. It seemed unimportant. It was like the night before the *France* sailed. It went on and on, and though portions remain bright, where it happened is unknown. I've looked for the street a number of times; it is gone.

UKIYO

Fʀᴏᴍ ᴀ ʙᴀʀ called the Seven Seas—less wondrous than its name, where every fifteen minutes a panorama of distant boats and harbors painted on the walls would darken to the sound of thunder with flashes of lightning, and heavy rain would begin to fall on a false tin roof—we went back to our suite.

In the hotel—it was a secondary place called the Hollywood Knickerbocker—was a livelier bar filled with laughter and noise, grinning faces, the euphoria of the postwar era. It was like an impromptu party, with many dotted lines between pairs of eyes, while removed from it, upstairs and alone, a forgotten figure sat, D. W. Griffith, the famed director, living out his final years. He was a metaphor for the fabled life: staggering triumph, praise, Babylonian splendor, then age and rejection, a fallen king.

He had been the greatest of them by far. The adult world—this was 1947—was still populated by people who had grown up amid the flickering of his then tremendous films *The Clansman,* later to be titled *Birth of a Nation* (1915), *Intolerance* (1916), *Hearts of the World* (1918), *Way Down East* (1920), and *Orphans of the Storm* (1921), following which came gradual failure. He had created the syntax of the movies and had been one of the aristocracy, his dark Western hat, lean intent features.

I had seen none of these films with their cottony puffs of cannon smoke, their jerky movements and virginal young women dressed in white. When I saw them, much later, I thought back to that time in Los Angeles when Griffith was upstairs, and below the crowd drank and sang. Lillian Gish and Mary Pickford were two of his stars. By then they were old too, in their fifties and past usefulness. Their voices had never been heard, that was the thing, and the angels who followed actually spoke, laughed, and wept. The father of a young actress once confided to me wonderingly of his daughter, "She can cry *real* tears."

So it was like passing, that first time, over lost, sunken fleets. I had come into the city with our navigator, a stocky, powerful Hawaiian named Fred Hemmings. We behaved like sailors. We had nothing to do but find ways to be appealing. We jumped from place to place like fleas.

It was later that I had the first glimpse of a movie being made. I had met Samuel Goldwyn in Honolulu—it had somehow been arranged by my father—and he invited me to come to the studio when I was next in Los Angeles. Without his secretaries and beyond his domain, he was an ordinary-looking man with no particular authority. Unexpectedly he remembered me when I called, although of course I was not permitted to speak to him directly. The guard at the gate—the very emblem of the studios was the unsmiling guard—would have my name. I was directed to a sound stage where for an hour or two I watched an actor dressed as an eighteenth-century gentleman descend a flight of stairs and deliver some dialogue, never to the complete satisfaction of the director. The actor was David Niven. It all seemed tedious. It seemed—the artifice and repetition, the naked back of the set—false.

Seven years later, an officer still, in civilian clothes I sat in the compartment of a train as it swept through bleak German countryside, going from Bremerhaven to Frankfurt. Points of rain appeared on the window. In the bluish issue of a women's magazine in which the models, maddeningly prim, wore little hats and white gloves there was a curious article that caught my eye. It was a tribute to a plumpish Welsh poet whose photograph, taken outside the door of his studio in a seaside town, a manuscript stuck in the pocket of his jacket, was beguiling. John Malcolm Brinnin, perhaps excerpting it from his book, had written about Dylan Thomas and somehow the piece had appeared in *Mademoiselle*. There was a picture of Dylan Thomas's wife, children with Celtic names, and even a snapshot of his mother.

Brinnin's lyric description of seedy, romantic life was an introduction to the poem that followed, in overwhelming bursts of language, page upon page. It was *Under Milk Wood*, roguish, prancing, with its blazing characters and lines. The words dizzied me, their grandeur, their wit. In the soft, clicking comfort of the train I feasted on it all. The drops of rain became streaks as the dazzling voices spoke, housewives, shopkeepers, shrews, Captain Cat—the blind, retired sea captain dreaming of a strumpet, Rosie Probert ("Come on up, boys, I'm dead").

It was an unforgettable performance, singing on and on—the longest poem, though written as a play, I had ever read—and its imagery was such that I was enthralled by the unoriginal idea of seeing it as a film. It could be, and eventually *was* one, of course, though I was then incapable of realizing that even a perfect film would illustrate only one facet of all the glittering possibilities. The poem's power was greater than any alternate version of it could be, and in fact it would be limited by such translation.

With me in that Bundesbahn car that had, I suppose, survived the war—within me—was a certain grain of discontentment. I had never made anything as sacred or beautiful as the poem I had read, and the longing to do so, never wholly absent, rose up in me. I gazed out the window. It was 1954, winter. Could I?

As it turned out, my entry into films was by way of a cluttered back room, toppling with papers, in the offices of the prominent theatrical lawyers, Weissburger and Frosch. The most junior member of the firm, theatrical in his own right, large, soft, animated, the son of a movie writer and brother of another, was Howard Rayfiel. He performed the essential drudgery: completing contracts, drafting letters, laboring in the stables of kings. On his own time he was impresario of a phantom company. He wore a velvet-collared overcoat and an Astrakhan hat in which he appeared, like a sophomore Diaghilev, at Carnegie Hall, not in the auditorium but in the large-windowed studios above, reached by a majestic ancient elevator. He arrived not with a ballerina but with a paper bag containing Camembert and apples, lunch for those conferring with his partner, a theater director who had had limited success but was confident of his talents. Together they were going to make films. They invited me to join them, to write a script. Flattered, ready to believe I could put my hand to anything, I began what turned out to be a long affair.

The director already had a first film behind him. I recall it as having almost no dialogue, the endless, headlong flight of what seemed to be a fugitive or survivor through dense woods, a man pursued by demons or perhaps dogs. Well into the film, as he bent over to drink from a stream, there was the glint of something dangling from his neck. It was a pair of silver bombardier's wings, and the source of his agony—I forget how it was made clear—was that he had been one of the crew members who had dropped an atomic bomb on Japan. He could flee but would never escape the memory. I was certain I could write something less banal.

I worked in a quiet, odd-numbered house on Sutton Place, one of a pair that belonged to a devoted pupil of the director, convert would be a better word. She was rich but did not contribute any money to the venture, only part of her premises. This was wise in one way and foolish in another. She would have probably lost the money and been criticized by her bankers, but a year or so afterwards she died in a plane crash—on her honeymoon, as it happened—and what did it matter then?

One afternoon in the studio at Carnegie Hall I encountered what I took to be the genuine: a man with an accent and a long, ascetic face, dressed in the unmistakable manner of an artist— pants from one suit and a double-breasted jacket from another. Adolphus Mekas was his name. He was renowned both for a film he was then directing and also because his brother, Jonas Mekas, was the uncompromising judge of all film culture which, capitalized, was the name of his didactic magazine.

I was eager to hear and ready to embrace Adolphus Mekas's views, especially regarding scripts. There was a then current idea that one should work without them, improvise, allow the actors freely to create a story. Plot was the curse of serious drama, as Bernard Shaw had said.

Was he, I asked cautiously, working from . . . did he have a script? Yes. He had scripts, but he kept them locked up, Mekas said, not to keep them from falling into possibly rival hands but to prevent the actors from reading them—that was the way they formed preconceptions, he explained. When the time came for the scene, he gave them the necessary lines and those only. He said all this with assurance and European calm. I have no idea what the movie he made was like.

My own script was a sentimental bouquet laid, as it were, at the feet of a young, irresistibly cynical New York girl, the flower of every generation, in this particular case nurtured in such bygone hothouses as El Morocco and the Stork Club. She was seen through the eyes of an infatuated but unforceful man who is put off by certain incidents she expects will endear her, and in the end they part. She disappears into the swift currents of Manhattan. His voice perhaps offers an elegy.

The story, which was called "Goodbye, Bear," had no barb. It was merely a history and would have been better as a poem; it had some aching lines. It also had a kind of lonely dignity, which produced an unexpected result, in the manner of the Chinese fable of the mandarin who for years stood along the river fishing with, instead of a hook, a straight pin. The word of this curious behavior spread until it finally reached the emperor himself, who came to see. What could anyone hope to catch with such a hook? the emperor asked the mandarin. For what was he fishing?

The answer was serene. "For you, my emperor," the mandarin said.

The emperor, uncrowned then, was an actor just becoming known on the New York stage, Robert Redford. Somehow he had gotten hold of the script and we met for lunch, two naïfs in the sunlit city.

There come back to me many images of Redford when he was new and his aura that of purest youth. One morning in London at the entrance of the Savoy, three or four women came up asking for an autograph. As he signed he gave me a sort of embarrassed smile. "You *hired* them," I said to him afterwards. He broke out in a wonderful laugh, no, no, he hadn't. The car that was driving us to the airport that day broke down in the tunnel just before Heathrow, and we got out and ran for the plane, carrying our bags. That was how easy and unattended his life was then. He was very likable and straightforward.

Together we went to the winter Olympics at Grenoble in 1968, slept in corridors as rooms were unavailable, and rode on buses. I had been hired to write a film about a ski racer, which he would star in, and we traveled for weeks with the U.S. team.

At dinner one night I remarked that I saw for the main character, the role Redford would play, Billy Kidd, more or less, tough, in all likelihood from a poor part of town, honed by years on the icy runs of the East. Kidd was the dominant skier on the U.S. team at the time, and in the manner of champions somewhat arrogant and aloof—there may have been an element of shyness.

Redford shook his head, no. The racer he was interested in was at another table. Over there. I looked. Golden, unimpressible, a bit like Redford himself, which of course should have marked him from the first, sat a little-known team member named Spider Sabich. What there was of his reputation seemed to be based on his having broken his leg six or seven times. He was from California, however, and Redford was also, from Van Nuys, one of those vaguely appealing names of the Coast.

"Him?" I said, "Sabich?"

Yes, Redford said; when he was that age he had been just like him.

The film was meant from the beginning to be about someone who was the opposite of that nearly vanished figure, the athlete who was supremely talented yet modest, who had the virtues of both strength and humility. Paavo Nurmi, the Finnish runner, a legendary champion—I have mentioned him—had always been an idol of mine. I pictured an older Nurmi, though knowing nothing about his personality, as a coach who had worked for years to have one of his racers win a gold in the Olympics, and who finally found the chance but with an individual he disliked, even despised, a crude, self-centered Redford. Athletes like this existed, but perhaps not coaches like Nurmi.

I thought the film would be about something which, in fact, survived in one line of casual dialogue, "the justice of sport." The final moments were to show an exultant Redford at the bottom of the course, arms raised in acknowledgment of triumph, as meanwhile a little-known competitor, last in the seeding, is coming down, beating the successive interval times one by one, and as the faces of the crowd begin to turn in a great final tropism towards the mountain and the cheers ominously rise, he streaks across the finish line at the last moment to win. This was to be the greater justice, perhaps inachievable in life.

So easy, all of it, such play. To go into New York restaurants with him and his wife, in the beautiful filthy city, the autumn air in the streets outside, eyes turned to watch as we cross the room. The glory seems to be yours as well. There was a dreamlike quality also, perhaps because Redford seemed to be just passing through, not really involved. It was washing over him, like a casual love affair. There was, even for a long time after he had gained it, something in him that disdained stardom. He wore black silk shirts and drove a Porsche, disliked being called Bobby by eager agents, and more than once said, "I hate being a movie star." Nevertheless he became one, with the life of evasion that went with it, of trying not to be recognized and approached, a life of friends only, of sitting at the very front of the plane, the last to board, like a wanted man.

At forty, some years later, he looked better than when we had first known one another. The handsome, somewhat shallow college boy had disappeared and a lean, perceptive man stood in his place. From a kind of casual amusement and a natural caution he had made an astonishing success. His days had a form, he accomplished something during them. Everyone wanted to see or talk to him. As if glancing at a menu he was able to choose his life.

One night on a plane, crossing the continent, he showed me a letter he had received. It was typewritten, from a small town in Kansas or Nebraska—a young wife, separated from her husband, having arranged for a baby-sitter, had driven forty miles to see a film of his. I forget which it was—*Ordinary People,* perhaps—but it had moved her profoundly, made her weep, and revealed to her in a new way the path her life should take. The voice of the writer, who was down somewhere in the darkness over which we were flying, was there on the page, truthful and lonely. Unlike thousands of other letters, boxes of them, he had carried this one around for months, meaning to reply but never able to. *I'm still here*, he wanted to say, *I still have your letter*.

The longing, I thought, is so vast that barely a part of it can be acknowledged. An unmeasurable sum comprises it, like the sea.

Our lives drifted apart. I wrote another film for him but it was never made. "My presence in something," I remember him saying, perhaps in apology, "is enough to give it an aura of artificiality." He knew his limits.

The last time, I saw him at a premiere. A mob was waiting, many with readied cameras to capture the scene. Inside the theater every seat was filled. Then in the near gloom a murmur went across the crowd. People began to stand. There was a virtual rain of light as everywhere flashbulbs went off, and amid a small group moving down the aisle the blond head of the star could be seen. I was far off—years, in fact—but felt a certain sickening pull. There came to me the part about Falstaff and the coronation. *I shall be sent for in private*, I thought, consoling myself. *I shall be sent for soon at night.*

———

As I think of early days, an inseparable part of them appears: the thrilling city—New York was that—in which they began, and there seems to be, over everything, a kind of Athenian brilliance, which is really the light coming through the tall glass archways of Lincoln Center, where, in the fall, the Film Festival was held. It drew what I felt to be the elite, the great European directors—Antonioni, Truffaut, Fellini, and Godard—presenting a new kind of film, more imaginative and penetrating than our own.

The theater at Lincoln Center was spacious and elegant, unlike the dreary, cramped ones where the first Buñuel or Brakhage—an amazing minor figure—might be seen. The screen was immaculate, the faces that appeared on it tremendously large and bright. They had a lunar intensity, powerful and pure. The patina of art lay upon everything, and we were part of it, elevated by it.

The city seemed to be leaping with films, schools of them, of every variety, daring films that were breaking into something vast and uncharted as an icebreaker crushes its way to open sea. I was living in the suburbs and I had only recently met, just down the road, by chance, Lane Slate. He was irreverent and well-read, with a handsome face and a mouth that never opened in a smile, his teeth were so bad. When he laughed he would stuff his necktie in his mouth to conceal them. He was the talented companion I longed for. There were two or three old automobiles, ruined classics, a LaSalle and a Delage among them, stranded in the yard outside his small white house. Inside was a piece or two of eye-catching furniture amid junk, a wife, an Old English sheepdog, and two well-loved little boys, indifferently clothed.

He had been divorced, from an Italian woman he described as beautiful, whom I never saw. She had garnisheed his salary. Driving into the city together we would often stop at an out-of-the-way New Jersey bank where he was obliged to shelter his always strained assets. He worked for a television network in a division called Public Affairs. We helped ourselves to the rich supplies of notebooks and stationery and planned movies we would make together.

There is a language within language, a kind of code, and it was the joy of this that drew us close. I liked the way he spoke, the speed of his conclusions, the breadth of his scorn, the exactness of his references. Also his aplomb. He had not been to college—he had read his way up and somehow knew everything. Though I could not quite picture it, he had been in the navy. He retained none of its lore except for a belief that one could always make out with girls who wore little gold crucifixes.

We formed a company and began to make a documentary on New York called *Daily Life in Ancient Rome*, with a narrative taken from Livy and Sallust. Early morning. Shooting on Fifth Avenue. A car pulls up at the corner and a girl in an Air France uniform with a trim, tailored skirt gets out. The car has diplomatic plates, and a pale, spent driver leans across to bid goodbye and close the door behind her. She runs, hobbled by the skirt, towards the broad glass front: AIR FRANCE. The night has ended.

We sat on stools in the dark looking at the rushes, weighing cuts. Into the bright sunlight of West Fifty-fifth Street in the afternoon, to the Brittany for lunch. The film will have faces, illicit couples emerging from the "21" club, dizzying shots up sleek façades towards dark skies, while beneath it in calm tones the prophetic description, centuries old, of decay.

This was the New York of Balanchine, Motherwell, and Mies van der Rohe, as well as Jack Smith, Yoko Ono, and George Kleinsinger, performers whom the years had yet to deplume. Kleinsinger was a composer. In his rooms at the Chelsea Hotel he had a tropical rainforest, uncaged birds hopping from branch to branch, fish in pools, fountains. Nearby was a gleaming black piano at which he was writing the music for an opera called *Archy and Mehitabel*. His daughter stood beside him and sang parts of it in a great, passionate voice, then returned to stretch out on the daybed beside another young woman, Kleinsinger's fiancée.

Yoko Ono was married to an acquaintance of mine who acted as her manager and dedicated himself to her career. She had been married before. He was somewhat ingenuous; she was not. They lived in one place and another, always struggling for money, and had a little daughter to whom he was devoted. I would see him in the Village with the baby in his arms and her bottle in a musette bag over his shoulder. His wife was above this. A performance artist, she radiated ambition. She was determined to have her chance, and in the end, in a very unexpected way, she found it.

Daily Life in Ancient Rome was never completed. We did make ten or twelve other films, documentaries, scraped together, some of them eloquent. We traveled over the country together, flying, driving, checking into motels, in the mindless joy of America, beer bottles lying by the roadside, empty cans tumbling light as paper. I can see his hands moving in small, inviting circles as he explains himself and his requests to someone. He sketched broadly and only lightly filled things in. He could so quickly make himself liked. It is his curious charm that I am remembering, the pockets with money crumpled in them, some of which often fell to the floor, the migraine headaches, which eventually came in clusters, the familiarity with names of all kinds, the cars in need of repair, the essential loneliness.

His older son, named for him, was hit by a car while riding a bicycle and died a few days later. It was at a time when we had already begun gradually to separate. Perhaps we had lost the power to amuse each other. We made one final film, on American painters: Warhol before his real recognition, Rauschenburg, Stuart Davis, a dozen others. From the small, asbestos-shingled house in Piermont he moved to Sneden's Landing, an exclusive enclave where the houses, though passing through the hands of various owners, had their own traditional names. Disasters followed, principal among them the death of his wife.

On envelopes addressed in his beautiful handwriting the postmarks moved west, to California, where, if it was to happen, he would at last become a director. He lived for a time in a house owned once by Greta Garbo, came back East for a third, unsuccessful marriage, and then retreated to Arizona and a ranch with the unlikely name of X-9. There the trail came to an end.

I had a friend, knot-jawed and earnest—Hurley was his name—who lived in a snug, orderly apartment like a captain's cabin on Sixty-first Street and who always used to ask, "But how did you meet them?" as if it were inconceivable. He also accused me—a cut slow to heal—of writing down everyone's address in a little book as soon as I met them. Was there really a time when I was trying to meet people? Oh, yes. I was ecstatic at the chance, in about 1963, to meet Peter Glenville, an Englishman, a director who had directed *Rashomon* on the stage and the film *Becket*. He had an undeniable gift and lived like a prince.

There were four of us at dinner, all men, in his New York town house. The meal was served by a uniformed maid. Glenville asked if I would be interested in writing a script, an Italian story he wanted to make. The mere proposal seemed a reward. He was showing his faith in me; he had tapped me, as it were. It was easy to see that he was discriminating—the house, the fine clothes, the tall, soothing companion, Bill Smith.

I was sent a typewritten outline and felt, upon reading it, disappointment. It was trash: A young man in Rome, a lawyer, meets and falls in love with a beautiful girl who is strangely evasive about her personal life. She is either only uncertain and innocent or— the evidence is flimsy but his suspicion mounts—a call girl. He marries her anyway, but incidents recur that are disturbing. I have forgotten the cliché climactic moment, but it causes her to attempt suicide and there is a final reconciliation amid the white sheets of the *ospedale,* or perhaps she dies.

No matter what was done with it, I told Glenville frankly, it would never possess the least merit. He understood my misgivings, but still the theme of jealousy was interesting and the locale . . .

The producer called from California. They were all "fans" of mine there. He had talked at length to Glenville. They were confident that I was the one to write the film. Forgetting everything, I inhaled.

There is the feeling that directors are dependent on you. In reality they are only attendant, waiting to see what is brought back, with luck something plump in your jaws. You are at most a preliminary figure. Their view extends past yours to meetings, cajolings, intrigues. They are the ones who actually create things. How reassuring it is to be drawn along by their energy, to linger in their so-

ciety, which seems luxurious and perhaps elevated, intimate with
that of the stars themselves.

I once sat near a victor at Cannes. He was in a buckskin coat
and a sort of black peddler's hat. The party was all young, and as
he spoke, the girl beside him took his hand, fingers intermeshed
with his, raised it to her lips, and began to kiss it in devotion. He
continued to talk, his free arm extended like a pope's.

———

In Rome, ochre and white, uninterested in me, I had the name of
a Count Crespi; Glenville had supplied it. He was cool on the telephone. I had to wait several days for an evening appointment.

He came out of his office to introduce himself, tan, handsome
face, ears close to his head, shattering smile. "I am Crespi," he
said, taking me into a small, plain room where he sat down across
from me.

As well as I could I told him the story of the film and he began
without hesitation to suggest things. The girl, instead of being a
model, which was rather a commonplace, might work at *Vogue*,
where his wife's former secretary, a very clever girl who spoke four
or five languages . . . but *Vogue* was already a little too fancy, perhaps, he decided. A salesgirl in a boutique, he thought, or perhaps,
yes, even better, a mannequin in one of the couture houses—
Fourquet on Via Condotti, for example. "She may earn only eighty
thousand lire a month but it's interesting work, she meets people,
a certain kind of person with money, taste. If she has something to
attend, Fourquet will probably lend her one of his expensive
dresses."

With heroic charm he began to describe the man in the film, the
young, proper lawyer. Politics slightly to the left—"In Italy, everybody is, everybody except me," he explained. The lawyer has a
good car, he goes dancing, to the beach. He loves sport, like all
Italians, though not as a participant, of course, and there is also

something traditional—he still goes home every day to eat with his mother at noon.

Crespi's enthusiasm and willingness to provide details increased my confidence. There might be a tone, a manner in which it could be presented, which would redeem it. As we talked on, in response to certain things I said, Crespi began to shift his view, to see the lawyer as less sophisticated, not part of the new Italy where people in Rome, as Fellini had shown, had seen *everything*. Perhaps it might take place in a more provincial town, Piacenza or Verona. Yes, he said, he saw it as a really romantic story. The women would all be crying, he predicted.

"But could all this happen in a town like Verona?" I said. "Are there call girls there?"

"Of course. Everywhere," he said. "It's in all the papers. It's the scandal of Italy. They advertise as *manicure,* with a chic address, *senza portiere.* Columns of them. Look in *Il Messaggero."*

It was true. In *Il Tempo* as well. I sat reading the papers in a noisy hotel on the Piazza della Rotonda, the recommendation of which had also come from Glenville. The furniture seemed to be from an old orphanage. The floors were bare wood. *Giovanissima*—very young—the ads all said. Via Flaminia, Via del Babuino, *senza portiere.*

As it happened, I didn't go to Verona or Piacenza. I met other people and then others. I took the apartment of an Englishwoman—her pretty, botanical name, Lyndall Birch, was on a small white card beneath the doorbell—on Via dei Coronari, a narrow, homely street in the old part of the city. The apartment was an *attico,* three rooms and a terrace, reached by climbing six flights of worn marble stairs. Across the rooftops, hot and becalmed, the Crespis' terrace could be seen, bounded by furled blue, palatial drapes. It was late June; the city was a furnace, the sun beating down on the ceiling. In the months that were to come I wrote lying prone on the apartment's cool stone floor, the burning air above my head too thick to breathe.

At dinner one night in a country restaurant I tried to follow the conversation and bursts of laughter. It was all wicked and in Italian. I could make out occasional coarse words. We were in the the garden, grouped around an animated woman named Laura Betti. She was a singer and actress. Pasolini and Moravia had written lyrics for her songs and she performed all the Kurt Weill–Bertolt Brecht repertory in Italian. She talked constantly that night, a cigarette between her fingers. Her laugh was irresistible. Smoke poured from her mouth. She was blonde, a bit heavy, perhaps thirty years old, the sort of woman who proudly wore a latent sadness.

We were in the ancient world, it seemed, in the cool air, the darkness beneath the vines. The empty carafes of wine were replaced by others, the green bottles of *minerale*. There were six or seven of us. They were talking about everyone and eating from one another's plates: about the famous actress who liked to make love in two ways at the same time, you could always recognize such women, Laura Betti said, by the way they looked over their shoulder with a knowing smile; about the madwoman who walked the streets singing in a ruined voice, a confused song about her great love who had taken her in his arms, the beauty of Jesus, and the little boy's dove she touched with her tongue. It was all about love, or, more properly, desire. Rome to them was a village that had no secrets. They knew everything, the names of the four countesses who had picked up an eleven-year-old gypsy girl one night and brought her to the house of a noted journalist to see him have his pleasure with her.

The script I was writing, they asked, what was its nature? Though feeling it sounded naïve, I described it. Perhaps it should not take place in Rome, I suggested—someone had mentioned Piacenza.

"Bologna," Laura Betti said. "That's where it could take place."

"Bologna?"

"It's marvelous," her husky voice declared. It was the city she was from.

"Bologna is famous for three things," she said. "It's famous for its learning—it has the oldest university in Italy, founded in the twelfth century. It's famous for its food. The cuisine is the finest in the country. You can eat in Bologna as nowhere else, that's well known. And lastly, it's famous for fellatio." She used another word.

"It's a specialty," she said. "All the various forms are called by the names of pasta. *Rigate,* for instance," she explained, "which is a pasta with thin, fluted marks. For that the girls gently use their teeth. When there used to be brothels there was always a *Signorina Bolognese*—that was her specialty."

The girl who worked in a publishing house and the one from Milan gave no sign of having heard. At nearby tables couples were talking in the darkness. I was impressed by Laura Betti's cool frankness, her poise—it was my novitiate.

I went to Bologna. Beside the wooden doors of the main station as the train pulled in, a woman was waiting. She nodded and smiled. I knew her name, Camilla Cagli. She was Bolognese; her husband was a lawyer. Laura Betti had called her and asked if she would be able to show me the city, and of that long day it is her smile I remember, the ease of her company, the natural grace. We walked beneath the arcades, talked of life in Bologna, and visited the huge house, the *palazzo* now become apartments, in which she had been born. For a few hours one is wrapped, even enraptured, in intimacy.

She had been married before, to a man of good family, but it was an empty marriage of bridge games and idleness before the war. She had been lucky and gotten a divorce—almost unheard of in Italy—during a brief period when the Communists were in power.

In the end, however, it was not in Bologna but in Rome itself that it all unfolded.

In Rome, the heat bore down. Dark Sicilians rose at two in the afternoon. The Tiber was green and stagnant. On Sunday mornings the highway to the sea was jammed with cars, the music from hundreds of radios beating the blue, exhausted air.

Three or four times a week I traveled up via Flaminia and across the bridge to the apartment of an American woman who was giving me Italian lessons. Her children closed the door to the living room and left us alone. Dorothy Brown was my tutor's name. We sat on the couch and studied. The vocabulary was not that of school. "The Italians are more interested in the *culo* than the *fica*," she told me, writing down the words. "There is even a verb for it, *inculare*. The girls all prefer it to preserve their virginity." Her boyfriend, she said, had done it this way with his cousin since they were both fourteen. Molten images: the dark, shadowed room, the youthful limbs, the faint smooth rustle of sheets.

At noon the boyfriend comes, an aristocrat from the south, small and self-assured, friendly with the children. We have lunch *en famille*. A maid serves. On her bare upper arm is a vaccination mark the size of a plum. "Marco, *mangia*," the boyfriend coaxes the youngest child—eat. "*Come fa crescere?*"—How are you going to grow big? The sun has emptied the midday streets. Around the Pantheon the cats are dozing beneath parked cars.

Like so many in Rome, Dorothy Brown seemed in a kind of exile. I somehow connect her with California. She had a chance in Rome—there is always a chance, even during revolutions and hard times—though good looks are hardly a guarantee.

Women seemed drawn to Rome, perhaps because of its decadence and the famous avidity of the men. There were women in expensive clothes at the Hassler or Hôtel de Ville; women traveling with their husbands and without; young women who claimed to be actresses—who knows what became of them; pairs of women in restaurants reading the menu very carefully; women stripped of illusion but unable to say farewell; women who owned shops and went to Circeo in the summer; divorced women who had once had a life in Trastevere; English girls who said, Oh, not this week because they weren't quite right—the doctor was sure it was nothing; girls who looked unbathed, filthy even, sitting in skimpy dresses in the restaurants, with young white teeth; *principessas* born in Vienna, living in the solitude of vast apartments; and aging fashion editors who seldom strayed far from the Hilton.

Against them, the legions of men: the handsome scum; men whose marriages had never been annulled; men who would never marry; men of dubious occupation; men from the streets and bars, of *nullo,* nothing; men with good names and dark mouths; swarthy men from the south, polished and unalterable, the nail of their little finger an inch long.

Amid this cast there were somber sights: the English prime minister's daughter, who was an actress, walking unsteadily through the restaurant, bumping into tables. She had narrow lips and an actress's always available smile. She was living with a black man on the Via del Corso in an apartment with high ceilings, no furniture, and the smell of incense. The front doors were lined with steel and had well-machined locks.

The apartment belonged to a Mafia figure, the black man confided, a very important man. "You know all those statues around Rome that have no heads? Well, he has the heads."

But it would be very comfortable when it was fixed up, she assured me. She had long red hair and pale skin on which there showed clearly a bruise on her cheek and another on her arm. Churchill, her father, was still alive. She sat down on the lone sofa with a drink.

"You've really got one there," the black man commented.

"No, I don't," she said.

"Oh, you sure do."

"Have I?" she said sweetly.

On a magazine cover on the floor was a photograph of her that had him in the background. She picked it up. "It's the best article we've ever had done," she said, "really, the most sympathetic, the most truthful. It's awfully good." In the light her hair seemed thin and wrinkles surrounded her eyes.

They were going to open a club together in Tangier. He was a musician and painter. Africa was the place, he said. "You just set foot there and the earth, it goes right through you, like you start trembling." His hands, infused, vibrated upwards. "Ain't that right, Mommy? Maybe I'll be prime minister someplace."

She didn't answer; she liked the idea of Africa, herself, someplace where it was easy to get money, she said, "I mean, that's all over, here, you know." It would be nice to have a summer crowd in someplace that was amusing; then in the winter, Lobo—that was his name—could paint. It would probably be a mistake, she decided in an added foresight, for him to become known as a singer or club owner first and a painter second because then, you know, people never quite erase that first impression.

———

It was a city of matchless decrepitude: muted colors, fountains, trees on the rooftops, beautiful tough boys, trash. A southern city—there were palms on the Piazza di Spagna and the sun incandescent in the afternoon. A venal city, flourishing through the ages—nothing so often betrayed could retain a shred of illusion. In the day it was beautiful. At night it became sinister.

Slowly, street by street, in fragments, it became familiar, like an immense jigsaw puzzle, one piece and a little later another fitting snugly into place. I recall it as a period when I had plenty of money. Eventually I was driving a white Fiat convertible bought brand-new, darting through the piazzas, swinging up ancient, wide avenues, peeling façade on one side, breathtaking view on the other.

On a June evening I had been introduced to a woman whose apartment might be for rent—I had not yet found one at the time. She was small, well-dressed, and untrusting, French-Canadian as I found out. In her brow was a furious vertical crease. Gaby was her name—Gabrielle, I suppose. She was seductive and at the same time disdainful; life had taught her hard lessons, among them to think always of money and to hate men.

She had been convent-educated in Canada, at Ursulines des Trois Rivières. I pictured gloomy buildings amid legendary dark pines. Her mother had gone there and her grandmother before that. She had slept in the very same bed they had, on a narrow mattress of straw. Girls were supposed to do that, she explained. To this day she slept as if in a coffin, straight and unmoving. Bathing at Trois Rivières was supervised—a white sheet fastened to a sort of neck ring was draped over the tub to defeat curiosity and assure modesty. She washed the linen collar of her woolen uniform every day and studied religion and religious history, accompanied by prayers. Many girls married millionaires, she said, as if the rigors of their confinement made sensuality and the desire for material things increase, even grow wildly. One girl married a Canadian Croesus, another, Georges Simenon.

In her own case the result was a passionate interest in human frailty. She rejoiced, somewhat bitterly, in the weaknesses and secret vices of Moravia, Italy's most famous writer; Visconti, the two handsome boys he had taken into his house after they had been in his *La Terra Trema,* they were dressed in uniforms and posed as servants; John Cheever (who had lived for a season or two in Rome); Pietro Germi, who left his wife for a young actress and had been betrayed by her in the most humiliating way; Thyssen, the rich art collector; countless others.

She told me with satisfaction the story of the singer who had begun as an actress, a shy, sweet girl who was given the chance to sing in a revue. She had to sleep with the star of the show, of course, and afterwards the producer, but they kept cutting her part. She went to bed with the star's brother because that might help her, and finally it had to be the stage manager. He took her to some house, a large one, and upstairs into a room. It was dark. "Take off your clothes," he told her. When she had done this, he said, "Put these on," and handed her a pair of high-heeled shoes. Then he had her get on her hands and knees on the bed. Suddenly the lights came on. There were other men in the room, all the previous ones, the star, the producer, the electrician. It was to be a kind of party and they came towards her laughing.

Gaby had been pursued, of course—that was one of the roots of her obsession. The workmen on the street who, seeing her pass, raised their hands as if forming them around her buttocks and cried admiringly, "*Beato lui . . .*"—blessed be the man to whom that belongs. The Sicilian prince who, as they were dancing at a ball, took her hand and said, "Here. What do you think of it?" having placed his naked member in it. The lecherous journalists and lawyers . . . it was unspeakable, though a moment later she wished she were twenty again, she would do all the things she had been afraid to.

She mentioned Corinne Luchaire, a prewar French star. "She was Göring's mistress."

I vaguely recalled a slender, beautiful blonde. "His mistress? Not really?"

"Of course!" she hissed. "Don't you know *anything?*"

Corinne Luchaire, she said, had been arrested in her apartment in Paris by the French Resistance and kept there all night while forty-one men raped her. She spent three years in jail. At her trial, her lawyer read aloud the entire Maupassant story of collaboration, *Boule de Suif*—the whore, the soldier who came to see her, didn't she know he was a German? "No, he was naked." I had never read the story, which was the first Maupassant ever published, and even now I am not sure if her version was correct, but it is the one I remember.

What she was exactly, I never discovered—writer, publicist, researcher of some sort, but withal, a Scheherazade who colored Rome for me with stories told in a slightly accented English; she hadn't learned it until she was seven and the "th"s were missing. "Ortodoxy," she pronounced it, and for "with" she said "wid." She rained images on me, some of them so intense they remain in my flesh like wounds.

She introduced me to Fellini, with whom she collaborated in some way. She brought him stories. "Talk to me, talk to me"—he wanted nothing in writing; he was inspired by listening, he said. It was often remarked that there were, at the time, only two real artists in all of Europe, Picasso and Fellini. Picasso was ancient and remote. Fellini was a man who sat in shirtsleeves and resembled his photographs, rumpled, with black hair growing out of his ears, like a lovable uncle.

I met him at the studio where he was working. The conversation began in Italian; he did not speak English, he apologized, but soon we had drifted into it. I had recently been to the Vorkapich lectures at the Museum of Modern Art in New York. They were essentially a tribute to Slavko Vorkapich, the master of the kind of montage used in the 1930s and '40s: pages of a calendar falling away to indicate days or months passing, the wheels of a train, then a car, then perhaps an ocean liner to show travel over great distances. The entire film world of the East Coast had attended the lectures, I said. It was difficult to obtain a seat, and of all the directors whose work had been chosen to illustrate concepts, Fellini was the one most often used, with Eisenstein second. Fellini gave a modest nod. He seemed grateful, the honor. He had only one question. "Who is Vorkapich?" he wanted to know.

On a slip of paper he wrote his telephone numbers—if there was anything in regard to which he might be of some help, he urged me to call him. I was not in Rome long enough, however.

She introduced me also to Zavattini, the dominant writer of Ital-

ian postwar films—*Shoeshine, Umberto D, The Bicycle Thief*—
whom I was prepared to greatly admire. He was bald, and wore a
baggy blue suit of the kind that has buttons on the fly. He was disheartened. "The cinema has failed," he said.

I was particularly interested in another person Gaby presented,
Nany Columbo, who owned a boutique and had been a mannequin in Rome and Genoa before the war.

"Do you speak English?" I said.

She shook her head. A pity.

The Italian girl I was writing about and whose reality, as on a
sheet of photographic paper, was only slowly forming—for a while
I imagined a younger Nany Columbo in the role. What ruined
girls, she explained in Italian, was all the luxury around them. She
said it as if she had lived through it herself, with easy resignation.
Everything about her seemed authentic, every word the bare truth.
When her husband came home from the war, she said, she was living in the country with her son. He came walking down the road.
She looked awful. Her hair was awry, her dress shabby. She
pushed a bed in front of the door, she said, and ran upstairs to fix
herself up before he could see her.

In the countryside a few hours north of Rome there were vineyards below the big houses; a man with his dog working in a field;
wood piled up by the doorway. The serene terraces of land with
their views of hills and groves were unchanged since the twelfth or
thirteenth century. In ancient churches the Piero della Francescas
were slowly fading, like the close of an act, from dark walls.

The thing I failed for a long time to understand was the connection between the vineyards, the great houses, the cloisters of
Europe and the corruption, the darkness, the riches. They have
been always dependent on one another, and without each other
could not exist. Nature is ravishing, but the women are in the
cities. There was one night in Rome, one morning really, about
two, when a man walked into a café near the Piazza Navona with

two women, one blonde in a blue-and-green silk dress, the other girl even better-looking. He was in evening clothes. They sat down; the waiters began to stir. He smiled and after a moment he uttered two words, but with his entire heart: "*Beaut*iful party."

———

I am turning the pages in a small, greenish notebook, half the size of a postcard, with a Spencerian *Notes* printed on the cover, bought probably in a dimly lit shop near Via Bocca di Leone in the summer of 1964. In it are the invariables: people, telephone numbers, restaurants, clubs, places to dance, piazzas, beaches, wines, unique things like the location of the cardinals' door through the keyhole of which the dome of St. Peter's could be seen floating above the edge of the garden, exceptional streets, and the names of two Italian whores who worked at the bar of a large hotel—actually one was a South African.

From these ample hints I can almost re-create the period, many dialogues, faces.

I was at the Hassler one afternoon and the women were talking about travel and food. A director's wife had her coat draped over the back of her chair. In proud black letters behind her neck, the words: GIVENCHY, PARIS. She was not the same one who, in Sophia Loren's apartment, admiring a wall of ancient frescoes, said, "Your decorator really did a fabulous job." The star said afterwards, in Italian, to another woman, "What can you expect?"

In a hotel one evening I sat with Scott Fitzgerald's onetime mistress, Sheilah Graham, and two magazine writers. Money was the sole topic, how much they earned, how much it cost to live. I tried to visualize the younger, unhardened woman Sheilah Graham had been, the unexpected gift for the broken writer. *Love is your last chance. There is really nothing else on earth to keep you there.* Nothing of that seemed to remain.

One of the writers was a film critic, the other was a tall woman in her forties who had braces on her teeth. She didn't like Italy. As for France, it was hideously expensive, she said. She hated France. It dated from the time she saw the French army leaving Indochina, "My dear, that was something, I assure you." France was not even a beautiful country; she had never seen a view there that she remembered.

"Where have you seen views?"

"Oh, India, Ceylon. That's where you see views," she said.

I was seated one night in a restaurant and two women sat down at the next table. One was American, older, with thin hands, and the other young, blonde, with a striking figure. Her first words were a complaint that she was "sitting downhill." The waiter hurried to bring her another chair and smiled at me in an aside.

They had just been to Capri and were talking with animation about it. Soon they were tasting a dish I had ordered and I was testing their wine. The younger one's glances were open and friendly. I could read palms, I told them—I found myself eager to touch her, to hold her hand. "Tell me your name," I suggested.

"Ilena," she replied. In the riches of that smile one would never be lonely or forgotten.

I examined her palm with feigned authority. "You will have three children," I said, pointing to some creases. "You are witty—it shows that here. I see money and fame." I felt her fingers pressing mine.

"You are an ass," she said gaily. "That means nice, no?"

Ilena may have been her name or it may have been the name she simply wore like a silk dressing gown one longed to peel back. Warmth came off her in waves. She was twenty-three years old and weighed sixty-two kilos, the absence of any part of which would have been a grave loss. She was, I learned, the mistress of John Huston, who was in Rome directing a film. She had also been the companion of Farouk, the exiled king of Egypt, and in that sense one of the last of an infinite number of royal properties reaching back to the pharaohs. She had met him at the dentist's office. He was there with his lawyer, she said, a detail I felt no one could invent. They discovered they lived not far from each other and began going out.

Farouk's days started in the evening. Like a true playboy, he rose late. She described him for me. He was amusing. He liked fine cars—he had a Rolls and a Jaguar. He loved to eat. I thought of the large men I had known, many of them good dancers, graceful, even dainty. Was it true of him? "Darling, we never danced," she said.

It was clear she had been fond of him. They had traveled to Monte Carlo together, to the *chemin de fer* tables where, a prodigious gambler, he was known as the Locomotive. The night he collapsed and died in Rome in a restaurant on the Appia Antica she was allowed to leave by the back door before the press arrived.

Whether or not she was an actress or ever became one, I do not know. Of course, she wanted to be—she had already played great roles.

We had a drink, the three of us, at the Blue Bar and a *gelato* on the Piazza Navona. On Via Veneto she stopped to talk with a group of elderly Italian businessmen. It was lovely to watch her. Her legs, the silk of her print dress, the smoothness of her cheeks, all of it shone like constellations, the sort that rule one's fate.

We dropped the American woman at her hotel, the Excelsior. Sitting in the car, in the driveway, I turned to Ilena and said simply, "I adore you. I have from the first moment." In response she kissed me and said, "To the right." It was late and she had an early appointment at Elizabeth Arden's; she wanted to go home.

"Are you married?" she asked as we drove.

"Yes."

"So am I."

It was to a man in his eighties, she explained. I recognized the story from the newspapers—she had married him to get a passport. He was in an old people's home, an *istituto*. She went to visit him there, she said. Then, agreeably, "Would you like to come?"

We stopped that night on a street near a dark piazza, across from a little place where she had often gone with Farouk at four or five in the morning for apple strudel. It looked closed, and I waited while she ran across to say hello to the woman who was the proprietor. After a while she came back. "She was *so* happy to see me," she said animatedly and added, "She's very nice."

We went on to Parioli, where, in a somewhat dubious building on Via Archimede, Ilena lived. The apartment was small and drearily furnished, but on the wall was a large picture of John Huston that had appeared in *Life*. Lying on the floor were books that Huston had given her to read. He might just as well have given her a chemistry set or a microscope. "You must *never stop* learning," he told her—she could do him perfectly. I could hear his rich, rolling, faintly cynical voice pronouncing "Mount Lungo" in his documentary on the battle of San Pietro, a village in ruins after the war, given over to weeds and sheep droppings. There is a cemetery atop Mount Lungo from the heights of which one can see twenty miles, all the bare stony slopes up which men fought.

"Never stop learning," he repeated. "That's very important. Promise me that."

"Of course, John," she answered.

In an album were many clippings of the two of them, Huston with a white, patriarchal beard. He was a *coccolone*—someone who likes to be babied. He was also crazy, she admitted, and very tight. "To get a thousand dollars from him is *so* difficult," she said.

The portrait she painted over a period of time was of an indomitable man who nonetheless was lonely. He would call on the phone, "What are you up to, baby?"

"Nothing."

"Come *right* over. Right away."

He was in the autumn of a life of activity, a life that had not always been lived in accordance with reason. He had no friends, she said, and hated to go out. He was living in a suite in the Grand Hotel on a diet of vodka and caviar. She would call him. "John, do you want some girls?"

"Bring them around," he said. "We'll have some fun."

She brought three, one of them eighteen years old—she liked young, tender girls, she explained, in the late afternoon was best. "Darling," she said to me after describing a scene that might have taken place at Roissy, "you're a writer, you should know these things."

Huston had fought at Cassino, she told me, as if in justification.

"No, he didn't."

"But he *did*. He's told me stories."

"He was a film director. He never fought."

"Well, he *thinks* he did," she said. "That's the same thing."

I liked her generosity and lack of morals—they seemed close to an ideal condition of living—and also the way she looked at her teeth in the mirror as she talked. I liked the way she pronounced "cashmere," like the state in India, Kashmir. Her cosmetics bag was filled with prescriptions, just as the shelf in her closet was crammed with shoes. Once we passed a big Alfa Romeo that she recognized as belonging to a friend, the chief of detectives in Rome. She had made love with him, of course. "Darling," she said, "there's no other way. Otherwise there would have been terrible trouble about my passport. It would have been impossible." I only learned in time that there was, besides Huston, also an Italian businessman supporting her.

She didn't like Negroes, Arabs, or certain cities, often that she had never been to. Above all, she hated bohemians. "Darling, they're so filthy." I admired her poise. On the telephone, to someone she did not know who had been given her number, she merely said, "I'm sorry. I have to go." I heard that on several occasions.

The things she said seemed to come straight from what she

knew or felt, as easily as one might pick up a fork. There was no hesitation or propriety. She said things I wished I might have, things more direct.

She was also, I hardly need add, difficult, especially about eating. "I have to have something to eat," she would say, becoming more and more nervous. "If I don't get something to eat, I'm going to cry." And reading the menu in a kind of desperation, "What shall I order?" When it came, she was likely to send it back. "I can't eat this." The restaurant never made a fuss. The crucial question was whether or not the dish contained butter or had been cooked in it. She absolutely could not eat butter. She had to be extremely careful, she said.

Once we sat down in a restaurant and while she went to the ladies' room I read the menu. As I did, I realized there was nothing on it she would like, and besides, the place seemed dull and nearly empty. I rose as she returned, and said, "Come. This is not good." She obeyed without a word.

There was a film festival in Taormina she went to. She had looked forward to it for days. I languished in Rome. The week passed slowly. I heard her distant voice—I did not know where Taormina was, exactly—on the telephone. "Oh, darling," she cried, "it's so marvelous." She was going to have the same agent as Monica Vitti, she said excitedly. A director had promised her a part in a James Bond film. She was not staying at the San Domenico Palace, she was at the Excelsior. Tomorrow she would be at the Imperiale—I understood quite well what all that meant—and on Sunday she was going to receive a prize.

"Which prize?"

"I don't know. Darling, I can't believe it," she said.

At last there was a telegram—I had felt I might not see her again—*Coming Monday Rapido 5. Afternoon,* and signed with her name. It was sent from Ljubljana—Yugoslavia.

I met the train. It was thrilling, almost miraculous, to see her coming along the platform, a porter behind her with her bags. Some things are only good the first time but seeing her was like the first time. I knew she would say "darling." I knew she would say, "I *adore* you."

The exciting days in Sicily, the festival, had left a glow. At a big reception, among scores of faces, she had seen, directed at her, the brilliant unwavering smile of a young man in a silk foulard, a wide smile, "like a killer's." She was wearing a white, beaded dress. Her arms were bare. Fifteen or twenty minutes later she saw him again.

The second barrel, as the lawyers say, was fatal. She said only, "Let's leave." Without a word he offered her his arm.

He had a beautiful car. The steering wheel was made of gleaming wood. They went somewhere but found it closed. That was enough. "Let's go to bed," she said. He said simply, "Yes."

At the hotel the *portiere* would not let him go up to her room, "*Non, non, signorina,*" he said. She began to make a scene. She was going to another hotel, she threatened loudly. Finally the *portiere* asked, "Where is he?" and allowed them to go up. Thirty minutes later he was ringing the room, to no avail.

I listened with some unhappiness but without anger. They say you should not tell these things to the other person, but in this case it meant little, faithfulness was not what I expected.

"You'll get to the top," I told her almost reluctantly, "but you shouldn't . . ."

"What?"

"Nothing," I said. "I'll tell you later."

"If I don't become too much of a whore," she said.

We drove up to Paris. I remember the hotel and the first evening. We were at the window; I was behind her, standing close. Across the river the lights of the city glittered, as far as one could see.

We had come up through the Rhône valley and many small towns. Past Dijon we were on a back road along a canal and came to a wide dam from which the lines of fishermen dropped forty or fifty feet into clear green water. The dark shapes of fish—I took them to be pike—were coasting lazily about. We watched the biggest ones approach, ignore the bait, and move off to lie motionless. "Like sultans," she commented. I felt she knew.

———

What I remember is a kind of glamour and sleekness. Travel, the great hotels. James Kennaway, the Scottish writer, coming into a suite at Claridge's one January in a belted, supple black-leather coat—he had time for just one drink before catching the night train to Edinburgh, not alone, my impression was. He was sharp-nosed, laughing. I knew him only slightly, though I had once gone for a weekend to his house in Gloucestershire. One of the other guests was a lively old woman who had been his father-in-law's governess and, at the appropriate period of youth, mistress. She remained close to the family. "Traditional," they assured me.

I remember, in Santa Monica, beneath the palm-lined bluff on the beach, the brief row of houses, one of which—a large, imitation Normandy farmhouse—had been rented by Roman Polanski and his young wife, Sharon Tate.

I had met Polanski through Redford. A call had come from London, in a warm, faintly accented voice—the producer, Gene Gutowski. Could I come there to talk about writing a film, the film about a ski racer? Somewhere in the whirl of London nights—restaurants so in fashion that their telephone numbers were unlisted, headlong drives through parks and narrow streets—Polanski gave me in a single sentence his idea of the movie: It was to be something like *High Noon*; the sheriff has been killed—in this case the lead racer on the team has broken a leg—and they have to send for a replacement. I was impressed by the succinctness.

Polanski was already famous, in his early thirties, although he

appeared younger. He had a small, speedy car with a telephone—
innovative then—a large apartment, and an air of freedom from
the dullness of being always and only oneself. With pride, but
hastily, he showed me photographs of Sharon, to whom he was not
yet married. There was something that both drew one to him and
cautioned one—his eye seemed to skim over so many things. Beyond the shrewdness and candor, he gave the strange impression
of not playing for anything real, as if chips were certain at some
point to be redeemed. His banter was filled with confidence. One
night in a restaurant we sat with Nureyev, who was eating a dish of
magnificent strawberries with his fingers. "See? I told you he ate
like a peasant," Polanski said. Nureyev didn't bother to smile.

He had passed, as a child, through the terror of massacre and
war. He had seen a column of men being taken from the Krakow
ghetto, doomed, his father among them, and had run alongside
like a calf, wanting to go. His father ignored him and finally muttered threateningly, "Get lost." The small boy of ten stopped,
stung, and watched them leave him behind, to life, as it turned
out, although, astonishingly, his father survived also. For such a
miraculous escape and the rich life that followed, was there a
price to be exacted?

That summer in Santa Monica—it was 1967—at the Mori
Fencing Academy, Polanski was a prize pupil. He was also rehearsing an important film he was about to direct. In the enormous cav-
ern of a sound stage, the floor of the apartment which would be in
Rosemary's Baby had been laid out with white tape. Polanski's instructions to the actors had the same verve and precision he
showed with the foil.

At the oversized beach house Sharon wore white pants and a
long-sleeved black polo shirt, the buttons open. Her hands stole
around me affectionately from behind. Polanski was weary from
the long day with actors. We ate in the kitchen, steaks Sharon had
thriftily bought at the post exchange in San Francisco—her father

was an army officer—and just as Roman had shown pictures of her to me, she showed one of herself in some film magazine to him. An army brat, I was thinking, although I had never seen one like her. The ease and devotion of their life seemed plain.

For reasons not worth going into, Polanski was dropped from the movie I finally wrote, and thus I never lost the admiration I had for his energy and charm, a charm that was not learned but came from some deeper source, as well as his power to command. I could not imagine him being unable to reply to a question or think quickly. He had an instinct for the visceral; in his hands even familiar material could become interesting.

As for Sharon, she remains for me a kind of Hera, the emblem of marriage. If she was not a very good housekeeper, she was pure of heart and her flesh was a poem. One felt that she could be enjoyed in all the ways that one can enjoy a woman, looking at her, talking, touching, as well as other ways.

August morning. In a white nightgown, barefoot, with lovely arms and long hair she comes to the table in their suite in the Essex House. Polanski, barefoot too, has been watching television. We sit down to breakfast together. May I have the syrup? Mmm. The butter? A hand passes it. Would you like any toast? A crisscrossing of plates and offerings, together with his and her concealed smiles. It was a duet from Noël Coward. The suite was on the south side, high up. All of downtown New York spread before us. The previous night had been frenzy and excess, the morning freshness and reason. On top of the building were large red letters that spelled its name in neon, at night visible for miles. They were a landmark, like a lighthouse, at the edge of the park, and also a schoolboy legend when for a time, inexplicably, the first "E" and "S" were burned out. In the ambience of pleasure and art we talked about the ski-racing script. He was at the time shooting the movie he had rehearsed in California. Ours would be the next.

I saw them at Cannes a year later, together, for the last time. He was serving as a judge at the festival. He was wearing a dinner jacket when we talked and a white, ruffled shirt. She was in a matchless gown. They were to come to the country for lunch, but never showed up.

When Sharon Tate, along with four others, was senselessly murdered in Los Angeles one night, there was, in addition to horror and disgust, the shame. America had slaughtered one of its innocents. It was incomprehensible, God would not permit it. Perhaps Polanski, who had been in Europe at the time, had overreached himself, achieved too great a happiness, and it had been taken from him. His child, unborn, had died, too—the karma his father had given him was not to be passed on. I felt the sorrow for him that one feels for kings. His powers defied simple grief.

I thought of the bedroom in Santa Monica. It was spacious, on the second floor, facing the sea. I had stood in its corner. The sun was burning the floor. The large bed in which they had slept was unmade, the sheets rumpled, the pillows tossed. In the drawers of the built-in dresser were narrow glass windows to enable one to see the color of the shirts in each. There were Matisse drawings in the beautiful bath.

Among the road maps, cards, old addresses—the lost world never put in order—there is, I know, a photograph: the brilliant, almost demonic director on a couch with the tall, graceful girl. It was taken one night when we had dinner. I envied him his wife. It is difficult now to imagine the woman she would have become. She remains as she was, as if among all the herd there had been this exceptional creature, slightly awkward perhaps, but without blemish and carrying in her person the essential traits, the true heart of the paradise he had somehow bargained for.

———

In first-class cabins, paid for with movie money—a good portion of the money, as it happened—in the warm autumn of 1967 we sailed on the *France*. Tremendous departure, crowds on the pier, the water widening, the ship assuming life. In the blue, oceanic evening, waiters brought drinks and packs of cigarettes to the table.

We dressed for dinner. Madeleine Carroll and her daughter were aboard, and Edward Albee en route to Paris and Leningrad for the openings of his play. As they entered, the bartender called out greetings to familiar couples by name. At afternoon tea there was an orchestra, and miniskirted girls without partners sat slumped in chairs. A theater producer told stories of Ireland—men who approached him in the street crying grandly, "Sir John!" He tried to correct them but could not. "A little something for charity," they pleaded.

"What charity?"

"Sir John!" they wailed.

The second night at three in the morning, I woke abruptly. Someone was throwing gravel against the port-holes. It was heavy rain; we had run into a storm. The ship rolled, soared ominously, slid down. The steel shivered and creaked. We had three state-rooms and four children, most of whom became seasick. His twin sister, Claude, was smiling and unaffected, but in the empty dining room I could see my son's face—he was five, Fidi was his pet name—changing color as food was brought to the slanting table.

There was bingo in the calm of the next afternoon. Amid the old couples and children sat a dark-browed Edward Albee, two cards in front of him. The handsome blond boy he was traveling with we saw little of.

We were going to France for a year, to a village in the south, not far from Grasse, where we had rented a large, sparsely furnished farmhouse—a *mas* in the regional dialect—solidly built with walls two feet thick. It had been occupied the year before by Robert Penn Warren and his wife, Eleanor Clarke. I wrote to ask if they recommended it, and a letter came from her in reply. It described a paradise, from the windows of which the sea could be distantly seen. You will have the most wonderful year of your life, it concluded, if you don't happen to freeze to death. The house, of course, had no heat. In the worst months of winter the sheets were so cold we could not turn over in bed—we lay like statues of saints, rigid, arms crossed.

La Moutonne, the house was called, the female sheep. The long, descending driveway was bordered by great eucalyptus trees, whose bark hung in sinuous strips. The front of the house more or less faced empty air. There was an embankment, the roofs of a few houses below and, far off, the tinfoil sea. The most wonderful year of your life—the simplicity of that promise.

All through the summer, to prepare them for regular French school—*école communale*—our two oldest daughters had been taking French lessons. In the Manhattan apartment of a professor, several times a week they sat and talked for an hour. The amount they learned, it turned out, was limited by a large wart the professor had on the tip of his tongue, visible when he spoke and absolutely mesmerizing to two little girls.

It was a long, beautiful fall. Many mornings I rose before dawn and went out on the bedroom balcony to read. Grasse rose blue in the distance. Its buildings had the luminous form and serenity of palaces. The only people we knew in the first months were Harvey Swados, the writer, and his family, half an hour away in Haut de Cagnes. It was they who had persuaded us to come to France—he was on a sabbatical.

Haut de Cagnes was on top of a hill, overlooking its then sleepy sister, Cagnes sur Mer, where Modigliani once lived and the gypsies used to come and bathe their horses in the sea. The Swadoses' small house belonged to a sculptor or perhaps his children—he had abandoned his family, and his wife had died of drink, with empty bottles piled on the stairs. There were hundreds of books, many moldy, and often inscribed by famous figures from the

1920s, when a disheartened Scott Fitzgerald had sat in the square not far from the house and moaned, "Ernie's done it," of *The Sun Also Rises,* which had just come out.

The village of which *La Moutonne* was part was less distinguished, able to claim only some years when Renoir, the painter, had lived there. There was a stucco church and a restaurant or two, and beneath our olive trees with their silvery leaves a white goat danced on her hind legs, striving to strip the lowest boughs. This was Lily, sweet-smelling, graceful, and deeply unaffectionate. The children adored her, though treating her with caution. Her face offered little in the way of expression other than satisfaction at eating, and her yellow eyes, set high on her head, were as cold as those of a serpent. It was impossible to estimate what she knew, but whatever it was, we came to realize, was firmly ingrained. At night she was kept in a roomy stone shed attached to the house. During the day she would graze, often climbing onto the red-tile roof of the shed, from there stepping onto the balcony where I worked, and even, if they were open, through the french doors into the bedroom. It was only at milking time that she disappeared.

In memory my forehead is pressed against her round side and I am listening to the thin, metallic sound of milk shooting into the pail, which at a certain point, with seeming inattention, she will step in with a dirty rear hoof. I can only guess why this gave her pleasure.

She was, for a long time we hoped it—we had taken her in the car to her "wedding"—carrying a kid. Finally it was apparent. She was provided with a bed of fresh straw, to which she seemed indifferent, and one winter morning before school the children came running into the kitchen to say that there were four extra legs in the shed!

I have forgotten what we named Lily's child, but in a matter of a day or two she was climbing the stone walls with her mother and learning the fundamentals of disdain.

I had my picture taken with Lily, holding her close while she looked the other way. One leg with its blackened, worn knee is visible and her mouth has the trace of a triumphant smile.

We were living in isolation. I had no one to talk to aside from my wife, no one whose opinion I could seek about what I had written. Late one afternoon I finished a story—it was about a man whose imaginary life slowly consumes his identity until ordinary events become fantastic—and in the panic that followed I gave it to my wife to read, desperate for a response. It was compelling, it was not. I went for a walk in the dusk. The path was desolate late in the year, but the house was lighted and alive as I returned. She was in the kitchen preparing supper. "Well, what did you think?" I asked.

"About what?"

"The story."

"I couldn't make head or tail of it," she remarked.

In time we met people, among them John Collier and his wife. He was, at that time, essentially a scriptwriter. He had strong leftist convictions, though they did not affect his manner of living, which was lordly, if thinly funded. He had come through everything, marriages, leaving England, the blacklist, financial ruin, and somehow made it to shore near Grasse in a huge country house said to have once been the property of Pauline Bonaparte. He readily admitted his mistakes, they came bobbing along behind. He had been offered *The Treasure of the Sierra Madre* to write when he was working in Los Angeles, but failed to see a film in it. He was luckier with *The African Queen* and had a profitable interest, even though his script was not used.

He was in his sixties, smiling, cherubic, not old, still quite green in fact, virtually a youth, he concluded. Nimble and rosy-cheeked, his thrusts were light as air. One time he came to ask if Harriet, his wife, could borrow some birth-control pills. My wife apologized, she was sorry but she didn't have any extra. "Well," he said unperturbedly, almost gaily, "I guess I'll have to come over here."

The Colliers belonged to a small beach club—there were many of them—to the west of Cannes, where Picasso sometimes came; the owners possessed a napkin on which he had once sketched a fish. We swam there and farther along where there was nothing, only a lengthy strip of bare sand. The sea was our chief pleasure. Fleeing from the waves or dashing into them, lying up by the rocks, wind-sheltered, there was the sense that time and events had stopped. We drove back, wearied by the sun, at day's end to the immemorial house where the goat waited, a sentry on the roof.

The mail, when it came, was laid by the postman on a table in the entrance hall. The telephone, with its shrill, disquieting sound, rarely rang. I sat on the balcony at a worn wooden table and wrote. Racers breaking their legs on icy runs seemed far away, but page by page I assembled lines to be typed by a woman in Grasse. I cannot recall if the Mediterranean was visible from where I sat, but from the floor above it was, in the afternoon, blinding and white.

The sea remains, the dense fragrance on the road past the perfume factories, the daily *Nice-Matin* with its glaring stories of crime and car accidents. Otéro, penniless and aged, the Venus of the century before, died in Nice that year. She is mentioned in Isak Dinesen's *Out of Africa*: old Mr. Bulpett announces that he appears in La Belle Otéro's memoirs, as a young man who went through a hundred thousand for her sake within six months—this was pounds, when the pound was tremendous.

"And do you consider," he was asked, "that you did have full value?"

After a moment's thought, he replied, "Yes. Yes, I had."

One night in May I had a dream of intense power—my daughter had become ill. I could not believe the seriousness, it was so sudden. In the dream she died. I was numb with sorrow. I told her brother and sisters. I went into the room where she lay, her beautiful face now closed, her long hair. Suddenly I was felled by it, brought to my knees. Tears poured down my cheeks. She was dead.

You cannot believe in dreams and yet, at some level, you must. The pharaoh dreamed. Macbeth.

The next morning there was a boil, like a stigma, in her left nostril. By nightfall she was desperately sick. The doctor pronounced it serious, an infection. The danger was that it could go to the brain. There was a vein that ran here, by the nose, he said. An infection on the face was not bad, but here . . . Above all, it should be energetically treated.

By the next day, pus was running. The nurse who was to give an injection didn't come. We drove to town. My daughter was eleven, the age of perfection. By now her lip was swollen, as thick as my thumb.

In the hospital they placed a lead shield over her eyes. She lay inert on a white table, two small pillows on either side of her head. My hand was held tightly by hers, I wanted to pull her back, to this world, to my desperate embrace. A square of light from an ominous machine was being moved onto her face with a shadowed + in the center of it.

"Don't move," the doctor said in French. "You must remain perfectly still for two or three minutes."

Behind the lead shield I could see her very blue, open eyes. The doctor left the room. A sound began, a low, persistent sound of voltage. She was motionless. The muzzle of the machine was only inches above her face. The square of light was the size of one's palm. We were helpless. I was sure she was going to die.

At one time in my journals, beneath the date I had written, *Every year seems the most terrible,* but that was self-pity. Anyone might have written that. The most terrible thing is the death of a child, for whom you would do so much, for whom you can do nothing. I had heard of the death of children and seen them lying helpless, but it was an arrow that would never be aimed your way.

Nina, my daughter, lived, but twelve years afterwards her older sister, Allan, died tragically. I have never been able to write the story. I reach a certain point and cannot go on. The death of kings can be recited, but not of one's child. It was an electrical accident. It happened in the shower. I found her lying naked on the floor, the water running. I felt for her heartbeat and hurriedly carried her, legs across one arm, limp head along the other, outside. Thinking she had drowned, I gave her artificial respiration desperately, pressing down hard on her chest and then breathing into her mouth time after time. Nothing. I kept at it. An ambulance came. Someone pronounced her dead. I could not believe it.

I did not know what to do. In the house I laid my head on the edge of the bed and began reciting over and over the only recollected psalm.

Even if the rest get through, there is always the thought of that one.

———

"There has been an accident at Cape Canaveral." These words were repeated endlessly one night—it was in 1967, too—like the news of a great disaster, like war. Grissom and White had both been killed. Something lodged in my chest, a feeling I could not swallow. "There has been an accident . . ."

I had flown with them, each of them, in Korea with Grissom, in the war. I saw the two of them moving now, along the walkway, slow as divers, clad in the same cloth mail. Over the threshold they stepped, into their sepulcher.

The capsule had become a reliquary, a furnace. They had inhaled fire, their lungs had turned to ash.

A month after White died I wrote to his widow, from afar, in the silence of the afternoon. *Dear Pat.*

I had dreamed of him many times, I wrote. He was precious to me. I believed in him. In him I saw myself, what I might have been. More, I felt the pride one has when intimate with greatness. He was on his way to greatness, needing only, as Matthew Arnold said in a different context, that two things concur: the power of the man and the power of the moment. It seemed the procession of heaven would stop for him, that it already had. We were convinced he was going to make his mark in history, not the history of his country or even of flight, but the history of mankind.

He was great, I wrote, in his ability, his strength, his character. He was great in achievement and great in his goals. But the moment did not occur.

Sometimes—I never knew when to expect it—the image of it all would return, the disaster with which I had some vague connection. At those times all else became trivial. It could translate itself into a genuine despair. It had managed to enter my soul.

I remember lying in bed in Paris, late at night. The hotel was silent. I was thinking of White. I put one finger to my temple. I was practicing shooting myself. It was very hard to pull the trigger. I waited, I began to count, one, two, three . . . A tremendous explosion! Then utter relief. What would I look like, I wondered? One side, the dark side, completely gone, splashed onto the walls and door. Who would care? On three, then. Ready . . .

Slowly the illness passed and came back less and less often. It was like some unhappiness in childhood, annealed by time. The road was leading elsewhere, to what seemed a counterlife, if not in importance then in its distance from the commonplace—a life of freedom, style, and art, or the semblance of art.

In some mysterious way which I accepted without wonder, the films I had been writing with little more behind them than undamaged belief all went into production within a year.

The one in Rome—it was called *The Appointment*—was badly

miscast and had the wrong director. Because of his ability and reputation he had the unquestioning confidence of everyone, though he later told me he had agreed to make the movie mainly because he wanted the chance to learn something about color from the experienced Italian cameraman. Whatever the reason, he was ill adapted to the script which, like a poor garment, should have been ripped at the seams and completely refashioned to make it fit.

Lotte Lenya, old and nearly disregarded, had a small role, and it is she I remember best. We sat and talked—she was very approachable—with the intimacy of those who are inessential. Her physical sensuality was long gone but the history of it was still in her face. She was that unmistakable type, lower class risen, and comfortable in either world.

The ultimately ridiculous movie I had written was shown at Cannes the next year as the American entry. I found myself sitting with Helen Scott, a large, homely woman who worked in films, was close to what was called the New Wave, and whom I knew from Paris. The theater was packed with well-dressed people conversing in every language.

The screening was less than a triumph. The audience, at a moment when they should have felt fulfillment, broke into loud laughter. On the terrace of the Carlton afterwards we could not help overhearing the acid remarks. I felt the brief pleasure of having had my doubts confirmed, while Helen Scott, a veteran of the business, sat silent in embarrassment. She was afraid that I might burst into tears. The sole consolation was that I had been paid. I might, if I'd been more provident, have stuffed some of the money in my stocking.

You are, in the audience for a couple of hours, in the hands of the director, who may or may not be trusted. *The vulgar falsehoods of the cinema,* as someone has put it. Movies are like passion, brilliant and definitive. They end and there is an emptiness. They are narcotic, they allow one to forget—to imagine and forget. Looking back, I suppose I have always rejected the idea of actor as hero, and no intimacy has changed this. Actors are idols. Heroes are those with something at stake.

In the war, I remembered, we went to movies almost nightly. We laughed at them as the men and women in evening dress at Cannes had laughed at mine.

Nevertheless, filled with ambition, I was soon directing a film of my own. It was the one taken from the story of Irwin Shaw's, and I now can see that I was too restrained, to mention only one shortcoming, in both the scenes I wrote and the direction that I gave the actors.

In the course of shooting we worked our way from the south of France down to Rome, traveling always by car. It was like a campaign of Hannibal's. The days were long and exhausting. There was never a minute empty and almost no solitude.

The star—and she was that—had agreed to be in the film, then changed her mind, and at the last minute was persuaded again when we flew all night to Rome, where she was shooting something else, to meet with her. Visconti, she said—he was just then directing her—was a true genius. I tried not to be disheartened. I was judging her unfairly, by her conversation and personality, while there she was, flesh and blood and perhaps willing to perform. She refused dinner—to get back to a boyfriend, I was sure— and after twenty or thirty minutes raced off in a car. Her agreement to be in the film, however, enabled us to get the money to make it.

I was to learn many things about her: that she chewed wads of gum, had dirty hair, and, according to the costume woman, wore clothes that smelled. Also that she was frequently late, never apologized, and was short-tempered and mean. When she arrived in France to work, she brought an English boyfriend and his two small children along. She had told me she hated hotels, and in their room were soiled clothes piled in corners, paper bags of cookies, cornflakes, and containers of yoghurt. The boyfriend, a blond highwayman, was a vegetarian. He prescribed their food. "Meat," he murmured in the restaurant, looking at a menu, "that'll kill you." In the morning sometimes they danced maniacally in the street, like two people who have just become rich or had an enormous piece of luck. During the day, after every scene she flew into his arms like a child while he kissed and consoled her.

Midway through shooting—we were near Avignon—she refused to continue unless her salary was doubled and, equally important, her boyfriend took over as director. She got the money but the producer refused to back the mutiny and set me adrift. When I heard what had happened I found it hard to suppress my loathing, although in retrospect I wonder if it might not have been a good thing. The boyfriend might have gotten some unimagined quality from her and made of the well-behaved film something crude but poignant—that is to say compelling.

The truth is, in stars, their temperament and impossible behavior are part of the appeal. Their outrages please us. The gods themselves had passions and frailties—these are the stuff of the myths; modern deities should be no different. If the movie is a success, even if it is not, all memories are cherished.

In the end the film we made, *Three,* was decorous and mildly attractive. It was popular at Cannes and had some flattering reviews in America. A young women's magazine voted it the selection of the month and critics had it on their ten-best lists, but they were alone in this. Audiences thought otherwise.

There were opportunities to direct again, but I remembered, when we were close to finishing, lying on the stone beach at Nice late in the day in a pair of Battistoni shoes, utterly spent. I felt like an alcoholic, like Malcolm Lowry. I had forgotten it was Céline I liked, Cavafy. It seemed the morning after. The ball was over. I looked down and saw the white legs of my father. All of it had demanded more than I was willing again to give.

For its real adherents the life never ended. I liked the stories of producers driving down to Cap d'Antibes in convertibles with two or three carefree girls. I had had notes placed in my hand by the wives of leading men, bored and unattended to, that said in one way or another, Call me. I had seen Harry Kurnitz's Bentley and his accompanying girlfriend, and the actors emerging from the Danieli in Venice, wrapped against the fall weather in expensive coats, fur-lined within and cloth out. The fur was the luxury in which they lived, the cloth an emblem of the ordinary world from which they were removed. Off to Torcello for lunch, jolting across the wide lagoon, the wind blowing the dark green water to whiteness, past San Michele with its brick walls, the island on which Stravinsky and Diaghilev lay buried—the real and the false glory, one moving past the other, though there are times one cannot tell which is which.

I liked the producers best. It may have been because I had more to do with them or because their job was to always have money, or perhaps it was their resilience. They were like prospectors, optimistic, willing to toil for years in hope of a strike. They needed neither honesty nor education, although the one I came to admire most was hampered by both.

I first met him at a lunch high above Fifth Avenue. Some well-heeled investors had invited him to give his opinion on a proposal Lane Slate and I were making to form a small company. In a tweed jacket and with the air of having been taken away from more important things he calmly asked a few questions and then proceeded to chop us to bits. It was like listening to a banker give all the reasons for turning down a loan. Films, even documentaries, could not be made for the amounts we suggested; there were no arrangements for distribution or sale even if the films were somehow made; finally, he did not find the subjects we had chosen interesting. There seemed to be nothing to be said in rebuttal other than "You are wrong." It had a pathetic sound. I disliked this man intensely. His arrogance was enraging. I could not remember his name. Battered, Lane and I descended to the street.

Some months later my agent came across a producer he was certain I would like, a man of taste, imaginative, young. He would be at the bar of the Four Seasons and we could have an introductory drink. I was appalled to find myself sitting down next to the same haughty expert who had flayed us before. My recollection is that in his self-esteem he did not recognize me.

Thus began one of the truest friendships of my life.

Harvard, ex–naval officer, former curator, writer, editor, his name was Robert Emmett Ginna, the "G" hard and the last syllable rhyming with "way." Though it was through error mispelled on his birth certificate, he had been named, like his father, for the enduring Irish patriot Robert Emmet. He had acquired, it turned out, the rights to a drably written novel with a central, melodramatic idea. These were the days of unforgiving dictatorships in Eastern Europe. In one such regime the hated chief judge—the equivalent of minister of justice—an icy man of no mercy, is also, unknown to anyone, its most famous and revered dissident. Once a year, during carnival, when identities are masked and all inhibitions put aside, the feared judge, disguised, becomes a legendary clown. Women fall in love with his daring, and of course this is the path to downfall. I was to write the script.

We arranged to go to Europe for research. In the February dusk a limousine drove us to the Pan Am Building, where we rose, throbbing, from the windblown roof in a helicopter and glissaded across the river and far-reaching suburbs. In my pocket was a wad of traveler's checks he had handed me for "incidentals," though during the trip I had the chance to cash very few of them. In the first romantic darkness, on Lufthansa, we moved towards the runway, and soon after takeoff, trim stewardesses were moving slowly down the aisle with a huge roast, which they carved to order. We were in first class. In Ginna's attaché case were an eyemask and a pair of slippers. When, after dinner and fine cognac, the talk gradually ceased, he bade a pleasant goodnight, put on the equipment, and leaned back in the seat. We were companions.

He was a man of firm habits, intense loyalties, great knowledge of art—his only real knowledge, he called it—and a fierce temper. His mouth could set in a line as taut as if drawn by a scrimshaw artist. He was a writer himself, as I have said, a journalist of long experience. He knew countless stories, as well as the names of serious restaurants in a dozen countries. He was a passionate fisherman and a superb cook.

We went to the heart of Europe and the carnivals in Munich, Cologne, and Prague. Also Basel. In the ballroom of the Bayerischer Hof I was dressed as a rooster—elaborate costumes were for rent—and he as a Roman senator with a gilded laurel wreath. *Did we really see or did I imagine,* he later wrote, *kneeling girls naked to the waist being ridden like horses?*

The resulting script, written towards the end of the 1960s, acquired a long history. Over the years, six or seven, when the movie that might be made possessed some animation, a faint breathing or wan, unexpected smile, various actors and directors drifted in and out of involvement. Joseph Losey, a lofty exile, said he would like to do it. We met in his London town house. He sat in a chair near the window. He had the watcheye, as Ginna commented afterwards, pale and slightly bulging; ponies had it. He also had an indigestible idea, that the movie should be made not in Europe but in South America. They had dictatorships there, and the background would be fresh. "The arcades," he said mysteriously several times.

Later, to our great happiness, Paul Scofield agreed to be in it. A studio decided to go ahead, providing we could get one of three actresses they named to play opposite him. By now, three or four years had passed. We flew to London once again; the three actresses were all there. The black eyeshade had been worn out or lost. Ginna tied a blue, dotted handkerchief over his eyes and promptly went to sleep.

London was his refuge and his sea. He had gone to Europe originally only a year or two before I had, but with different eyes and inclinations. He knew literary as well as architectural and social London, people like Jane Portal Welby and Patrick Leigh-Fermor, Airey Neave. He knew the glories of the National Gallery and writers for *The Times*. The hall porters at Claridge's and the Connaught pronounced his name "Jinnuh."

I had grown to love him, his unbreakable spirit and style. He lived in beautiful houses, one year high above Salzburg, the ancient meadows falling away on either side. The first cathedral in Salzburg had been built in 774. Eight times it had suffered the great scourge of such edifices, fire. Finally it was demolished. I learned this listening to his wife, Margaret, giving their children lessons at home. Below us, Salzburg was invisible, drowned in a silvery mist.

He had lived with Margaret in Paris, in the old Hôtel Alsace, in a room with hideous wallpaper, the very room in which Oscar Wilde had died. He had lived alone in Rome at the American Academy, in Dublin, and New York. They had almost been married in Dublin, where, despite the romance of it, there were difficulties since he, a Catholic, had been married before. Friends interceded for them, among them Brendan Behan and his wife. Celebrating the nuptials in advance, Ginna, with Margaret in tow, unwisely began with the Behans what became a colossal binge. By noon they were, Margaret excepted, dead drunk. Ginna somehow managed after lunch to go up to his room in the Dolphin for a few minutes of rest, hands crossed on his chest. As a wedding gift that morning, Behan and his wife had given the couple a beautiful Waterford flask they had picked up somewhere for a few shillings as it had no stopper. It stood on the mantel. When Ginna woke, there was a note in the top of it. *So long,* it said. It was from Margaret—surveying the wreckage she had gone back to America.

They finally married. It had already been called off twice. In her family's view it was an unacceptable thing because he was a Catholic. His family saw it as impossible because they did not recognize divorce.

During the years we were closest he lived in painter's country, far out on Long Island; the flatness of the land, the incredible light. He had a small house in Sag Harbor—she did, actually; she had bought it before they were married with money she earned herself. The house had once been a brothel with men of every color lying in the street outside in the morning.

They lived in this house from time to time—from necessity to necessity, one might say—but also in fine houses on the bay or near the ocean, the finest of which stood at the far end of a long lawn that in back became pasture running unobstructed to the sea, a house they owned and that, tragically, burned. There was no place in the world I loved the evening meal as much as there.

He was then and remains the most successful man I have known, successful in his apprehension of life and in his values, untarnished after everything, even when reverses came and the tide was running against him, the phone in the office ringing and he not daring to answer. The secretary had been let go, the credit cards recalled. He would go through the morning letters. Like a gambler looking at cards, he glances, throws them unopened into the trash. But still a dinner for friends, which he prepares himself, fresh flounder fillets, a cold white wine. Outside it is winter and raining. The fire dies, the brandy is gone. We go to bed at two, the walls are icy but the bed soft and warm.

On a final trip to Europe we are sitting farther back in the plane, and as it lands and decelerates, he reaches around near his feet. His shoes have disappeared. "Anyway, *they're* in first class," he says wryly. They had been handmade, though now a nail was coming up through the sole of one.

We stayed for a time in London in the house of an old friend of his, Elizabeth Furse, beaming and unpredictable, in Chapel Street, sleeping in the coat-piled study like impoverished salesmen, the bath three floors above. Elizabeth Furse no longer had a restaurant—to which, above a small pub, one had gone, in any case, only by invitation—but the impulse survived. At Sunday dinner a crowd—there were members of Parliament, London editors, daughters of earls—sat in the basement kitchen with its large table, shelves of cups and saucers, piles of magazines, and flowers.

Flats, visas, jobs, were staples of her conversation. She was the fierce but generous matron of many lives, around whom animals purred and weaker spirits crumbled. "Robert," she had warned Ginna, "I want to know about any lady friends you plan to bring in."

She had earned her intractability, at the very least by her actions during the war, when she worked for British Intelligence in occupied France. Her son had been born while she was a prisoner, and she jumped off a train with him when they were on their way to the death camps. Later she had come to England. "Listen," she explained, "I learned languages." She'd been born in Latvia. She was instructing us all in the art of survival; the lesson was wide-ranging. "I knew all those people: Gide—he was kind, he was a kind man. Thomas Mann, God. His children . . . it was all incest, constantly."

She was like a figure from the Old Testament, her sternness, her prejudices. On a large plate being passed was the fruit for dessert. She had gotten it at Covent Garden. "Lying in the gutter," she said. "There were some bad spots on it but it was perfectly good. While I was picking it up they were insulting me and throwing fruit at me. Do you know what they did in the end? They came and began stamping on the fruit, crushing it! Perfectly good fruit. Wasting it. That's what's wrong with this country, I tell you. That's why the Communists will sweep over you!"

There was still the threat of this at the time. She was like a commissar herself, whatever her politics, and one felt the chill of her warning: The waste will come back to haunt you.

Ginna knew her well and had lived through too many prophecies to be disturbed. He had his own formulas. In the evening, looking through the refrigerator, he discovered a bottle. After reading the label, he handed it to me. *Polmos Żubrowka*, I read.

"It's vodka," I said.

"Keep reading."

It said something like, flavored by an extract of Żubrowka, the fragrant herb beloved by the European bison. I remember especially the word "beloved." "Have you ever drunk this?" I asked.

"Very well known," he assured me.

I did not know whether to believe him, but in such matters I hesitated to dispute his knowledge. I had seen him many times sign his name laboriously to bar checks late at night though in the morning he was always lucid and fresh.

The many nights and glasses. They were ritual, above all with old friends, Harry Craig, who had been, was it Beckett's secretary?, back from somewhere and signaling for another bottle of Haut Brion—Château O'Brien, he called it. His old friend, Jules Buck, at the Bibliothèque, over near the United Nations. It's late, the restaurant is empty, in a hush that its name suggests. They know the bartender, Roger, however; they recognize him and pound on the glass door. He unlocks it, polite and tough-looking, like an Algerian boxer. They greet him in French. At the vacant bar Roger asks, *"Que désirez-vous, messieurs?"*

"Cognac, Roger," they say.

"Oui, monsieur."

He lays three large brandy glasses on their side and fills them until the amber-colored liquid is ready to pour over the rim. Then he sets them upright and places them in front of us. A quarter of an hour passes, perhaps more.

"Cognac, Roger."

They have missed the place, they tell him. It's good to see him again—*c'est bon de vous revoir.* Jules Buck is wearing an expensive trenchcoat, the belt unfastened and hanging down. They are talking about Peter O'Toole, with whom Buck has made films and who starred in one of Ginna's. The deeply aromatic smoke from Ginna's French cigarettes tints the air. One last cognac. They are so drunk they are looking at things with great discernment, as if discovering them. Finally it is time to leave. The bill is thirty-five dollars. We tip him fifteen and thank him. At the door, hands are raised in warm farewell, "*Au revoir,* Roger."

He nods. "*Bonne nuit. Je m'appelle Gérard,*" he adds wearily.

We part with Jules Buck at the corner. Ginna's speech is clear, but his thoughts seem to slide off into the ditches. "What time is it?" I ask him.

"A lot," he mutters, then, "What the devil is this?" at something found in his pocket. He becomes difficult to steer. At last a cab stops. We head uptown. "Your old *copain* is torpedoed" are his final words.

You recall, perhaps, the three actresses the studio had named, any one of whom would have been a bottle of champagne across the bow, and down the ways, majestic and large, we would glide.

One of them was Maggie Smith. Ginna had given her one of her first movie roles in a film called *Young Cassidy,* taken from Sean O'Casey's autobiography. She would remember that—it was easy for him to transfer to her his own sense of loyalty. We went to see her and she turned him down. He managed to hide his disappointment.

We had moved to the Cadogan Hotel, the hotel where Wilde had been arrested, and on a June evening drove out to Chiswick to see Vanessa Redgrave. It was a house facing a small green park. The tall Greek Revival windows had no drapes. We waited in the large sitting room. There was a shabby couch with a huge framed mirror leaning behind it, books and records strewn about, seashells, toys, a kind of bar, and pillows on the floor by the garden window. It was the house of all suburban women with unraveling lives. Here and there a bare nail was driven into the plaster wall.

Then she came in, tall, very nearsighted, in a mauve jersey dress with no sleeves and a slit skirt. Near her shoulder was the glint of a white, embroidered brassiere strap. She was completely natural. She could not find ice to put in our drinks. One liked her immediately.

She was thirty-four years old and already at the pinnacle of a celebrated life, playing the lead in *Mary, Queen of Scots,* then being made. Her young son came in and began climbing over her. Glass beads and part of her drink spilled onto the floor. Later her two daughters, plump and with dirty feet, came to say they were going to bed, they wanted her to read to them. She promised them two chapters. We had imagined a smooth seduction but the distractions were hindering us. I asked about some reel cans stacked near the couch. They contained a film she liked very much, she said; "It's Italian. It's called *The Policeman.* It's about a young man from a village who becomes a policeman—is recruited—and how, slowly, bit by bit, he is changed and grows away from all the things that formed him, becomes less human, less kind, and in the end . . . well, the end is a little too much—that's not the point of it."

I felt that familiar moment of unhappiness; I realized I had written the wrong script. All one could do was not think about it or perhaps suggest some similarities between that one and ours.

She would read our script, she said, although the script she enjoyed most, she added cryptically, was one that was read to her, by the director.

Driving back to town, Ginna remarked how deeply the story of the movie she described had affected him. "Yes," I agreed.

"*The Interpreter,*" he said, naming the original story on which a movie he had produced, *Before Winter Comes,* was based, "was that kind of story. But we never made it," he confessed.

By now Max Schell had agreed to be the director. He, too, liked a script read to him, and in the luxury of his London house, rented from a maharanee, he listened, proposed changes, acted out portions, and told stories. One of his examples I remember, to illustrate character, was from *Anna Karenina.* In the railway carriage, he said, when the old woman comes in with her coat all bundled up and complains that it's cold. "It's cold, isn't it," she says, to one person after another, but they ignore her. At last she turns to Anna and says, "It's cold." "Yes, it's cold," Anna says.

His cook made lavish lunches that week, and often there were interruptions from visitors, telephone calls, unexplained matters. Late one afternoon a flawless Nefertiti appeared in simple, expensive clothes; long nose, perfect skin and hair. "Miss Bode," Schell introduced her in a low voice with pointed brevity. Work was over that day.

I wrote in the mornings according to what we had sketched out, variations on scenes, additional pages. In the end Vanessa Redgrave came to dinner. She was to give her answer.

She arrived wearing workman's overalls and a railroad engineer's cap, a woman of convictions. Over her shoulder was a large canvas bag filled with books on Chinese communism. She began talking about politics and the evils of bureaucracy. With his famed charm, Schell attempted to divert her from these subjects. He had only limited success.

At the table she ate very little—she was not hungry, she said—and continued along the lines of her interests. What was the political significance of the script? she asked.

Heads turned towards me. Though I knew every word and

meaning of the film we hoped to make, politics was not part of it. Falteringly I talked about human emotions and their greater importance and summoned up classics like *Les Enfants du Paradis*, though from the first moment I could see this was not the response required.

Ginna and I sat in gloomy silence for a long time until Schell, having seen the unfed Maoist to a taxi, came back up the stairs. We wanted to voice our despair, but like the good captain he was, perhaps springing from his role in *The Young Lions*, he prevented it. His face filled with warmth, in purest movie talk he said confidently, "I think the last goodnight kiss did it."

It did not.

There was still Ingrid Bergman, who was appearing in a play at the time, but for other reasons, including, I think, the health of her husband, she too said no.

The best scripts are not always made, just as the hardest fought campaigns may not end in victory. I say this merely as an observation, beyond any experience of mine. There are so many factors: timing, impulse, frivolity, accident. The films that are made are like menhirs, standing amid the rubble of everything broken or lost, the pure lines, scenes, the great effort lavished like milt over roe. The agents and stars kick through it idly. Perhaps it is this waste, this vast debris, which nourishes the glory.

As a producer, Ginna may have had limitations. He was scrupulously honest. He was a classicist—his interests were cultural, his knowledge large—and unequivocal in his statements and beliefs. His past was filled with figures who, rising on the wings of his telling, assumed legendary status: Behan, of course; the ballerina Pat McBride; Neville Cardus, the old writer of cricket; Carol Reed; Jack Nugent, solitaire-playing owner of the Dolphin; Kennaway; John Ford; and the two Swedish girls, sisters, who were waitresses at Durgin Park, fabulous girls, unattainable, as he said—they were picked up after work in large cars. There was a quality of Fitzgerald in his stories, of the romantic and unpossessed.

We never parted. I am going into the city on the morning train with him, the sun still flickering in our faces, people boarding sleepily at the stops, the beautiful coastal country, Southampton, Westhampton, Hampton Bays, Bay Shore. I guard his heroes, among them Jacques Callot, one of the greatest of printmakers— Rembrandt collected him also—Goya.

In the late 1970s, returning to journalism, he became a magazine editor. The circle was closing. Midnight. We return to the office. There is some final checking to do. He sits correcting the piece of a writer he likes whose telephone has been disconnected for nonpayment. The restaurants are being swept, beneath us the traffic along Sixth Avenue is thinning out. The life of reporters, writers. The night is their noon. On the couch, curled amid books and papers, a woman in a white suit, whom we have had dinner with, is sleeping.

Ginna gave me my first work in journalism, a field which eventually supported me. I was sent to Europe to interview writers: Graham Greene, Nabokov, Antonia Fraser. When I reached Paris there was a telegram from Greene, who was famously reclusive, saying he could not meet me. Then word came that Nabokov had canceled as well. Disaster loomed. I was more concerned with disappointing Ginna, who had faith in me, than with being rejected. Late at night I walked up a sepulchral Boulevard Malesherbes and slipped a note, humble though not abject, under Greene's door, and later I found the courage to call Montreux and plead with Mme. Nabokov. "Montreux Palace Hotel," a voice said in English. "Mr. Nabokov, please." "One moment."

I don't recall if I heard the operator ringing or not, but the next word was "Hello." It was Véra Nabokov. When, after consulting her husband, she finally invited me to meet him the following Sunday, she repeated his preference that interview questions be written by reminding me, "My husband does not ad lib." All my efforts were finally successful and Graham Greene, I think taking pity on me as a journalist, arranged to have a novel of mine, *Light Years*, published in England. His opinion of it was higher than the English critics'.

Ginna afterwards became editor in chief at Little, Brown. The offices of the firm faced the Boston Common and no city or location could have suited him better. Among the many books he published was one of mine, written at his urging and with his encouragement, *Solo Faces*. Although I knew enough about the subject, mountaineering, in the end I liked the title more than the text, perhaps because there was nothing ecstatic about the writing, as there had been in the two previous novels.

The place in the world he was made for he perhaps never fully occupied, but the places, Locke-Ober's, London, the American Hotel in Sag Harbor, the trout streams upstate, all the museums, the Scottish salmon rivers, he managed to make fabled. He read and saw, tasted and drank, and with him one knew the joy of doing the same.

Perhaps I have given the impression he was less drawn to work than to conviviality, but in fact the two in him were stunningly combined. Not all men are so handsomely made.

They are marching off without you, forming up. The faint, familiar sound of commands rises, far off.

I felt that, the confusion and panic, as I sat in a beautiful room watching the television. It was July but the room was cool and the streets of New York seemed silent. I was watching three white-clad men who were preparing my annihilation; they were leaving for the moon, the first flight meant to land there.

Aldrin is one of them, the one I know. He waves. Memories of being in the squadron together come back to me. His wife was interested in the theater. She was thought of as artistic, a damning thing. His hand grasps a rail as he climbs aboard the truck. I want to turn away but cannot. The simplest of his acts is dreadful to me.

They pass through a shadow and beneath the complexity of the enormous crane. They enter an elevator. A solemn commentator is explaining it all. The door of the elevator closes. They rise.

They arrive at the top, like the top of a scaffold. I cry out but there is no sound, I haven't the courage to cry, my life has already left me. I think of the long description of an execution, a guillotining, written by Turgenev, the unbearable ceremony.

A wreath of white smoke is leaking from the rocket. I am able to say nothing, not a word. I sit in the St. Regis with anything one might want there at hand. I feel hollow, as if I had lost everything.

They announce twelve minutes. I feel like the unknown crewman who is guiding them to the cabin, no, he is filled with excitement and pride, he feels himself to be an important figure. It is all a dream and yet intensely real. I can smell the smooth enameled steel. I can hear the radio voices, confident and brief. The camera is now under the engine bells, their openings vast as gun maws. The elevators in the hotel with their freight of well-dressed businessmen are moving up and down, the maids in the carpeted hallway are pushing their carts.

Five minutes. We are waiting, we hundreds of millions, staring intently at the faintly blackened site from which they will go. My heart is no longer beating, it seems to have stopped, to have prepared itself for the end. *Fifteen tons of fuel a second,* the announcer is saying. Fifteen tons, and its own weight besides is unimaginable. The morning is hot and airless at the Cape. Birds fly past the rocket, unaware of its potency. Three minutes.

The days of flying that have borne them to this, the countless, repetitive days. The astonishing thing is that we are empowered to bequeath history, to create the unalterable: paintings, elections, crimes. In fact they are impossible to prevent. One of the most memorable acts of all time is about to occur. Two minutes.

I had an Italian mistress, O very fine, who would fly places to meet me. She was slender, with a body brown from Rome's beaches and a narrow pale band, as if bleached, encircling her hips, the white reserve. She wore a brown leather jacket and had black hair, cut short. I had a luxurious corduroy suit, soft as velvet, from Palazzi on Via Borgognona. She had bought it for me as a gift. She was the antidote to, among many things, the sickening hours surrounding the launch and intolerable days after. I had taught her a catechism, or rather together we had composed one, which she could recite in perfect English, the flagrant words sinless in her mouth, the innocent questions and profane responses, and the low, inviting voice in which they were uttered. One minute.

We were silent that night with the television still on, light shifting on the walls in the darkened room. I was watching, transfixed by it, as well as by the cool, unhurried act we were engaged in. As a boy I had imagined grown men achieving scenes such as this. Tremendous deliberation. Reverent movement, oblivious, assured. She is writhing, like a dying snake, like a woman in bedlam. Everything and nothing, and meanwhile the invincible rocket, devouring miles, flying lead-heavy through actual minutes and men's dreams.

I have never forgotten that night or its anguish. Pleasure and inconsequence on one hand, immeasurable deeds on the other. I lay awake for a long time thinking of what I had become.

I was a *poule* for ten years, fifteen. I might easily have gone on longer. There was wreckage all around, but like the refuse piled behind restaurants I did not consider it—in front they were bowing and showing me to the table.

Robert Bolt, who had been a schoolteacher and then a playwright, was as talented as any writer of his generation. David Lean, for whom he did celebrated films—*Lawrence of Arabia, Zhivago*—had been known to bring him thousands of miles to discuss changing a single line, and honors were heaped at his feet. The best script I had ever read, he had written, an astonishing version of the *Bounty* mutiny and its aftermath, filled with original images and scenes. It was a work of high ambition. In the course of things it was never made.

Aging and far from his house in Surrey with the river drifting past, separated from his wife, he found himself in the derelict tropics, the occasional friend of a childlike actress, Mia Farrow, who was acting in a movie on a nearby island at the time. As an offering to her he rewrote pages of dialogue, and she was able to present them to the original writer as her own suggestions. In the end, tiring of this, she handed a sheaf of pages over, confessing all. The writer was a close friend of mine, Lorenzo Semple, and far from being annoyed, asked if he could meet Bolt, whom he greatly admired.

A dinner took place. It was in a shabby Chinese restaurant with unmatched dishes and a dirt floor. Bolt came wearing a palmetto hat. He was drunk. The talk was of writing, of course, though becoming less and less coherent as the evening went on. Bolt was somehow able, nevertheless, to bring out an important point. In writing films, he cautioned, in writing films, yes, there was one thing that should never be lost sight of.

"What is that?" Lorenzo asked.

"The money, my boy," Bolt said, "the money."

There were writers who made good use of it. In Los Angeles, on Summit Drive, I sat at lunch with an elegant man in his forties; I'll call him Edoardo. He came from the Veneto, the most civilized area in Italy, as he said, where even the farmers, though drunkards, were cultured after fifteen centuries of elevated life. Venice, the region's great city, had for ages been the light of the world.

A tall Swedish girl with a Russian name, Natasha, was serving us—veal *gratinée,* fresh garden peas, cucumbers in a sour-cream sauce. When she had slipped out, I asked casually, "Is she the cook?"

"Yes. Cook, everything," he said offhandedly, returning to the subject. "When London had two hundred and fifty thousand people, Venice had three hundred and fifty thousand. Shakespeare laid four of his plays there, *The Merchant of Venice, Midsummer Night's Dream, As You Like It,* and *Romeo and Juliet.*"

He was throwing in Arden and Athens as locations, but I was only hesitant about one. *"Romeo and Juliet?"*

"Well, in Verona, but that's nearby."

I was captivated by him, the grand house, the Rolls-Royce in the covered driveway, the gardens. He seemed like Uncle Vanya to me, a shrewder Vanya, hardworking, knowledgeable.

I happened to mention d'Annunzio. He knew everything about him, his uncle had been in d'Annunzio's squadron in the First World War and even looked like the poet, small, ugly, and bald. D'Annunzio had used him as a decoy. When he wanted to go to a hotel with some woman he would have the uncle sit in the villa, reading by the window.

We drank white Burgundy. The Swedish girl, graceful and silent, served a bowl of fresh raspberries and strawberries in cream. D'Annunzio, who died in the 1930s, had been the most celebrated writer of his time—the end of the nineteenth century and beginning of the twentieth—with a life of colossal breadth, the most notorious since Byron's. He was the lover of Duse and countless others. He had written Mussolini's famous speeches. Becoming old, he withdrew into a pantheon of his own design, the Vittoriale, above Lake Garda, where a kind of opera continued. He dressed in a monk's outfit and had his servants, all attractive women, dress as nuns. The next day he would be in a commodore's uniform and they were sailors.

"There are at least twenty d'Annunzio scripts in Italy," Edoardo said. "They've been trying for years to make a film about him. I remember the day he died. I was at school and a boy came up and said, 'No school today!'

" 'No school?'

" 'The poet is dead.'

" 'Hooray,' I said."

It was like Rome in Edoardo's house, Monte Mario, the terraces and pools. Sometimes in the evening, he said, they sat outside, he and the Swedish girl, looking out over the city. He was king of this Eden, gentle, wise, with a kind of classic ease and moderation, a single young novitiate beneath his wing—a man past the panicky appetites of youth, serene, able to savor, unhurried even if beset, like all men, by infinite desires.

"Edoardo?" said someone who knew him well when I mentioned his name. "He's the most unhappy, dissatisfied man I know."

"Impossible."

"He's an artist *manqué*. He thinks he's wasted his talent on movies, which he detests. Actually, he's never written any good movies—they're all trash except for one he did for Germi. Oh, he's a fabulous raconteur, especially in Italian, but he hates his life and is filled with self-disgust. He considers himself the only intelligent person in Italian cinema, and since he's the only one who reads, he's been able to make a career of taking de Maupassant stories and passing them off as his own. He's never married. He's the saddest man I know."

———

This was the Coast, the fabled Coast. Girls with hair blowing and sunburned limbs. Driving there in the summer of 1976, coming out of the desert, the crushing heat and emptiness on the road to Barstow. Then tired and heat-stained, along the freeways, into Santa Monica and up along the sea.

The house had a garden looking towards the hills, hibiscus and jade trees and a single huge palm, the fronds of which one could touch from a balcony on the second floor. Visible from the same spot was the bare, alluring corner of a tennis court. Silence. Birds fluttering in the branches.

Of the mysteries, the first I recall was a lily stalk bending over in strange, jerky movements to disappear into the ground, A small animal was gathering supper.

Cool morning mist and the sound of waves, cries of children in the street, the fronds plunging down from the heights of the tree. Malibu. Dank sand beneath one's feet in the narrow passageway that led to the beach, the vines overhead glittering with sun. A steamer basket arrived from my new agent, Evarts Ziegler; fruit and wine in a frock of apricot-colored cellophane. *Welcome to California,* the card read. It was signed simply, *Ziggy.*

Lorenzo, who was a favorite of his, had praised me and persuaded him to take me as a client. When I went to meet him he immediately told me how much he admired my work on a film I'd had nothing to do with. I nodded modestly, taking it as a good omen. He was, even then, an anachronism. His hair was gray; he wore three-piece suits and had gone to France for the first time in 1929 with his mother. Later he went back and forth across the country on the Super Chief, a train so luxurious it had a barbershop and waiters who would ask at dinner if you would like a nice fresh trout, caught in a mountain stream and picked up at the last stop.

In the bathroom adjoining his office were signed photographs of Sinclair Lewis and Hemingway, left to him by his father, and in the private sauna one of a naked girl ravenously drinking, water pouring down her chin.

He had a ravaged, sharp face which he was constantly working with his fingers, pushing it together, fixing it. He looked like a naval lieutenant who had been burned in a turret explosion. Over the decades he had acquired certain nervous gestures—I remember him habitually touching his right lower eyelid as he talked or thought. He was married to his second wife at the time, a blonde woman who seemed to hint society, but along the line he got divorced and after an interval married again. One had the feeling he was resigned to the idea of matrimony, that he regarded it as a necessity like good clothes. He was in his sixties though seeming to lack any mortal anxiety. "My health is innate," he confided to me one day.

"Innate?"

I had misunderstood him. "But my marriage is a two," he added.

He had a house in Pasadena, another in the desert, and a beach house near Santa Barbara. Business was conducted in his offices in Beverly Hills and occasionally over lunch, where he would discreetly point out various studio heads of enormous wealth. For me he performed the usual functions—negotiating, preparing contracts—but in many ways he was more of a companion than an agent. I could rely on him for unenthusiastic opinions delivered with the realism of a criminal-court judge.

I wrote during the day. At night as the sea disappeared, we drove, shooting past the canyons, along the coast. In the darkness the clouds were low over distant Santa Monica—beneath was a band of imprisoned light. Everywhere cars were speeding, not in urgency but in aimlessness, leisure. We drove in the redolent darkness, the undefined city drawing near.

California life, the film extra's life, cool night air and sea winds from the 1930s or whatever decade one's images of it dated back to. Despite my indifference, even dislike, there was something— the blue legend, the inexhaustible sea. On the cover of the telephone directory was a bit of description which explained that as late as the 1940s—the heart of my lifetime—such and such a part of the city had been almost all small ranches and now was entirely shops and homes. A melancholy came over me as I read it, almost sweet, a pang like thoughts of someone I had loved and would never see again. I envied those who had grown up here or had given it countless wasted days.

At the studios, like the gates of royal enclaves, one was waved through. There were huge blow-ups of famous movie scenes framed in the hallways at United Artists though no one bothered to look at them. The majesty of the present required scorn of the past, and movement was always towards newer and greater things. The hopeful came from everywhere, like suitors in a fairy tale, to try their luck. The appeal was irresistible. Even polished figures from the East, more like university presidents than hustlers, arrived with their dreams. I saw Peter Gimbel there. He had come with his wife, a blonde actress, Elga Anderson, and Billy, their dog. They had a script, of course, that they hoped to make. Now to business, he seemed to say, and from the breast pocket of a bush jacket drew a pair of gold-rimmed glasses to read over a list of possible agents.

Gimbel, his wife called him, with the trace of a German accent. I had met her in Rome years before when she was a gleaming colt, proud and indifferent to stares. She was still beautiful, European, with an occasional haughty expression of disdain crossing her mouth—an actress, with something of the word's meaning in the time of Molière or Goethe clinging to her, a natural mistress to the aristocracy with the requisite behavior.

She and Gimbel had no luck, then or afterwards. In a way she'd had hers, and he was like a gentleman drawn to the Regency gaming tables. He could afford to lose and would have been pleased to win, though there was not much chance of it.

It is beyond conquering. You may taste it, even reign for an hour, but that is all. You may not own the beach or the girls on it, the haze of summer afternoons, or the crashing, green sea, and the next wave of aspirants is outside the door, their murmuring, their hunger. The next tide of beautiful, uninformed faces, of perfect limbs and an overwhelming desire to be known.

They all, in a way, were like schoolmates, some popular, others to be avoided, some lazy though not without appeal. Like schoolmates, they scattered and found various fates.

Jean-Pierre Rassam I met first in Paris at La Coupole. He was there every night. It was a belief of his that in any city one should have a single restaurant, that way people always knew where to find you. For him in Paris, it was La Coupole. Later, in New York, it was Elaine's.

We had been talking about him, though I had not met him, Helen Scott and I. He had been at a film conference, she said, and standing at the podium had introduced himself, "My name is Jean-Pierre Rassam. I live with my mother." I admired the bravura and self-effacement. He was the brother-in-law, difficult and romantic, she said, of a director, Claude Berri. He was a mythomaniac, happy only in dreams, appealing and self-destructive.

As if summoned by the lure of her description, he came to the table. I should say someone came to the table and I recognized him immediately: the suicidal face, fine black hair, curved nose, thin lips, a face as perfect as an animal's, as sleek. He was urbane and unmanageable. His history was one of glorious tatters, yet he had the power to make one believe in him, in the infinity of possibilities he represented. For his university degree, the oral examination, he'd announced the work of a writer he had never even read, Charles Péguy, an obscure poet. He dazzled the questioners. They sat nodding in approval. At the end, one of them asked, as a matter of interest, which book of Péguy's he preferred. He didn't know, Rassam said, he'd never read any of them. They failed him for honesty, but the story would have been much less interesting if he'd lied.

Rassam had many friends at La Coupole. With some, passing among the tables, he sat a long time, with others he exchanged a greeting and a word or two. He was almost always alone. It was because of the dream that one night he would meet the woman of his life there, and he didn't want to be with anyone else at the time. It was a misconceived idea; you are always with someone else.

Helen Scott had been a mother to him—whether the one he had referred to or not, I cannot say—during a long year when he suffered from serious depression. He emerged from it at last. "In his own milieu," Helen confided, "he is unbeatable, and he always finds his milieu."

She drank that night and talked about the past, her father who had been an actor. When military music used to play, he would salute and march around the room. He didn't speak to her mother except through the children ("Tell your mother she's a murderous bitch"), and it was only at his funeral that Helen began to understand him, she said. His funeral marked his reentry into her life. We continued to drink. There was something of the coquette in her, unlikely as it seemed, beneath the heavy body and crude features. She knew Truffaut very well, and once in a hotel had come to his room in a negligée, hoping to seduce him. He had to lock himself in the bathroom. Before Paris, she had worked for the United Nations in New York, for the Polish delegation. Scottka, they called her. She had worked with Kropotski.

"Who was Kropotski?"

"Dr. Kropotski. His digestion was bad," she said.

She was big; she was lonely. She had tried to lose weight in a clinic near Grasse and had come to dinner with her food in a small paper bag—one meager slice of cold veal—but her main preoccupation was transportation, how to get places: she didn't drive.

When we left that night she was singing in the street, something from times even more distant, a vanished girlhood when her homeliness seemed perhaps like a mark of character. "You'll eat corned beef and cabbages," she sang, "and miss your Abie . . ."

Rassam remained remarkable, the most extraordinary person they'd ever known, people said. Unforgettable words. A few years later he was living at the Plaza Athenée and producing films, among them Robert Bresson's *Lancelot du Lac* and an outrageous, beyond category, so to say, obscene comedy called *La Grande Bouffe*. He married an actress and had a child, but his excesses were deeply ingrained and his talents inseparable from his flaws. Heroin was among his pleasures.

The last that I knew of him he was living on the Avenue Montaigne in a beautiful old apartment with hardly a stick of furniture. The living room was absolutely bare. In the dining room was a large table, able to seat sixteen, and two sofas. Not long afterwards he was dead, from an overdose of barbiturates. It was accidental, they said.

———

In the floating world, of those I knew, the one who seemed most to embody its contradictions was a prince of the blood, Christopher Mankiewicz, the son of not only a man but a family renowned for its talent. His uncle had written the film often named as the best ever made in this country, *Citizen Kane*, and his father's achievements were even more celebrated—Herman and Joseph Mankiewicz, borne by the immigrant tide but destined to become the purest of American voices.

His father was in every respect large, and Christopher inherited the dimensions. Tall, blue-eyed, and arrogant, he had the satisfaction of knowing, whatever misfortune, that he would always possess a distinguished name. Misfortune seemed unlikely. He had charm, intelligence, and, not unexpectedly, a good measure of self-indulgence. In the familiar way, he suffered from the long life of a powerful father, a man of prodigious appetite and wit, famous for his love affairs with stars, Judy Garland, Loretta Young, Joan Crawford, who fell on her knees and cried that the baby might have been hers.

His mother was an Austrian beauty, Rosa Stradner, an actress who had come to Hollywood to be a star but despite marriage to an important director did not achieve it. There were fierce fights at the dinner table; the father would storm out and the mother begin drinking. On countless nights she would come to her son's room to wake him and talk, sometimes passing out on the floor. She was still beautiful when she committed suicide at the age of forty-five.

Her son grew up to marry an Italian dancer. They met in Rome during the shooting of his father's momentous failure, *Cleopatra*, with the strange excitement of catastrophe on a grand scale somehow increasing the passion. Christopher was a romantic in every way. Devoted to classical music, susceptible to literature, mad about women, it was only the lack of wealth that in the end served to protect him. As a young studio executive in New York where we first met, he wore expensive double-breasted suits with the enviable aplomb of a fat man, spoke perfect Italian, used a cigarette holder, and possessed a failing, to me invisible, but which his wife saw clearly: the millions he promised her he would have before he reached thirty were not forthcoming. Perhaps, like Rassam, he was too brilliant for ordinary success.

Still, his shrewdness and the momentum of his early career carried him far. He had strong friendships, many based on his wit and taste as well as his outspoken opinions which, despite their validity, were often undiplomatically rendered. The confusion of letters strewn about a large desk; the heaping meals in restaurants, quickly devoured; the apartments and luxurious suites—these began to slowly slip away. He worked in Los Angeles, where, in his father's assessment, he ruined his chances on innumerable occasions. "Isn't it time you left town?" his father commented finally. "You're finished here."

In Rome, in the early 1970s, he was working for Grimaldi, an important Italian producer. His life had become nocturnal. At four in the morning the lights were still on. In an undershirt he sits at his desk doing a vast jigsaw puzzle. His mother-in-law, of whom he is very fond, is asleep, his young son also. This son, Jason, is six years old, beautiful and petulant, a compulsive talker with a slight lisp. Early in the morning he comes into the room. "Do you know what this is?" he demands. "This is my favorite book. In this book you can learn about everything. You can learn about the stars, and what is the deepest hole in the sea, and about thunderstorms and how to stop them. This is my best book. And this," he says, showing it to me but also to himself, "is a script I wrote. All alone. And this! This is a book—have you seen this book? This is about soldiers." He then begins to explain to me, with remarkable accuracy, how children are born.

Now he is still sleeping, however. The blue haze of cigarette smoke hugs the ceiling. The third act of *Aïda* is on. Christopher passes his hand over the table. "I've done all this section here," he indicates. His face is innocent, unweary, a face that will never show corruption.

We were working on a script, the odyssey of which had only begun. This was the best part, the freshness and hope at the start. There had even arrived an encouraging letter from his father, remarkable in that it was only the second, and turned out to be the last, Christopher had ever received from him. In addition to praise the letter went on to suggest an entirely different approach. Day after day we talked about it until it grew dark.

Once, late in the afternoon, there was a tapping at the etched-glass door to the garden. Pressed against the glass, arms spread, was a figure like a huge moth against a pane. "My God!" Christopher cried. "Bruna!" His wife, from whom he was virtually separated. In she came, out of the evening, smiling, her face filled with joy. She was working as a model. She had canvas luggage and a long, stylish coat. She went in immediately to surprise her young son.

A festive hour. All was laughter, excitement, familiarity. One would never dream they were a couple on the brink of divorce.

They had married too young, that was the trouble, Lydia, the mother-in-law confided. What did I think? "Bruna was too young," she continued sadly, "Chris was too young."

We dined, all of us, at a trattoria on Via Flaminia, beneath bright lights, as if on a stage. It might have been a play; the dialogue was polished, the actors had worked together many times. By the end of the evening they were at each other's throat.

The next scene: London, a year or two later. The Grimaldi days were over. Chris was living in the basement room of a friend, trying to put together the elements of the film I had written. He had a Mercedes and a black overcoat, chalky with stains, but little else. He was, he said, keeping up with events by reading the newspaper under the cat dish.

I like men who have known the best and the worst, whose life has been anything but a smooth trip. Storms have battered them, they have lain, sometimes for months on end, becalmed. There is a residue even if they fail. It has not been all tinkling; there have been grand chords.

We ate at inexpensive Greek restaurants with his associate, Ned Sherrin, who had considerable theatrical experience and had joined forces with him. We were definitely going to make the film; it was called *Raincoat*. "The deal is almost done," they said.

They were like revolutionaries. For the cause, even if dubious, one gave everything. Their feet were not really on earth; they were leading a visionary existence, the life which was to come. One day they would walk up wide steps to tremendous applause. What was I doing now? they asked indulgently. Finishing a book, I explained.

"Is there a film in it?"

"There's no film in anything I write, not even scripts," I said.

Things, however, take time. The tide of battle wavered. They had a star, Alan Bates, who had agreed to play the lead, and based on that, much of the financing. A few months later the star was gone, though the money was still there. Then a studio materialized and someone wanted the script revised and the location of it changed. The drama moved to Los Angeles. For a while there was a flaring of interest and a flight to Rome to obtain the commitment of another star, Donald Sutherland.

Months passed, an uneventful week at a time. Years. At some undetermined point the whole thing slipped into an unmarked grave, the common fate, as it were. We spoke of it less and less, finally not at all. It had simply perished along the trail.

It is probably the common touch that is crucial in movies, not only for their success but for their very existence. Without it, one is at a disadvantage. I think of a producer Christopher worked for at one time, the hero, like a mobster or corrupt politician, of many favorite stories—Bruna rather liked him, as it happened. He once told Christopher the actual secret. He had made ten movies, he confided, and not one of them, not *one*, had ever made a penny. But he would go on making them, he said, you know why? "Because I know how the game is played."

In Toronto, under amiable conditions, the last of the films I wrote was made. It was called *Threshold,* prophetically for me. Although I wrote other scripts, I had a deserter's furtive thoughts.

The movie was about a cardiac surgeon and the first mechanical heart. The writing, as one sees often in retrospect, was imperfect, but I could not at the time imagine how to improve it. The budget was too small and the actors were not all ones we wanted. Some of the best scenes were dropped or awkwardly played as a result.

The entire screen, I wrote, is filled with an image too immense at first to have shape, a gigantic sun—big as a city, grainy, raging—that in silence or to strange, unnerving music slowly opens to reveal its core, *for the heart is the sun of the body.* There were a number of other defining metaphors, only one of which rather startlingly survived.

When I finally saw the movie, feeling as always naked in the audience, I saw mostly the flaws, quite a few of them my own fault.

Sometime in here, perhaps a little earlier, I flew to London one final time. I was with a producer who was said to have been one of two heirs, the displaced one, to a great studio. We had taken a night flight from Los Angeles over the Pole, bringing a script I'd rewritten to a director who was about to begin shooting, a delicate mission. We arrived at five in the morning and fell into the illusory world of the Dorchester's luxurious rooms—rich woods, fabrics, carpet. I woke after a few hours, dazed, the winter light gray at the windows, muffled sounds in the hallway, an apologetic maid half-entering.

In the hotel's dining room we sat down with the director, Mark Robson, a wizened man in a little hat, vicuña scarf, and camel's-hair coat, far from what I heard were his Texas beginnings. The producer bravely introduced the subject. "The boys feel the script could be better," he said.

Robson inquired calmly, "Which boys?"

"The boys," the producer repeated, avoiding mentioning the name of the head of the company.

Robson nodded. That was enough; he understood completely, there was nothing to worry about. "I spent an hour on the phone with Robert Shaw this morning," he commented pleasantly, naming the star. "He loves the script. He doesn't want a word of it changed."

"James," the producer said to me, "will you tell him some of the proposals?"

The original script was weary cliché—no worse than many, certainly, and not difficult to improve. A large plate of pea soup growing cold before me, for twenty minutes, I described at some length the rationale behind the changes while Robson sat quietly. After I had finished there was silence.

"Well?" the producer asked.

Robson smiled politely with the gentle quality of a false priest. "I don't understand," he said simply.

"What do you mean?"

"It's just that I don't understand anything you've said." I could not but admire him.

He went on to make the original film. It has been forgotten, of course. It was designed to be forgotten. Its sole distinction was that the star, Robert Shaw, died during the shooting of it. It may be that Robson had been right in not wanting to complicate it or attempt to have it carry more weight. He may just have wanted to be done with it, like an ugly neighborhood one drives through on the way to something better. Perhaps he had run out of strength. The best is the enemy of the good, as my onetime agent, Kenneth Littauer, often cautioned me, and the same relationship probably exists between the passable and mere rubbish.

I wrote one (I thought) final script, years later—overwrote, I should say. Again only the seed of a story was provided: a reclusive star of the first magnitude who has not permitted an interview for years grants one to a very private, literary writer, one of whose books she happens to like. She has everything, he has almost nothing other than familiarity with the great dead and the world they define. Somehow it enthralls her, and for an hour or a week they fall in love.

Perhaps I dreamed I was the writer and the irresistible woman who had not, for years, had the least whim denied her was a symbol for film itself, though in fact the writer was closer to John Berryman, able to coax the birds with his cockeyed, intimate language.

I prepared myself—why, I cannot remember—by reading Bernard Shaw's *Man and Superman,* and in a stifling upstairs bathroom, then outside beneath the trees, attended by swarms of yellow jackets, and finally in the airless upstairs reading room of the village library, I wrote the script. Something might have come of it but never did.

I had the failing of being interested in subjects too iconoclastic to be undertaken. I labored for months on a script about a fantastic imposter, a high-ranking German SS officer, tall, blond, long-nosed, once head of Interpol and later governor of occupied Czechoslovakia who some believe to have been, incredibly, a Jew, Reinhard Heydrich, eventually assassinated.

I drove to Taos to try and interest an actor named Dennis Hopper in the role. His self-intoxication frightened me away. I listened as late at night in a cowboy hat he sat delivering to his girlfriend an unrecognizable summary of world history. His going around armed, for some reason fearing for his life, did not encourage me. In all likelihood the audience would have ignored *Heydrich* had it been made.

There was another final script, which in fact ascended a bit before crashing as the result of a director's unreasonable demands, and I suppose there might have been another and another, but at a certain point one stands on the isthmus and sees clearly the Atlantic and Pacific of life. There is the destiny of going one way or the other and you must choose.

And so the phantom, which in truth I was, passed from sight.

———

I have forgotten the names of the concierges at the Inghilterra and the Bauer au Lac, and they have forgotten mine. Images, though, remain, innominate but clear. Driving the roads of southern France—Béziers, Agde—the ancient countryside, husbanded for ages. The Romans planted quince trees to mark the corners of their fields; sinewy descendants still grow there. A woman, burnished by sun, walks down the street in the early morning carrying an eel. Many times I have written of this eel, smooth and dying, dark with the mystery of shadowy banks and, on that particular day, covered with bits of gravel. This eel is a saint to me, oblivious, already in another world.

And another time, in a brief recess from work at the end of summer, its very last hour, a few leaves already on the ground, in fields near Annecy. Huge poplars, solid as oaks. The sound of pears falling. Two thick-coated horses, full-grown and strong, stand near the barn, then slowly walk down to the fence to take an offered apple. One nips me, without malice, on the wrist.

And the old projectionist in the screening room in New York, whose name I knew, who had once been flyweight champion and had known Benny Leonard, Jack Dempsey, and K. O. Kaplan.

Harry Craig—there is a name I remember—a grand, bulky Irishman rich in literary knowledge who'd once read poetry on the BBC. Seeing a book on the shelves, he would reach for it while beginning to recite from it beforehand. He had written movies for De Laurentiis—*Waterloo* was one of them—and also an epic about Muhammad, in which the prophet's face could not be shown, and for which he was awarded the unforgettable and honorary title of Pen of Islam. A wife in Rome, many children, his hands held high and fluttering for emphasis as he spoke. He liked, even required, a hot lunch every day. I can hear his fine, sweet voice, "Do we have time for a drink?"

He was one of those prodigals—castaways, one might say—who find themselves, not undelighted, in the high-flying movie crowd. He was like a disgraced doctor or lawyer for criminals, brilliant but with a stain. His hand was capable of better things, but something within him—sad wisdom, surrender—allowed him to linger at the ball and find it entertaining.

Years before, in my youth, someone had made a remark to me that I had never been able to brush away. It was in Texas when we were lieutenants, confident and wild. At many parties I was among the loudest and most disheveled—the drinking and singing, the shouting of nicknames. One night a classmate I knew only slightly, standing beside me, asked in a quiet voice, "What are you doing this for?"

"Doing what?"

"This isn't really the person you are."

I looked at him as if in disbelief and made some evasive reply, but I knew the truth.

As he had spoken to me I sometimes felt like speaking to others. Harry Craig was older than I and in many ways wiser, but I wanted to take him by the arm and walk away from the crowd, the laughter and cycnicism, the veneer, saying only, "Come, Professor. We must go."

———

I loved you very much. I might say that of Paris; my memories are heaped there. Somehow I was constantly returning—the train gliding through the endless suburbs or in blue air the airplane banking as, face close to the window, I looked down. Far below the fabled city unifies itself, which it will not do when you are within it. The tangled, irregular streets create a kind of anatomy. A city which since Gothic times, as the poet says, has been ever increasing in deformity, and withal retaining more perfection than any other of its class.

Across the river to the rectangular, banklike hotel, the Palais d'Orsay with the no-longer-used station just beside it. It was there I often stayed. There was a restaurant, perhaps a bar. The hotel is no more, but by a happy chance the building still stands, as part of a museum, and is thus preserved without. The lobby has disappeared for me, and the hallways, but the large windows in the rooms I still see clearly and the long curtains sailing inwards as a storm, with terrifying thunder and bright electric flashes, came across the city one afternoon like disaster or the outbreak of war. The sky became dark. The curtains blew wildly and rain prickled us, sacred and unforgettable.

I loved you very much, that is to say, often and a great deal. Your slender back, leaning forward in the bath, your immense femaleness. I never met your parents, of course—just as well—though we did meet the mother and sister of one of your wealthy suitors, and the baron who was another, and eventually, when he entered your life, your husband. That was much later. You revealed a new world to me, something called the Old World: style, sensuality, and betrayal, in the end no one of them less precious than another.

To write of someone thoroughly is to destroy them, use them up. I suppose this is true of experience as well—in describing a world you extinguish it—and in a book of recollection much is reduced to ruin. Things are captured and at the same time drained of life, never to shimmer or give back light again.

There remains, though, in the case of those years in the movies, a kind of silky pollen that clings to the fingertips and brings back what was once pleasurable—too pleasurable, perhaps—the lights dancing on dark water as in the old prints, the sound of voices, laughter, music, all faint, alluring, far off.

DÎNERS EN VILLE

In MANHATTAN, in the lower right-hand corner, I had found a place in which to write, a room near the river, within sight of the cathedral piers of the Brooklyn Bridge. It was on Peck Slip, a broad street near the fish market, strewn with trash and ripped wood by the time I arrived each morning, but quiet with the work of the day by then over. I wrote in this room with its bare wooden floor and ruined sills for a year—it was 1958—struggling with pages that turned bad overnight.

I was thirty-three years old and knew no other writers. There were some artists in the neighborhood living in lofts with girlfriends or wives, and around the corner, up dank stairs smelling of urine and landings heaped with rubbish and torn mattresses, was a dedicated sculptor, Mark di Suvero. He had the entire floor. The windows were unwashed and a few bare bulbs provided light. Sculpture of ambitious scale stood here and there. In one corner, up near the metal ceiling, was a bed mounted on four tall columns. It was warmer up there, he explained, and you couldn't, if you were tired, just casually flop down. Also there was nothing devious about venery—you had to help her up, there was full complicity. Nearby was the potbellied stove, which supplied heat and on which, comrade-like, we sometimes cooked dinner, fish usually—he swept the store downstairs in return for food—sautéed with onions.

Di Suvero had been, glamorously I thought, born in Shanghai, the son of a diplomat, and the family had lived there until just before the war. There was the hint of aristocratic background, a palazzo in Venice that unfortunately they no longer owned.

"It was sold?"

"The Fascists," he calmly replied.

He had a saint's face, lean with a blond beard and blondish hair, "so handsome and understanding," a museum woman explained, and he lived as a young animal lives, above the impurity of his surroundings, working only—he was a good carpenter—for enough money to get by; the rest of his time he kept for himself. We walked the streets after dark searching for the discarded things, barrels, scorched beams, rusted chains, that his sculpture was made of. The pieces had lofty titles, *Orpheus and Eurydice*, bent nails and splintered boards. I was not in a position to recognize their parentage in constructions like Picasso's *Mandoline et Clarinette* of 1913, unpainted scraps stuck together, or *Violin*, exploded and crude, and they were far more abstract, but I liked to talk to di Suvero. I was certain of his authenticity, probably because I felt I had none myself. I was from the suburbs; I had a wife, children, the entire manifest. Even in the city I found it hard to believe I was working on anything of interest. Di Suvero was the opposite. Unburdened and inspired he could do as he liked, see no one, work until dawn. His face remains before me, the face of that year, energetic and pure.

Over New Year's I was away for a few weeks and when I returned he was not there. His door was locked. In the evening the windows were dark.

There had been an accident, I learned. He was in Roosevelt Hospital, badly hurt. It had happened in an elevator, he'd somehow been crushed. They had him on a cot, face down, his forehead supported by a canvas strap and he could see a visitor by means of a small mirror on the floor. He was paralyzed from the waist down. All the youth and pride. It was like going to visit the gravely wounded.

When I came into the room I did not notice the mirror. Then I saw his eyes which were waiting for me in it. One could see the violence of the injury in his eyes—the whites were gone, they were beet red from hemorrhage. His spine had been broken but not his will. He had vowed that no matter what the doctors said, he would walk again. He talked about a major architectural competition he was planning to enter, he had even begun building a model.

In another hospital on the other side of town my father was dying. It was months before I saw di Suvero again. His legs in steel braces, unsteady, threatening to fall, he nevertheless managed to come to the Peck Slip room which I was just giving up. The book I had been writing was finished. *The Arm of Flesh*, it was called. I was confident of its title. Two women in cocktail dresses, brittle, chatting women, were having a drink with me to celebrate. Their talk flowed around a restrained di Suvero. I had the impression his opinion of me was being revised.

I did not see him again. I heard about him occasionally. His work was now in museums; he had become unpredictable and angry. On a panel at the Guggenheim he had suddenly gone wild, cursing the audience, crying, and threatening. Perhaps it was the result of painkillers, narcotics; he broke up the presentation. I thought of the beautiful god he had been. *There are men who feel they are owed nothing.* He exemplified that so completely. His self-denial encouraged me.

He had given me a book of Rilke's poems in which there was one, "Torso of an Archaic Apollo," that seemed to have been written for me to read it. The poem described, in a restrained way, a beautiful statue in what I remember as the quiet green of a park, the perfect limbs, the grace. It came within a moment of going on too long until its final surprising line which was simply, *You must change your life.*

It was a difficult process, the changing. Only a few people offered any encouragement, even unknowingly. Kenneth Littauer was one. Littauer and Wilkinson was the firm, its name printed on the frosted-glass door. Down on the street were clothing stores and traffic. White-haired by the time I knew him, a former editor like his partner, Littauer knew France well. He spoke French perfectly, at least inside the door of the St.-Denis, a small restaurant in the East Fifties that he favored, where, teeth blackened from his pipe, he chatted in slang with the headwaiter. He wanted to *se débarbouiller*, he said, to wash up. *"Oui, mon colonel."*

He liked to talk about flying—his own experience of it had ceased around 1918. At his house in Connecticut he had a piece of glass about the size of a theater program with a bullet hole in almost the exact center of it—it had been the windshield of his plane when he flew with the French in the First World War. He had been an observation pilot. The bullet had only grazed him. Decades later he was invited with other old pilots to a screening of ancient footage. The film was disintegrating and the historians wanted to know who, in random scenes of various fields and swiftly moving figures, was who and what was worth preserving. "Well, Colonel," his partner airily greeted him when he got back to the office, "how did it go?"

"All right, I guess," Littauer said. "It was nice to see the golden boys come alive again for an hour or two." He was referring to the fighter pilots, the now antique aces.

My being a flyer tipped things in my favor. He liked to hear my stories. If I were a passenger, he wanted to know, and the pilot and copilot of a jet airliner were both incapacitated by, say, a bird crashing through the windshield, would I be able to land the plane? I imagined myself calmly calling the tower and asking for someone to be summoned who could talk me through it step by step, flap setting, power, final approach speed. Made confident by the wine at lunch I assured him I would be able to, not a perfect landing perhaps, but good enough.

"If this book isn't accepted . . . ," he said, to help prepare me for the possibility.

"I'll start another."

I felt he expected me to say it. He was a man of integrity, diligent and pessimistic. Max Wilkinson, in contrast, was a sport. Small finger extended, he would stroke his nose during conversation in a characteristic gesture of disbelief and thought. He dressed well, blazer, pearl-gray slacks. He was interested in shares, wealth, unconventional men, scoundrels.

There was something surrendered about him, the ghost of an earlier, finer world. His people had come here in 1623, he remarked carelessly. Doomed gallantry, vain hopes, it seemed to imply. He liked to tell of going, when he was a magazine editor, to see Scott Fitzgerald. "I had a manuscript of his that I wanted to sit and go over with him. When we arrived he was drinking a water glass full of gin."

We were at the Century Club or Toots Shor's, the drinks beginning to have an effect. Fitzgerald, he said, had disappeared that night, gone upstairs, and then come down again, completely naked, saying, "I know what you really want. You want to see me take my dope. Well, I'll show you."

I was inclined to believe his stories which were seldom repeated. They were like accidental memories.

"I want to be forgotten," he would mutter. "My whole purpose in life is not to have lived. Just say . . . just say, he loved flowers, he used to stop on Third Avenue and buy their wretched blooms." His voice trailed off.

The next day, as with men of long experience, he would be well turned out and unrepentant. By lunchtime there would be the springiness of a boxer who knows he will not have to fight. "One never gets old in here," he would say, patting his chest. It is hard to think of a man for whom that was truer.

Of the agency's other clients I knew little. Some were journalists, including faded ones, others wrote detective stories or westerns. In the office one day I was introduced to an Australian with a round, lively face and brown-edged teeth.

"My dear fellow!" he cried enthusiastically.

His name was Lindsay Hardy. He was a prodigal and to Wilkinson like a son.

He'd been in the war, in New Guinea and the desert.

"What was it like?" Max asked.

"We polished our rifles," Hardy intoned, "and killed the Hun in the hills of Jesus."

He was in New York to try to write a film script from a book of his that had been sold to the movies. Meanwhile he was living lavishly, a delight to women. They were crowded into his past as well. "The widow Woods," he recalled, "in Brisbane. I was her lover. One day she said to me, 'Lindsay, do you know anything about pruning?' She'd an enormous apricot tree behind the house, a great thing, its branches touching the very sky. 'Of course, my love,' I said. I was eager to please her. 'Will you prune my tree for me?' 'Anything,' I replied. I went to the library and read up on pruning. Then I came back and cut the tree.

"It was disastrous. The tree bore not a single piece of fruit the whole year, it even shed its leaves. It finished me, of course," he moaned. "She cut me dead when I saw her in the street."

I don't know what happened to his script. When the money ran out he would swim for the Narrows, he always claimed, and eventually he went back to England. A few years later I heard that his luck had gone bad. His wife had died of alcoholism and he had no money to pay heavy fines for speeding and reckless driving. "He was tough," Max Wilkinson reminisced, "fond of drink. He had an old Rolls-Royce that he loved." There was no word of him, however. He had vanished completely.

His name brought happiness, though, even to the children of those who had known him. I was talking to one one night, listening in awe to the story of her girlhood. She and her mother had been devoted followers of Wilhelm Reich and had experienced many sessions in an unconventional device that was called the orgone box. I knew only that it had something to do with sexual energy. She had also, perhaps as a corollary, been intimate with a man when she was seven, a lover of her mother's. She had been openly flirting with him and her mother had finally told her to go and join him in bed.

I tried to imagine this mother but could not: a thick-wristed woman who loved pleasure and, dying, might whisper, "Burn my diaries," or a woman with a splendid throat and pure face battered by years; in any case a woman, I knew, who had no difficulty attracting men, though most of them, her daughter told me, were no good. There was one, however, "A great guy. He was a writer." Had I ever heard of a book called *The Grand Duke and Mr. Pimm?*

"Lindsay Hardy," I said.

"You know him?" she cried ecstatically.

"Yes."

"I can't believe it! Whatever happened to him?"

He swam for the Narrows crossed my mind, but I said only, "I'm not sure."

———

Kenneth Littauer remained my agent as long as he was alive, or nearly. He was seventy-four when I had lunch with him for the last time. It was at the Century Club and I had a presentiment it was the finale. He'd been obliged to give up his work—he forgot things, had no strength, he fell three times in one week, his wife had written to me. I expected to meet a broken figure, but he seemed the same as ever, stooped, untrusting, alert. We talked about travel and other things. We had often planned to meet sometime in Paris and have dinner at the Grand Véfour, which was high on the list of places he did not disapprove of, but we had never gotten around to it. I wanted to ask certain questions, those I had neglected to remember the answer to over the years: his favorite daughter's name, her husband's, the title of a book he had recommended to me, details of his father.

When we finished lunch he insisted on seeing me to the door. We walked down the five flights and in the entrance said goodbye. He had been a lieutenant colonel at twenty-four, in France. They had wanted him to stay in, but he decided not to. I would understand the reason, he said. "There was no one to talk to."

In the street I jotted down the name of the book, *Disenchantment,* by C. E. Montague.

He died a few months later, on Bastille Day, as it happened. I was in France at the time and felt a shock as I read it in the paper. In the obituary there was something I had forgotten or never knew: He had the DSC.

———

In a black shirt and Texas tie with a beaded steer's-head holding it, John Masters appeared. It was in the country, New City, on South Mountain Road. He was tall and stern of appearance as befitted a former English officer. High on his cheeks were clumps of long, untrimmed hair, a mark of caste. "Bugger tufts," he explained without elaboration. He had served in the British Indian Army. Eventually, in a history of the war in the Pacific, I came across an account he had written of a battle in Burma, his battalion in defense of a hill in the jungle against overwhelming Japanese attacks, an episode, like many others, of which I never heard him speak. They were part, perhaps, of his authority. It was to his house one would hurry in case of grave danger. He would know without hesitation what to do.

There was a night we had invited people to see a film never shown in theaters but nonetheless legendary, the hymn that Leni Riefenstahl had created of the Nazi rally in Nuremberg in 1934. It opened with Wagner, and a Junkers transport flying through ethereal clouds, bringing the German leader to the ancient city. Masters and his wife arrived late. They were standing in the doorway as Hitler was seen, deep in his thoughts, looking out one of the aircraft windows. "I don't think I want to watch this," Masters said, and with his wife he turned and walked out.

Behind his best-selling books, *Bhowani Junction* and *Nightrunners of Bengal*, there was the organization of a military campaign. On large index cards were written detailed descriptions of his characters—date of birth, schooling, color of hair and eyes. On larger paper the chronology of events was laid out. He had studied the business of writing in a very methodical way. He had worked out firm principles. Never lose focus or take the spotlight from where it belongs, he told me. If a main character is a woman, say, and she is going up in an elevator, don't begin to describe the elevator operator. That would loosen the grip.

My own methods seemed negligent when I listened to his. Their failure might be predicted. On the other hand, I was not trying to write *Bhowani Junction*. I had the rapturous dreams of an opium addict, intense but inexpressible. I wanted—someone in Rome supplied the words for me a few years later—to achieve the *assoluta*.

I was still thinking in this immodest way when I met, entirely by chance—it turned out he lived in an apartment next door to one I was using in the city—a writer who I at first felt was traveling, though in a different manner, a similar path. He lived alone, with a small dog, in a long, darkened room pricked with white lights, pinpoint lights, strung along the bookshelves. There were expensive art books piled on the tables—he would go to Scribner's on

Fifth Avenue and buy them whenever he happened to have some money—and high on the wall three or four large framed photographs such as one might see of movie stars except these were of a woman's gleaming black *chose,* as Pepys liked to call it, her furnace, as if what lay beneath the satin evening gowns and soft skirts of *Vogue* were made bare.

His name was Davis Grubb. He had written a book called *Night of the Hunter.* One of the first things he asked me was whether I had read an article—an entire issue of *The Nation,* I think it was, had been devoted to it—denouncing J. Edgar Hoover and the FBI. I had to read it, he said in a low voice. The FBI had been involved in the assassination of Kennedy. Surely I knew there had been a conspiracy? Had I read Mark Lane, who provided proof? No, but I had seen him on television.

"When?" he asked.

"Oh, a couple of months ago. It wasn't here. It was in Toulouse."

"Toulouse."

"You know. In France."

"I know. I was there last night," he said. There was the stare of a man willing to be thought mad.

His dog, a Lhasa Apso, may have been named Laddie. They often went together, late at night, to Clarke's, a bar where Grubb drank with men who were unquestionably off-duty policemen. How did he know they were? I asked. "White socks," he said. I could see the dog sitting patiently near his feet, Grubb, the drunken father, careless but loved.

It was said that he was an addict. Looking back, it makes sense, the nocturnal habits, the surreal remarks, the continual need for money. One morning he asked me to help him carry a suitcase filled with remaindered copies of his book. He was going to try to sell them to a store a block or two away—did I think he could get a dollar apiece for them? I did not give an opinion. The store was not even a bookstore.

I believe he was lonely. I never saw visitors. I saw him in the hallway, poorly dressed, locking the door to his apartment. He was in desperate shape, he told me. He needed money for the rent, otherwise he would be evicted. I had thirty dollars and gave him twenty; he thanked me with some embarrassment. We walked out together, down Park Avenue, then over to Madison. There was a luxurious restaurant on the corner.

"Do you have time for lunch?" he asked casually.

"Lunch? Not here," I said.

"Another time, then," he replied, adding that he thought he'd go in for a bite. I watched in disbelief as he passed through the doors of shining glass.

It was his final image, though I saw something that made me think again of him once in England: a footpath across wide fields and on it, gray-haired, alone, with a staff in his hand and a pack on his back, a man walked, a soiled dog trotting behind him. The years were gone and all possessions. The villages did not know him, nor would he ever be known. He had only what was crazed and unbroken inside him, and he would be well as long as his dog was alive.

———

Of those years, the 1960s, I remember the intensity of family life, its boundlessness. It was an art of its own—costume parties; daring voyages in an old sailboat, a leaky Comet, far out on the river; dogs; dinners; poker on Christmas night; ice skating. We were in a world of families, all young, unscarred: the beautiful Dutch girl and her husband; the painter and his wife who unexpectedly opened a restaurant on the highway, named for one of his heroes, del Piombo; the psychiatrist and his wife who were our first close friends. It was all an innocent roundelay, a party of touching originality being carried on in the midst of real-estate transactions and countryside that was slowly falling, field by field, to builders.

We lived, for the most part, in a half-converted barn near New City, about thirty miles from New York. Of all the houses this remains the clearest—the cozy room that was made into a study just off the front door, the long bright bathroom with a row of windows above the sink looking down on trees and a shed that served as garage, the stone fireplace, the rough wood floors, the huge kitchen. There was a terrace of large squares of slate that had once served as sidewalk in Nyack, and in back, through woods, was a stream. Still farther one came to a long, slanted field planted each year with tomatoes, the mere gleaning of which was a harvest. Fingernails black with earth we brought basketfuls back to the house in the fall.

Not far away, on South Mountain Road, was the aristocracy. The early artists had settled there, and Maxwell Anderson, the playwright, had owned a house designed by Henry Varnum Poor. Of the latter I knew only that his name was attached to certain structures like a particle. The one I was most familiar with had blue walls and rooms of inherited art, Bonnards and Utrillos, Vuillards, and Cézannes. "Callas just left," they might have said.

The seasons passed in majesty: summer's inescapable heat, the storms of winter, the leaves of autumn which in a single night fell from the elms along the road. A few days later I drove through. In the great arcade a wave of yellow leaves was rising, driven into the air again by wind, as far as one could see. It was, unknown to me, a foretelling of what was to come, the time still far off when the beautiful debris would rise again and I would write about those days.

———

The famous figures, writers who taught at universities and were nominated for awards, were still lofty to me and remote from the path I was beating between country and town, diurnal in, nocturnal out, listening to the car radio and watching the black, familiar road unreel before me.

I had written a third book, some of it during a summer in Colorado, some in the Village, fragments of it scribbled on the empty passenger seat while driving to one place or another reciting to myself, rehearsing. It was not a maiden book. It was the book born in France in 1961 and 1962. Not a word of it had been read by anyone. I had a letter from Paula written at the time that urged, *the important thing, and I go back to what we used to talk about when we were twenty-one and twenty-two, is to do the things you believe you can do, and want to do and will do.*

It was my ambition to write something—I had stumbled across the words—*lúbrica y pura*, licentious yet pure, an immaculate book filled with images of an unchaste world more desirable than our own, a book that would cling to one and could not be brushed away. During its writing I felt great assurance. Everything came out as I imagined. The title was partly ironic, *A Sport and a Pastime*, a phrase from the Koran that expressed what the life of this world was meant to be as against the greater life to come.

I was at the time under the spell of books which were brief but every page of which was exalted, Faulkner's *The Sound and the Fury* or *As I Lay Dying*. This sort of book, like those of Flannery O'Connor, Marguerite Duras, Camus, remains my favorite. It is like the middle distances for a runner. The pace is unforgiving and must be kept up to the end. The Finns were once renowned for running these distances and the quality that was demanded was *sisu*, courage and endurance. For me the shorter novels show it best.

This almost perfect, so I believed, book was turned down by my publisher out of hand. Other publishers followed suit. The book was repetitive. Its characters were unsympathetic. Perhaps I was mistaken and in isolation had lost my bearings or failed to draw the line, emerging as a kind of hermit with skewed ideas. At last the manuscript was brought to the attention of George Plimpton, the editor of *The Paris Review*, which had a small publishing capability, and he at once agreed to take it.

That year, in the autumn evening I hurried towards corner newsstands, their light spilling on stacks of papers, to pick up the just arrived issue of *The New Yorker*, which was running, in four long parts, the entire book that turned its author, Truman Capote, from a kind of pet into a blazing celebrity.

In Cold Blood filled me with envy for its exceptional clarity and power, and my admiration was all the greater since I remembered the original chilling article in the *Times*, the prosperous farm family brutally executed in their own home in safe Kansas. I had even cut it out of the paper, it seemed so monstrous and foretelling. Capote, to his great credit, had done more. In a terrific gamble he had set out, flagrantly daring and astute, with nothing besides his talent and a notebook, to lay bare every facet of the crime he could discover. It was a gamble because the case might never be solved and all his time and energy might be wasted. As it was, the murderers were for a long time uncaught.

Blood, sex, war, and names—the same bouquet goes for the *Iliad* and the front page. *In Cold Blood* was somewhere between the two, an enormous success. Capote soared to the heights. He was clever, his tongue wickedly sharp. He had already swooped through the bright lights developing the diva persona that was to prove irresistible, and now there was money, too.

That November he gave a great party, a masked ball, at the Plaza. The guests, in the hundreds—the list of those invited had been kept secret—were a certain cream. Many came from prearranged dinners all over town, movie stars, artists, songwriters, tycoons, Princess Pignatelli, John O'Hara, Averell Harriman, political insiders, queens of fashion, women in white gowns, men in dinner jackets. They were going up the carpeted steps of the hotel entrance, great languid flags overhead, limousines in dark ranks. The path of glory: satin gowns raised a few inches as they went up on silvery heels. Stunning women, bare shoulders, the rapt crowd.

They woke, these people, above a park immense and calm in the morning, the reservoir a mirror, the buildings to the east in shadow with the sun behind them, the rivers shining, the bridges lightly sketched. There were no curtains. This high up there was no one to see in.

In the small convertible I had bought in Rome I was driving past that night and for a few moments saw it. I knew neither the guests nor the host. I had the elation of not being part of it, of scorning it, on my way like a fox to another sort of life. There came to me something a nurse had once told me, that at Pearl Harbor casualties had been brought in wearing tuxedos, it was Saturday night on Oahu, it was Sunday. The dancing at the clubs was over. The dawn of the war.

In the darkness the soft hum of the tires on the empty road was like a cooling hand. The city had sunk to mere glowing sky. My own book was not yet published, but would be. It had no dimensions, no limit to the heights it might reach. It was deep in my pocket, like an inheritance.

———

At the very end of 1969, *A Sport and a Pastime* having been published with sales of a few thousand copies, I received a fan letter, long, intelligent, and admiring with, although I was unaware of it until afterwards, the title of one of the writer's own books woven secretly into a line. *I would like to ply you with questions*, it read. *Sincerely, Robert Phelps*.

So it began.

We met a month or two later in the Spanish restaurant—it was his suggestion—in the Chelsea Hotel. I have never passed it without remembering, in the manner of a love affair. He was then forty-seven years old but very youthful, almost impish, lean, soft-spoken, with a wonderful smile. From the first moment I recognized him for what he was, I saw in him the angelic and also something, call it dedication, for which I yearned. I longed to know him.

He was fond of books; steak tartare; gin from a green bottle poured over brilliant cubes each afternoon at five, the ice bursting into applause; cats; beautiful sentences; Stravinsky; and France. I also liked France, that is to say I was in its thrall, but I did not know Colette or Cocteau except for their faces. I did not know Jouhandeau or Paul Léautaud who, when he was an old, forgotten man wrote, *Écrire! Quelle chose merveilleuse!* The France that Phelps revealed to me was a cultured world in which literature endured.

He also loved movie stars, money in the abstract sense, and glamour—at least he liked to think about them. With a colleague he had founded Grove Press and then sold it, vowing to live by his typewriter. He told me of coming to New York one of the first times to interview James Agee, so nervous he'd had to write the questions on the palm of his hand in ink, and of hearing the slow, mortal steps of Agee, who had heart trouble, coming up the stairs.

He had a keen appetite for gossip, without which most conversation is flavorless, and a great personal modesty. I have said "angel" though he was not a gentle, swooning one. There was a call one day from a woman in California who was writing her thesis on Cocteau and wanted advice. She had gotten his telephone number from his publishers. Could she write to him? she asked. "Yes, perhaps you can get my address from my publishers," he said.

More typically he made one think of Satie, shy, unshined on, true, if not to himself, to the things he knew mattered. His life was like pure notes, unhurriedly played. Seldom did he talk about his own writing, usually with the impression that it was more or less an illness he was trying to get rid of. He wanted to write novels but could not. Instead he wrote articles and reviews, and books that were for the most part compilations. He delighted in stories, remarks, outrageous acts—the uninventable—and believed in a moral principle that was like the law of gravity: Things had their consequences, including fame. *"Il faut payer,"* he would say. All around him great Babylon was roaring, the city was pounding out wealth, celebrity, crime, yesterday's newspapers were blowing in the streets, and amid it he led his singular life. He owned neither house nor car. His expenditures were for the essentials. On his publisher's—Roger Straus's—desk he once saw a list of advances that had been paid to writers and his name led all the others, he said rather proudly; they'd advanced him more than anyone else. Philip Roth had gotten five thousand dollars for *The Professor of Desire.*

"Did that do well?"

"Oh . . ."

"What would you guess?" I asked. "Twenty thousand copies?"

"Twenty or twenty-five."

"It was on the best-seller list."

"Was it?" he said coolly.

Pinned above his own desk were photographs—Glenway Wescott and a boyish Phelps walking down a dirt road together, heads down as if talking, tennis-shoed feet in unison; a picture of Gertrude Stein with the quotation *I am coming to believe that nothing except a life-work can be considered*—drawings, lists, five Italian words to be learned that week, a carefully drawn astrological chart for the month, and Auden's comment *We were put on earth to make things.* In the hallway was a pile of books to be thrown away, those that, in going through the shelves, he had found of little merit. His was an existence completely focused, and he himself *one of the last fanatics of a religion that was dying out.*

He once mentioned—after dinner, table half cleared, his wife asleep on the couch—two books he was engaged to write. One was called *Following,* about people he followed on the street or others whose lives or careers he traced, essentially his voyeurism. The other was *1922,* the year of his birth, divided into 365 parts, not all with entries, he explained. The book was to be about everything that happened that year or was in progress or had ended, and that would be part of his life, bits about Walter Benjamin, Proust, Colette, in short, the matrix of his world. It would begin at the moment of his conception and end after his birth.

Early on he pressed on me the single book he loved best, and a model, I think, by another unfulfilled critic, Cyril Connolly's *The Unquiet Grave*, its dedication being from *A never writer*, as Connolly called himself. Phelps had read it, he said, twenty times.

———

The apartment was on Twelfth Street, off Fifth Avenue. It was on the fourth, the top, floor. The door had no buzzer; someone had to come down to let you in or fold the key in a piece of paper and drop it from the window. Up those stairs had come Marsha Nardi, who had been the mistress of William Carlos Williams and Robert Lowell—her letters were famous—throwing out her arms and reciting, as she climbed, a poem of Baudelaire's. Up also had come Ned Rorem, an intimate friend he admired and envied; Philip Guston; Richard Howard, and Louise Bogan, as well as other writers and painters. Ned Rorem, he said, had once proposed to Gloria Vanderbilt. Her reply was worthy of a queen: "But you'll have to fuck me, you know." Phelps talked about a friend who had been in France just after the war and with chocolate and cigarettes, unobtainable luxuries, had gotten remarkable signed editions from Cocteau and Colette. "It wasn't Ned Rorem?" I said.

"Oh, God, no. He wasn't in the war. He was busy changing lipstick," Phelps said.

The larger of the two rooms, in front, had a fireplace. Phelps's wife, Becki, who was a painter, had taken it for her studio. Passing through a small rectangular kitchen like a cottage of its own, one came to the back room, in which they ate, slept, and entertained. It was filled with books and with talk of them.

At their table one night someone mentioned storms and the pleasure of sleeping during them. "Absolutely the favorite thing I know!" Phelps cried. "There's a wonderful storm in Hardy, do you know it? In *Far from the Madding Crowd*." Hardy was the greatest writer of weather, he said. Next came Turgenev and Colette, and Conrad, of course. But where were there other storms?

"*Huckleberry Finn*," someone said.

"Of course. Is there one in Joyce? Proust? No," Phelps answered himself, "all of Proust is indoors."

"Pavese, in *Devil in the Hills*."

"*Rain*."

"*The Grapes of Wrath*, at the end where they . . ."

"*Pnin*, at the beginning."

"*The Wild Palms*."

"*A Farewell to Arms*."

"*Wuthering Heights*."

On and on it went, titles batted back and forth without hesitation, like a shuttlecock. I soon ran out of them, myself. It was long afterwards, in his copy of Sherlock Holmes, that I came across a word written inside the cover, *Weather*, and beneath it, with the page number, the title of a story, "The Five Orange Pips."

That night, later, Becki read my astrological chart. She held—they both did—to the Aristotelian belief that this world is bound to the movements of the one above and everything is so governed. Leo was ascendant for me, she said, "and the sun in the eleventh house means powerful friends." There were hidden relationships and a great deal of promiscuity, unrelenting. "Tell me," she said, "have all your dreams been realized?" I burst into laughter.

"A great renown awaits you finally," she said consolingly. "What is it you want?"

"To be an immortal," Phelps said impatiently, it being fundamental.

Though they did the charts together they never agreed. He was exact, she was intuitive. "Oh, my God," he would protest, *"that's not there."* There was a single, deep furrow in his brow, between the eyes, the sign of a divided life, perhaps, and I noticed a slight trembling in his long, intelligent hand.

———

"Read these," he directed me one day. It was in the cramped front room that served him as a study on the second floor of the building. The book he handed me was the collected stories of Isaac Babel. He had marked three, "Guy de Maupassant," "Dante Street," and "My First Goose." I had never read Babel. His name was one of those vaguely floating around. The opening paragraph of "My First Goose" was stunning. I examined every word over and over. They were straightforward but at the same time unimaginable, and set a level which it seemed the rest of the story could not meet but astonishingly did.

From time to time, when he was not using it, I myself worked in the room and read the books he had there. Maugham was one.

"Which book?" Phelps asked when I mentioned it.

"The Summing Up."

"Of course. That's his best."

His opinions, honed by years of reviewing, were confident and direct. The novels of Elizabeth Hardwick were "like old wicker chairs." Faulkner was a terrible writer, "He may be a genius but he's a disgraceful writer." Of a prominent editor, he remarked merely, "He's a drunk." His favorite English writer was Rayner Heppenstall—I had never heard of him—and, of course, Henry Green. I immediately read *Loving*.

"The nineteenth-century form of the novel is dead," he told me, "it no longer works. It died in 1922 with *Ulysses*—the writer pretending he is not part of the work, is invisible, above it. But then, whose voice is it? *Perfume of embraces all him assailed. With hungered flesh obscurely, he mutely craved to adore.* Bloom," he explained, "looking in at ladies' underwear—it's Joyce's voice, of course, but he doesn't admit it.

"The second form," he went on, "is when the writer speaks through someone, inhabits them, as it were, as Henry James did or Fitzgerald in *Gatsby.*"

"Berryman's Henry."

"Yes. That's perhaps a great work of the second half of the century. Prose or poetry," he added, "it's the same.

"The third form of novel is the confessional, the first person, the writer standing there before you, Henry Miller in *Tropic*, Genet in *Notre-Dame-des-Fleurs.* Colette wrote a marvelous description of the execution of . . . who was it? In Genet, the very first sentence . . ."

"Weidman."

"Yes! Now he's immortal. Gertrude Stein said no life that is not written about is truly lived, and there it is."

It was the voice of the writer, he insisted, that was the first and definitive thing. I had, around this time, seen a van Gogh exhibition, paintings of his and his contemporaries discussed in his own words, and was struck by his saying, in a letter to his brother, *What is alive in art, and eternally alive, is in the first place the painter and in the second place the picture.* Phelps would agree.

"The original form of storytelling," he said, "is someone saying, I was there and this is what I beheld, as in Shakespeare where who was it says something like, I saw her on a public street, fourteen paces, or something." It was Enobarbus in *Antony and Cleopatra* he was thinking of. "Now we are coming back to that again.

"Think about what I've said," he advised.

I had heard similar ideas from a writer in London, Andrew Sinclair, who felt the novel, the psychological novel that began with Richardson and explained motives, emotions, and feelings, had ended with Proust. Sinclair couldn't read Proust. He didn't like to hear what the writer said about his characters' thoughts and actions, he preferred to see and hear the people and decide for himself. The Proustian kind of novel had coincided with the rise of the middle class, its prosperity, and ended with the class's decline—something he regarded as self-evident. Anyway, it was a tributary, not the main stream. The main stream was story, like the Bible, like Homer.

Sinclair had a deep voice and was, for me, unfathomable. I ran into him from time to time, sometimes when he was married and sometimes not. His first wife, who was part, or perhaps entirely, French, had been very beautiful. She'd gone to Cuba and given herself to Castro. "She taught me a lot," he mused. "She taught me that everything I'd learned in England was irrelevant."

Sinclair had some unusual views, among them that anecdotes were the real history. In this leaning towards the fragmentary he was not unlike Robert Phelps, who liked startling glimpses, lines, unexpected details. "Do you realize," he asked me once, "Freud had no sexual intercourse after forty?"

"Where did you hear that?"

"On the radio," he said, unembarrassed.

I had a memorable lunch with him on his forty-ninth birthday. We drank several martinis, and enlivened by them I could see, in the light, his good-natured, countryman's face, the long nose and sensitive mouth. His hand was shaking. "*Mia zampa*," he murmured apologetically—*zampa*, paw. He was telling stories of Glenway Wescott drinking at a party with the Duke of Windsor. He married the duchess, the duke remarked, because she was the finest fellatrix in Europe.

We were in a restaurant filled with flowers, fresh napery, the faces of women. "His problem," Phelps said of the duke, "was quite well known. It was premature ejaculation, poor boy. They had gotten him women from everywhere. He was miserable. He'd

never known the male glory that comes from giving a woman pleasure. Gloria Vanderbilt's aunt was coming back from Europe—this
is what started it—and met Wallis Warfield in New York. 'Neddie
is such an unhappy boy,' she said, 'take care of him.' 'I will,' Wallis
said. She knew what society was: One did everything but one didn't
talk about it."

"The Duke of Windsor didn't actually say that?"

"According to Glenway," Robert said.

———

In the bedroom he was packing. He was going to France that week
and also Italy. On a map of Rome I located hotels for him and the
best place to change money. Velvet pants were folded in his suitcase, sweaters and shirts, books. As an afterthought he added a
bottle of scotch.

On the desk was a letter in black handwriting from Colette Jou-
venel, Colette's daughter, with whom he was going to drive to Italy.
Cher Robert, I read. They were thinking of doing a Hollywood film
of her mother, and someone was needed to represent the daughter's interests in discussions. That was the subject of the letter.
"She's a *baronne*," Phelps commented offhandedly. "Oh, nothing
important—created by Napoleon III, looked on with amusement
by the real aristocracy."

He looked forward to dining on eels with Janet Flanner and accompanying an eighty-four-year-old Marcel Jouhandeau on one of
his regular Thursday afternoon visits to a male whorehouse near
the Place Pigalle. I later had a letter from him, from Paris; he'd
had a meal in the bistro owned by Jouhandeau's ex-lover, about
whom Jouhandeau had written a masterpiece, *Un Pur Amour.* It
was in this letter or another that he told of his delight in discovering that he was able to walk from his hotel, tucked in the corner of
Place St.-Sulpice, to the Seine, the entire way, on streets named

for writers. He may have exaggerated slightly—I have never been able to duplicate the feat.

Cher cadet, he would often address me in his letters. He was older, it was true, but it was not for wisdom I was drawn to him, rather for his presence, which confirmed all I sought to feel about the world. In the books he gave me to read, in the long conversations, the lines of Joyce, Connolly, Virginia Woolf, stuffed, as it were, in his pockets, he was one of the most important influences in my life and in whatever I wrote afterwards. Would this interest him, I often wondered? Would he find it deserving?

"Do you use vermouth?" he asked sweetly one evening as he brought out the gin, his right hand shaking, almost with a life of its own. "Katharine Hepburn has it too," he commented. "She had to sit on it during a television interview."

"Why does it only affect one hand?" I asked. "Why doesn't it affect more?"

"My God!" his wife cried. "Please!"

Phelps himself moaned.

———

He had loved books from the beginning. His father had been disappointed, wanting him to be a real boy, go hunting with him, play ball, while all he wanted to do was read. The plant, his father called him, the houseplant.

He was an only child, born of an unhappy marriage. His father had married his mother because she was pregnant—he hadn't wanted to, he'd been in love with two other women at the time. When Phelps was eight or nine his grandfather, whom he loved, shot himself. It was during the Depression. The old man had lost everything, including in the end his house, which Phelps's father had bought and in which they all lived together while the sharp-tongued grandmother, in scorn, ate her husband's soul. There was a long argument that began over some tiny windows. The grandfather, who was a cabinetmaker, had fashioned two little windows to be set in doors—in those days housewives were being assaulted by roving, jobless men who came for a handout. No one wanted to manufacture the miniature windows, however, and they sat in the workshop. Robert loved them, of course. For his birthday his grandfather installed one in the room, little more than a closet beneath the eaves, where Robert slept. The grandmother noticed it while she was raking leaves and was furious. Here the house was again to be sold and he was marring it with this foolish window.

That night there was a bitter argument at the dinner table. His grandfather went outside and soon afterwards Robert heard his name being called. He went out to the garage where his grandfather had his workshop, and just as he drew near, there was a shot. The old man had put a rifle to his chest.

Robert's father came running. He began to shout at his father-in-law, who was lying on the floor. A few hours later, in the hospital, the grandfather died.

There was more to come. In the offices where his father worked was a man who had seven or eight children and who the times had made desperate. His co-workers banded together, each to support a child, and Phelps's father sponsored one of the daughters, a girl of twelve or so.

He gave her money. He bought her clothes. And somewhere along the way she became his mistress. Her name being completely familiar there, emboldened, he brought her to stay in the house. Why, his wife wanted to know? He found some explanation. It was uncomfortable, however, the invisible currents, the instincts. She didn't remain. Then, needing a go-between, the father confessed everything to his son. For two years Robert served the pair, hiding it from his mother, trying to protect her.

In the end she found out. She had seen them together or someone had told her. Robert was walking with her behind the house, coming up a path, when suddenly she fell to her knees, weeping. That night there was a terrible fight and his father confessed it all. His mother tried to kill herself by slashing her wrists. Two years later she died. It was breast cancer, metastasized everywhere. Phelps's father married the girl.

After college, Robert never returned home. He had adored his mother, he was deeply attached to her. He drew the curtain. I asked him once about his years in Cleveland; he remembered very little of that, he said.

"But you lived there. You wrote for the newspaper."

"I used to write obituaries for the *Cleveland Press* during the summers," he said.

"Then you do know it."

"I knew certain people who died in the forties" was all he would say.

He had resected it from his life. He never saw his father again. One day there was a telephone call; it was from his stepmother. Daddy was very sick—she had always called him Daddy—could Robert come? "No," he said.

Instead he wrote his father a long letter saying that their parting was forever; there was nothing between them anymore. A friend called the next day to say how awful the effect had been and pleaded with him to come home; his father was dying. He did not go. Nor did he go to the funeral. There was a half-sister he had never seen.

One is drawn to lives achieved in agony. His beautiful scrapbooks and letters. *Earthly Paradise,* his assemblage of Colette's writing to form an autobiography, her own intimate descriptions with his knowing linkage. He wrote another book on Colette, *Belles Saisons,* in a form he liked, photographs with extended captions, which surpassed most longer works. It had a unique shape, a bit wider than ordinary books with endpapers the blue of Colette's stationery. When the first copy arrived his wife sat up all night reading it.

"Such a beautiful book," she cried to me worshipfully the next day. She loved what it represented. I opened it and began to read. I was so overwhelmed I kissed him.

Colette, as it turned out, was his chief subject. He edited her collected stories and translated her letters. I had an inscribed copy of *Earthly Paradise*—it was the favorite book of my daughter and was buried with her.

The long, fluttering hand, its helplessness becoming worse over the years, could no longer write. It was Parkinson's disease, psychosomatic, he knew or at least said, the result of rage, self-condemnation, and self-betrayal, in the end fatal. I could barely hear his voice, a whisper leached away by illness.

A long leap forward now to the last time I saw him. He was lying beneath a single white sheet in the heat of July. Very ill, he could no longer speak. He held my hand for a long time and occasionally gave me what I can only think of as canny glances. It was a sweltering afternoon. His torso and legs lay bare. The lean body and beautiful feet, I would have bent and kissed them were it not for the black nurse sitting silent, watching.

———

When I think of him I think of France, the appetite we had in common. He knew the world of its writers. I knew the provinces, the beautiful, empty roads, the faded rooms. The French figure I knew best was, of course, Napoleon. I remembered that he had married Josephine when she was thirty-two, and that she had subtracted five years from her age for the occasion, while he gallantly added one to his. Robert had gone to the Larousse to see if it was true, but about Napoleon I was confident, I had led the class in military history, I knew his life.

In Phelps's book about Cocteau, *Professional Secrets,* there is Cocteau's confession *Every morning I tell myself, you can do nothing about it: submit.* A suitcase contained his unfinished novel, left for months on Fire Island; the abandoned attempts—I write and write, he said, but it's fiction, I don't believe what I am saying—and short stories begun ten years earlier until, *I have a strickening sense of waste, of important days of my life slipping away without being marked, or used* . . . He did submit, unhappily, year by year. To me it seemed romantic, like a sophisticated alcoholism. Whatever his failure, he made me faithful to him and to the things he believed. He is woven for me into the stuff of literature, the literary life.

At someone's memorial a few years later, during the tributes, while girl photographers skipped along the front row to shoot well-known faces, a man rose slightly in his seat and looked back, a young man, intelligent, unsure, in dark glasses and a camel's-hair coat. I recognized him instantly but with a shock: Robert Phelps at twenty-four, undamaged, ignorant of what he would one day come to know so well, *il faut payer.*

———

In January 1972, the year's beginning, smooth blank pages lay beneath my hand, and in hours of undisturbed solitude I began an outline. No, this is not exactly right. The outline, sixty-five pages of it, was scribbled on the back side of leaves of an old loose-leaf desk calendar. The smooth blank pages came three days later during a huge blizzard, the temperature very low, the snow fine as salt. The roads were closed, Denver airport, Loveland Pass.

I was nervous and elated. I knew what I wanted: to summarize certain attitudes towards life, among them that marriage lasted too long. I was perhaps thinking of my own. I had in mind a casting back, a final rich confession, as it were. There was a line of Jean Renoir's that struck me: The only things that are important in life are those you remember. That was to be the key. It was to be a book of pure recall. Everything in the voice of the writer, in his way of telling. I had a list of sufficiently inspiring titles, *Nyala, Mohenjodaro, Estuarial Lives*. I was writing to fit them, though in the end none survived.

This was in Colorado, in Aspen when it was only a remote town. Behind the old wooden house with its linoleum floors was a building that had been a garage and was now a studio with blue, stenciled boards high up on the ceiling, a fireplace, and a counterlike desk along the wall. Writing is filled with uncertainty and much of what one does turns out bad, but this time, very early there was a startling glimpse, like that of a body beneath the water, pale, terrifying, the glimpse that says: it is there.

In the spring, confident, I sent the first seventy-five pages of what I had written off to publishers. Absolutely must have it, I imagined them saying. The replies, however, were at best equivocal. Farrar Straus turned it down. Scribner's. As rejections came, one by one, I was stunned. I lay in bed at night wrapped in bitterness, like a prisoner whose appeal has failed. I tried to think of the books that amounted to something only after having begged, so to speak, at many doors.

Finally a well-known editor whom I had met once or twice agreed to take the book. This was Joe Fox.

He was then in his late forties—Harvard (swimming team captain), divorced (man about town), backgammon player, also squash, and acquainted with almost everyone. He was a Philadelphian, though he had lived in New York for years among, with other things, irreplaceable pieces of furniture that had been in the family since Colonial times. He had the prep-school habit of referring to himself by his last name. "Fox here," he would announce on the phone when he called. I do not mean to say he was snobbish or Anglo, however. He did have his systems and rules and was eligible for any club, but he was also supremely democratic and loyal, a man who did his work in a shirt and tie, the work that God and class, not to mention the publishing house, expected. He liked travel, the ballet, and, without the appearance of it, parties. He was somewhat deaf to argument.

The book was ultimately called *Light Years*. I remember his final comment when the editing had been completed—the manuscript had blue pencil, his, in one margin and red, the copy editor's, in the other—"An absolutely marvelous book in every way," he said, adding, "probably." I had the exultation of believing it. I wanted praise, of course, widespread praise, and it seemed somehow that Fox might assure it—he had been the editor for many admired writers, Paul Bowles, Capote, Ralph Ellison, Roth. I wanted glory. I had seen, at the Met, Nureyev and Fonteyn in their farewell performance, one of many, of *Swan Lake*—magnificent, inspired, the entire audience on its feet and wildly applauding for three-quarters of an hour after the curtain as the deities appeared, together, then one or the other, then again the two, on and on, bow after bow in weary happiness as armfuls of roses were brought to the stage.

Such tremendous waves did not fall upon writers. On Victor Hugo, perhaps, or Neruda—I could think of no others not poor Joyce, or Pushkin, or Dante, or Kawabata. For them a banquet or award or something on the scale of the scene in the restaurant at midnight when the star is preparing to leave and stands before the mirror near the bar, drawing tight the belt of his trenchcoat, watched by enthralled waiters.

When was I happiest, the happiest in my life? Difficult to say. Skipping the obvious, perhaps setting off on a journey, or returning from one. In my thirties, probably, and at scattered other times, among them the weightless days before a book was published and occasionally when writing it. It is only in books that one finds perfection, only in books that it cannot be spoiled. Art, in a sense, is life brought to a standstill, rescued from time. The secret of making it is simple: discard everything that is good enough.

I love Nabokov interviews, Ben Sonnenberg wrote. *May I see it before it appears?*

I knew him only from correspondence. I had just come back from Montreux and meeting with Nabokov. *I recently read twenty-two of them before falling asleep,* Sonnenberg went on. *They are all in* Strong Opinions. *In my dreams that night, he was persecuting me with his high opinion of* Ulysses, *which I do not share. He scoffed at my liking Cervantes and Genet. Fortunately, before I woke up we found a common ground in the movies of Max Linder.*

He had read ten books by Nabokov that year, he said, including *Lolita,* which he had reread and which was still his favorite. The letter was dandyish but I was reassured by the straightforward choice.

We were in touch because of the theater. He had a job reading plays for Lincoln Center and had written to me about one I had submitted that he unsuccessfully championed. We finally met for dinner in a restaurant on Division Street in Chinatown. I arrived a little late to find him in a small room with bare tables, four bottles of Japanese beer in front of him, waiting. He wore a flowing bow tie and his hat, overcoat, scarf, and—I had not seen one for years—cane were hanging near the door.

"Do you know Fukienese cooking?" he asked. His voice was clear and soft with a faint whiff of England. "Permit me to order for you. It's not so spicy as Szechuan but more distinguished than Cantonese."

After discussing it with a waiter, whose name he knew, he ordered soup, pork chops, and sea bass. I liked his epicurean nonchalance and the intelligence in his voice. Both of his eyes had a slight cast so that he never seemed to be truly looking at you. They were dark, possessing eyes. His formal education, it turned out, had ended in prep school. The life that followed was devoted to women and art.

We talked about his marriages; he discussed them as one might discuss ships. Somehow, in listening to the recounting, I was filled with a sense of strength. It was of Ford Madox Ford I was reminded, the sleek Ford, in the sense of being properly nourished, who all his life remembered the words of an uncle, told to him while strolling through the fields: Always help a lame dog over a stile.

Sonnenberg's father was well known. He was one of the early lords of publicity and image-making, an art collector and a man whose every outward appearance, including a great moustache, was proof of success. The family house was a mansion on the south side of Gramercy Park, where extravagant dinners were given and the guest list was thick with famous names.

Formed by all this and at the same time contemptuous of it, the son made rebellion his guiding principle. Like a Regency sport he took pride in distressing his family, his father in particular. What redeemed him was the high level of squandering. The evil companions were books.

That first night, on the street, he handed me a stack he was carrying while he went to use a rest room. I looked through them. Some plays, a book on Elizabethan drama, a novel of Naipaul's, the Sunday *Observer*. While I waited I read four or five pages of the novel, my first taste of Naipaul.

Sonnenberg was a prodigious reader and had a powerful memory. These qualities later served him well as an editor when he founded, with inherited money when his father died, a literary quarterly, *Grand Street,* and ran it for ten years until illness and exhaustion of funds forced its sale. It was the chief work of his life.

His most noticeable trait apart from taste was a polite but remorseless candor. He could be counted on to speak his view in few words. I recall, among other things, his dealings with a manipulative and troublesome writer, Harold Brodkey. For the first issue of *Grand Street,* Brodkey had submitted a very long story, which Sonnenberg didn't like, tactfully suggesting that perhaps ten pages of it could be published. Brodkey, indignant, refused and in its place offered a poem, which Sonnenberg rejected with a note he later was sorry he'd sent, to the effect that he liked the poem rather less than the story.

Over the years, as the magazine flourished, there were some infrequent letters exchanged between the two, as well as an occasional encounter at a party. Finally a letter came from Brodkey in which he proposed, for whatever reasons, that they might resume their friendship. Sonnenberg wrote back civilly that he preferred not to, he didn't want to be in a state of watchful cordiality, he said.

The play of mine that originally brought us together eventually had a staging in an avant-garde theater converted from a church. The director was a bantam of a man with bold Celtic charm. John Beary was his name. His father had trained horses for Aly Khan, who in fact was Beary's godfather, recalled as strolling through sunflecked mornings near the track, *My Old Man* mornings, in casual clothes, the kind one carries wood in, Levi's and a worn sportcoat.

Beary was passionate, articulate, and somehow lonely, though he was married. Domesticity he described as "the other life—the child, home, all of that." He meant it in contrast to life in the theater, art. I remember his stories which were the true pay for the years he had spent, his great love affair once with a leading actress. The night she played at the Abbey. The affair had passed its zenith, and at the reception she was with another man, a pathetic figure, someone to be detested, Beary said. They were bickering and suddenly she tired of it and left.

Beary followed her to her room. In the darkness she said only, "Well, then. You've come," and heartened, he lay down beside her. In the midst of things the door flew open and in came the rival, his arms filled with bottles from the reception. He was drunk.

"Why don't we have a drink?" he cried, standing there.

"Why don't you throw that stuff right out the window?" Beary, sitting up, growled.

There was a pause and the man went to the window, pushed it open, and the bottles crashed in the street. Within minutes the hall porter was up, banging on the door. He threw them all out.

The theater is unto itself, artificial and grand, trailing a magnificent pedigree like a fur coat behind it on the ground, extravagance, pretension, little biting lives. Tyranny abounds. Beary, himself, was arbitrary in many of his actions, probably because he so rarely had the chance to be. One actress he chose on the spot, the audition having lasted less than a minute. "The role is yours," he said grandly. I suspected it was because of her good looks. He was sure she could act.

The play, "the best thing you've ever done," as I was told, was too ambitious, with some startling moments but weak in structure. It was called *The Death Star* and focused on the vain belief that the death of a legendary military figure, a repentant one, could still the human urge for war. Those days will return, it said, the chaos.

There were more than thirty roles, played by twenty actors, some talented, and Beary, in a state of nerves, alternately praised and nipped at them through the rehearsals. The stage manager, a cooperative girl, he had in tears. She seemed to thrive on it. Plainly, he knew more than I.

The evening of the first performance arrived. From the lighting booth I could see faces I knew pass below. In the crowded dressing room there was excitement. One of the actors, I noticed, a strange man with a hyphenated name, seemed almost drunk. Playwrights, I knew, often were. I drank nothing, however. It was too late for anything except resignation. I was fearful and attempting to be calm.

From the earliest moments, when the curtain was raised, I saw it was wrong. The mood in the theater is something one can feel like heat or cold. Everything that had gone before, the preparation, the belief, was suddenly of no importance—the play was like a ship put to sea; whatever mattered before did not matter now. Before the indifference of the audience, the many people seated and silent, the whole enterprise was transparent, as if x-rayed. My stomach was turning over. I was in literal pain. There was a moment at last when the play came to life, the attention rose to meet it, there was a swell, like being brought up by a wave. A powerful speech—Kevin McCarthy delivered it—closed the act.

I lay on the floor in a small upstairs room, alone in the dark, for fifteen minutes.

The second act was better. McCarthy, in his closing lines, was chilling, a glimpse of what might have been. The play had an epilogue. As it was being read, a lone remorseful figure appeared behind the speaker, head down, ashamed. It was the drunken actor.

I was too embarrassed to be seen afterwards. Finally I went down the back stairs. I was greeted by enthusiasm and beaming faces. They had loved it, the power, "I'd buy a ticket anytime." I did not believe them. I was more inclined towards the comment of a friend that he had liked it better when he had read it. The two scouts from the Public Theater had left during intermission, along with a couple of black whores who had wandered in from the street, probably for warmth, and then sat bored. They were the hard-hearted audience I coveted.

Sonnenberg telephoned the next morning. "Well, how does it feel to be famous?" he asked. "All the actresses calling?"

"Not really."

"How did you feel about the play?"

I said I thought it wasn't too bad. How did he like it?

"I didn't like it," he said simply, "not at all. All the directorial choices were wrong, casting, staging, everything. It was much too slow and certain actors"—he named the girl Beary had instantly picked—"were hopeless."

Sonnenberg's illness, which proved terrible beyond description, had first showed itself in the most trivial way: the toe of a shoe caught for an instant in a sidewalk crack. I did not see that, but I watched the cane slowly become more than an item of dress and then change to two canes as their owner struggled to emerge from a taxi and shuffled slowly towards the door of a restaurant. Inside he fell across one of the tables. A waiter and people sitting nearby tried to help him to his feet but he grimly declined.

"Is it a matter of balance?" I asked when we had sat down.

"Yes, largely."

"Do you have feeling down there?"

"Yes. It's just that the nerves won't control," he said calmly.

It was multiple sclerosis, a disease that attacked the nerve sheathings. It progressed relentlessly. He lost the use of his hands. At the bottom of typed letters was a scrawl—he could barely sign his name. The pleasure of food was gone, so much of it had to do with the satisfaction of cutting, the holding of utensils, and so forth. He mentioned this at dinner at his apartment more and more rarely did he go out—and, as if to prove it, spilled a glass of water over himself when he tried to drink. Pieces of food had fallen around his plate, dropped from dead fingers.

He appeared not to notice. His calm behavior, his lack of complaint, were a kind of scorn. He was proud of the torment, as if it were part of the price of the expensive clothes, the girls he had known, the exotic names. Stupidity and death must not alarm you, he seemed to say. The illness was a mark of superiority like his faint, forbearing smile. The useless fingers, the disobedient limbs, were a sign of aristocracy. We who did not have them were inferior.

Year by year it grew worse. The New Year's birthday parties were abandoned. The magazine, in which I had been published a number of times, was gone. He was reduced to the inexhaustible, the life of the mind, but without relief. Memories, yes, but from the rest he was removed except as people came to tell him of it, the city that lay all around in dawn and darkness, the traffic floating at night on the streets below, the crowds, the avenues and shops, women with their daughters in department stores, long elegant noses, tumbling hair, the floor of cosmetic booths with scores of salesgirls, cheeks smoothed with color, white smocks, bright mouths, beckoning, counseling, smiling. He had known all this in the days when, as someone said, the life of reason was not in itself sufficient. Now he had stoicism, essential but useless. I think of the plea of Sonnenberg's father when he was ill and dying, which echoed something my own father had said near the end. "If you have a son," the old man said, "teach him to shoot."

———

It is the evenings one remembers, the end of the day, dinners in the Fifties, dinners downtown.

Dinners with Fox, beyond counting. He lived on the south side of the park in a luxurious building that had originally been painters' studios. His apartment was lofty with a curved, white balcony above the main room and bookcases everywhere. He was the ultimate New Yorker. In the city he invariably wore a suit. He had worked first for Alfred Knopf, the legendary publisher, and was related by marriage to the Canfields and Burdens. His best friends, in all likelihood, were women, to whom he attached himself with little difficulty.

Dinners with him at Caravelle, Remi, Petite Marmite, smoked salmon in slender coral sheets, lamb, expensive Pauillac. Dinners at a hotel in the country, a table in the bar. Winter night, black as ice. The warmth of the room, a fire burning. The Japanese woman hostess, the bartender in vest and white shirtsleeves. Mussels *à la barque*. Bacala. Women taking off their coats at the door and being shown with their escorts to tables.

The fragrant smoke rose from his after-dinner cigarette. He told of famous parties, the one of George Weidenfeld's in London. The invitation in beautiful calligraphy said *Exotic dress.* Weidenfeld himself came as a pasha. There were three orchestras, one of them on the stairs, and the most beautiful women Fox had ever seen. Couples would disappear into the garden or splendid upper floors and return after long intervals. There was that English phenomenon, an upper-class wanton who, though dropped from the guest list, came anyway. As an act of disdain she pleasured nine of the guests, one after another, in a bedroom. Marie Antoinettes and Japanese samurai lay collapsed on the sofas at dawn.

Through him one met many writers. He was like an old courtier who understood and could arrange almost anything. His nostrils were large, sometimes with hair in them. He hadn't gone to his twenty-fifth reunion at Harvard, he told me. He'd looked over the list very carefully. There were fifteen hundred names, only forty he knew, twenty-five of whom he didn't want to see again, ten, for a few minutes, and only five he liked. The figures were probably inaccurate but they were stamped with his self-confidence; his ancestors preceded Benjamin Franklin. One of them contemptuously shook Andrew Jackson's hand with his own wrapped in his coattail. At Random House his position was secure. He was not one of the razors. He was protected by his ability and by not having an ambition to run things.

Dinners on Park Avenue, the Schwartzes' apartment, comfortable and serene. Their two children, sons, coming in and out of the room, the younger one in various costumes. He is handsome. There can only be envy of him, his intelligence and future. His father, Alan, is a lawyer who married the most beautiful girl at Bryn Mawr; people would talk about it for a generation.

In the kitchen everything is laid out, thick ribs of beef, fresh loaves. There are cookbooks, stacks of china. Pinned to a corkboard: notes, cards, addresses, the order and complexity of this life. A scene that never fails to draw one in, the heaped green of the salad, the dark bottles of fine Bordeaux, the abundance and preparation. Halberstam is coming, Alan tells me, Hope Lange, Helen Frankenthaler. Drinks in the living room. The women are well dressed, at ease. They have traveled, been admired; one longs to hear their confessions. I do not know that Hope Lange, blonde and clear-faced in the audience, once caught the eye of a man on the stage reading—it was John Cheever, a fateful glance—or that she had been Sinatra's; her allure I could see was powerful. In the dining room, filled with books, I sit next to her; Halberstam is across the table. In Vietnam—his name was inextricably linked with it—the war is finally over.

"Did you know John Vann?" I ask.

"How do you know him?" Halberstam replies.

"I don't."

"The most extraordinary figure of the war."

Halberstam then summons him up, the military adviser of the early days, a lieutenant colonel who was an idealist, educated, spoke Vietnamese. The extensive writing about him had not yet appeared, I had only come across "John Vann" and a few telling lines of description. I was like a woman who fixes on a horse because of its name.

In the beginning, Halberstam says, the correspondents all sat at his feet, they could talk to him and he spoke frankly to them. "He knew more than anybody. The war could never be won by weapons, he continually said." He had incredible energy and instinct. At the time of the Tet offensive he smelled something funny, and it was he who was responsible for pulling back certain units before the enemy struck and avoiding complete disaster. "He never had anything to do with Vietnamese women." I feel an odd mixture of elation and disappointment. "It was beneath his image and belief, and it was taking advantage of them." Halberstam himself had a beautiful girlfriend in Saigon. "Everybody did."

The lone and perhaps foolish figure whose fate it was to believe in something with all his being—something stirs in me as I listen, something dusty and forgotten, struggling to its feet. Halberstam is manly-looking with big hands and a strong, resonant voice. I feel I know him and also Vann.

"But he was killed, wasn't he?" I say.

"He died in a helicopter crash."

We leave the table. Cognac and coffee in the living room. A fire of small, city logs is burning in the fireplace. The hostess and Helen Frankenthaler are lying together on the sofa, feline and content, beneath a quilt. My mind is still on the conversation at dinner, which has somehow removed me from the present. It has opened a gap like the narrow band of water that appears, in the first moments of departure, between the ship and the dock, designating two worlds. The uniform of the dead lieutenant colonel seems to lie there, ghostly, on the floor, my own size.

Dinners on Shelter Island at Max Wilkinson's, first at his house and later, when it was sold, in the little house that belonged to his new wife. She was repetitive and scolding. "Oh, Max," she said at the table, "you are so stupid! You talk and talk and talk and talk."

There was silence. He had been summoning up the image of his old partner's wife, in Arizona in the thirties when he first saw her, Helen Doughty, in a white linen dress. She was so beautiful, he said.

Finally he answered his wife. "Yes," he said quietly, "I suppose so."

Dinners in Europe. A small restaurant, perfect, well lit. The feeling of attentive service, fresh white cloth. The face before me, Buddha-like and wide, is an older woman's. She is the widow of a man who was still older. He was her second husband, she was in her late thirties when she met him, he had already broken up with his wife. "I didn't steal him from her but she hated me."

There were two children. "I didn't want to be their mother, after all. They were always welcome, but she was the mother. 'Look,' I said, 'come. If we are friends, good. If not, then we are not.'"

The European lucidity and understanding. "It's more difficult for a woman," she says. The wine bottle has become empty and another unobtrusively appears. "A man can always, at fifty or sixty, start a new life, but a woman is used up. It's not fair, but that's the way life is."

There is something very appealing about her, the lack of sentimentality, the frankness. She had an earlier marriage and a child, she reveals. He died, she says simply. A brain tumor. He was two. I calculate quickly, sometime just after the war. "He was only two," she says again. That is the extent of self-pity. "He was absolutely normal and then it began. He would fall and hit his elbow, for instance, and cry holding his head—it hurt him there."

One cannot say she is a stronger woman because of it, she was always such a woman. She has gone through the most difficult thing of all. She speaks three languages, perhaps four, and if she dreams of marrying again does not bother to confess it. Not surprisingly, the ex-wife and stepchildren are very close to her now. The ex-wife lives in Lugano. "She always comes to see me. She likes me to come there."

I think of her and of Jonathan Swift's mistress, Stella, a symbol of Europe, justly admired, as the stone that covers her says, for many virtues as well as for great natural and acquired perfection. One thing stands out: I have never heard her complain.

Drunken dinners, parties, really, where the food is ignored and they are jammed at the bar. At midnight the music is pounding; in the street the thin sleet of winter drives down. For some reason I think of the Village, where Pat Kenny lived when we were fifteen. Her parents were gone for the weekend, or at least the night. I did not know how to begin. We sat on the couch. She was pleasant. There was a copy of Robert Briffault's *Europa*, a thick novel of the 1930s, in the bookcase. "Have you read this?" I asked.

"No," she said.

She knew nothing of the passage that had electrified me, the gown torn from the back of the sumptuous woman who had cheated at cards and her hands quickly tied to a ring above her head. I did not know how to connect this to the two of us; it did not illustrate what was intended but it shared something. I wanted to see her wrenched from the vague, infuriating conversation we were having. I saw only the victim beneath her clothes, I wanted it revealed.

The years have their closure. Many of the people upon whom I had based characters passed from sight. It was only in part an accident. They had been consumed, my interest had waned. There were exceptions. The girl of *A Sport and a Pastime* I was always curious to see again, what had become of her, the details of her life, the closet in which her dresses hung, the drawer with her folded things, the bottles of perfume, shoes. I wanted again to lie there watching her prepare as if she were alone in the room, before the performance, as it were, putting on makeup, slipping into heels. She would be twenty-eight, thirty, completely changed. In fact she was married and living in Los Angeles. There were children. It was very like the book.

I had met her at Kennedy when she first arrived in America. She came through the crowd, innocent in her beauty, filled with joy. She was eighteen. Counts had coveted her. I met her also in dreams. I went through someone's empty room and knocked at her door. "Yes, come in," she said without asking who it was; I sensed she was expecting someone else. She looked up. Everything about her. I pulled up her dress in a single motion. The incredible nakedness. Laughing, she pushed it back down. In the dream I had lost the photograph of her, I didn't have an address. "You say you adore, but I think it's something else you like," she said. She was curled up, wearing nothing. At the end of a crowded road under gray clouds my ship was preparing to sail. There was traffic, the imminence of departure. My heart was sick.

Nedra, the stylish woman of *Light Years,* I sometimes saw again, usually in the city, the last time in the house she now lived in alone—true to the book, she and her husband had eventually divorced. I loved her, her frankness and charm, the extravagance and devotion to her children. I never tired of seeing her and listening to her talk. She smoked, drank, laughed raucously. There was no caution in her.

Her old lover, one of them, sat with us that last night. Nedra had aged. The years had seized and shaken her as a cat shakes a mouse. Her jawline was no longer pure and there were small pouches beneath her eyes. Her nose had gotten larger. Her still-long hair had traces of gray. In her face, which I loved, was my own mortality. The lines at the corners of my mouth, which were more terrible than an illness—I jumped up to look each morning; they were there.

She was going to give him her father's old tie pin, she said impulsively, it was the best thing her father had owned. "Do you still have the pearl cuff links?" she asked, pulling up the sleeve of his jacket. "No. They're on the other shirt," she guessed. He lived in a small house behind hers. I had no idea if they were still intimate—she was capable of every appearance of it without the thing itself.

Hers was a singular life. It had no achievements other than itself. It declared, in its own way, that there are things that matter and these are the things one must do. Life is energy, it proclaimed, life is desire. You are not meant to understand everything but to live and do certain things. Despite all I had written about her, there was more, and the carnal scenes, a minor element, I imagined entirely. It would have been gratifying to know if they were appropriate. Some things, however, she did not talk about.

She is gone, and the other wives, too, it seems, the ones men had; they are widowed or divorced, wise from intimacy, strong-voiced. The families, like old temple columns, are broken, never to be restored. When the world was young it seemed impossible. The unions were too firm, the comfort of an open, loving heart too great. I stood on deck one winter morning, coming back from Europe by boat, near to docking, the unawakened city in gray light. A family came to the rail nearby. They were German; they'd been in first class. The woman's face was beautiful, that clarity, composure, and breeding that make one long for one more chance at life. I felt a burning, terrible shame. Everything I valued was suddenly made worthless and I was plunged into confusion, trying to imagine what this marvelous woman said, how she argued, sat down at the table, slept, dressed. I could not picture a single detail of her life. I was like a desperate young boy, kept from, not even knowing that the test of elegance was close inspection, and that to her husband she was quite a different person than she was to me.

"Moritz!" she called to her child. He was as handsome, with a white hat made of crudely sewn leather and square earflaps. He was seven or eight, well-mannered. He came and stood by her, near her side. Suddenly the concept of virtue as strength was real.

I often came across her opposite, the heroine of all our books and films, still young, divorced. In a bar she was wearing a kind of toque made from a colorful scarf, tight jeans, a turtleneck shirt. How had she been, I asked.

"Hello! I'm fine. I'm settling down."

Though she was still broke, as she said. She was the daughter of a writer I knew who had reversed the usual sequence—he had published some novels first and then came the list of other roles: restaurant owner, bandleader, policeman. His daughter had been working as a waitress; she had her father's unorthodox spirit. She was going to get another job when her complexion cleared up, she said. "It's hard being alone. Will you buy me a drink?"

In fact, she hadn't been alone. She'd had a guy for a month, very straight, she explained, but nice, Notre Dame, all that. He left.

"He said I was taking up too much of his time. I wanted him to move in, but he didn't love my children enough. He said he did, but he didn't. Well, you know, it's difficult. I should take the time to write down twenty lines a day, shouldn't I?" she asked.

Yes, like putting pennies in a jar, it would add up, be valuable some day, perhaps salvage her life.

That was some years ago. I don't know what became of her.

There are certain houses near the river in secluded towns, their wooden fences weathered brown. Near the door in sunlight, stiff-legged, a white cat pulls itself up in an arc. Clothes on a half-hidden line drift in the light. It is here I imagine the wives, their children long grown, at peace with life and now drawn close to the essence of it, the soft rain flattening the water, trees thick with foliage bending to the wind, flowers beneath the kitchen window, quiet days. Men are important no longer, nor can they know such tranquillity, here in perfect exile, if it can be had that way, amid nature, in the world that was bequeathed to us.

———

At the end of the summer in 1980 we drove East. I had been living, toward the end divorced, in Colorado and after the death of my daughter decided, more or less, to go home. I was drawing a line beneath ten years. It was late August. In the morning the grass was cold and the topmost leaves of the trees had begun to yellow. I took my last walks along the river, which was teeming with light. I had a dog, a Welsh corgi named Sumo, white-footed and clever. I used to compliment him on his behavior, his ears. He would look away, yawn. We walked together. Mist rose from the brow of the bank, a solemn, ennobling mist. Not another soul.

We passed through Denver, where I used to go often—it was like an equatorial city, steaming, inert, we were dying of the heat— and went on to Red Cloud, the town in Nebraska where Willa

Cather lived as a child. The Republic River, in which she once swam, was stagnant and dark. The sun was murderous. Mosquitoes light as ash drifted onto us as we sat.

In Ohio was a lesser shrine, Louis Bromfield's Malabar Farm. Bromfield had been a best-seller in the years before the war. In the beautiful old house we were the lone visitors and the attendant's knowledge was limited to the names of movie stars who had been Bromfield's guests decades before.

The long drive ended far out on Long Island. We rented a house near the sea. It was the beginning of off-season, the warm fall days. We could walk down the road to the beach; over a ragged dune the Atlantic lay, a collapsing line of surf. The bathers were in a group, men, children, and a sprinkling of young women gleaming like seals. The heavy waves rose, scattering them amid shrieks.

It was the season of bleached telephone poles and hordes of black sparrows perched on the wires. In the afternoon haze the sea burst white where bluefish were feeding. Inland were fields of rye. It was the country where I had written parts of books and where legends existed as they did in Tahiti and Key West the blind caretaker who lived with his wife and knew all the houses, and some of their occupants, by feel. He went around and attended to whatever needed care, even in the dead of winter. He had fallen off a roof once. "Well, that happens," he said.

I first knew the region when I came in the 1950s and was stationed at Westhampton. The airfield might have been in North Africa, it was that desolate and open to the sky. In the metal alert hangars at the end of the runway we slept in our flying suits with boots laced, ready to sprint for the ships when the klaxon blared into sound in the dead of night. Heading out over the black water in a sky without stars, talking in pilots' shorthand with the radar station.

My wife and I had lived in an apartment near the bay. The town was quiet, like a failing country club. We were friends with the mayor, who was a doctor, and his good-looking wife. Their circle seemed sophisticated and a little bored. There was the feeling that there were lives ready to be capsized, a vague feeling of unseen fracture. It was exciting.

I saw my first Stanford White houses, and the ocean on every kind of day: frothing with huge waves in the distance; green and veined like marble; calm, with the waves far out and a slow, majestic sound. In the fall the geese flew over in long, wavering lines, sometimes breaking apart, drifting into wedges, great-hearted leaders at the apex.

If I look back and try to locate the center of my life it must be those days, I should probably say that decade. I had come through the early storms. I had a young wife. My idealism was at its height. I remember trying to write and being unable to—the atmosphere was wrong, the intimacy, the lack of solitude. Also, no one read. We were at the opposite pole from reading. Even at West Point there had been apostates, but not here. I had the seed within me but it was not yet time.

On the surface one might say I was thwarted, and perhaps that is true. Nevertheless I was happy then. I can only compare the feeling to being loved.

————

Now it is fall, a long time afterwards. The geese are dropping down to the ponds. The sea is huge, a storm coming. We had been swimming in it, exalted. Then drinks at Fox's in his new house. Gloria Jones is there, her capped teeth and rich, vulgar voice, *"Jamais de ma vie!"* she cries, never in my life. "How did you two meet?" she asks, it is her quintessential question, "You met, how? Just like that, as they say?"

The then and now are intertwined, the dimming past and the

present. Like an enduring disease there are the dreams. I am flying with someone, wide open, on the deck. The sky is cloudy, the
flak terrifying. We are going at top speed, flashing past storage
tanks, along a river on the way to the target. Suddenly ahead in the
mist, steel bridges! Too late to pull up! We hit them! A great wave
of heat sweeps over me. I have crossed—it is completely real—
over into death.

I wake in the darkness and lie there. The aftertaste is not bitter.
I know, just as in dreams, I will die, like every living thing, many of
them more noble and important, trees, lakes, great fish that have
lived for a hundred years. We live in the consciousness of a single
self, but in nature there seems to be something else, the consciousness of many, of all, the herds and schools, the colonies and
hives with myriads lacking in what we call ego but otherwise perfect, responsive only to instinct. Our own lives lack this harmony.
We are each of us an eventual tragedy. Perhaps this is why I am in
the country, to be close to the final companions. Perhaps it is only
that winter is coming on.

One night in the darkness, outside, listening to the distant
booming surf, "Isn't it strange," I say, "how you want different
things at different times? Now all I want is a house by the sea.
Hawaii was like this, still empty then, still beautiful. We used to
make love in the cane fields."

"Who? Who did you do it with?"

"A naval officer's wife, I remember. Her name was Sis Chandler."

"Whew! That's a hot name. She must have been something. Was
she blonde?"

"No."

In fact I could not recall what she looked like, but I remembered her and one or two things she said. It was her name that
mattered, especially after so long a time. Pronouncing it had made
me feel a long-vanished warmth towards her.

I have not forgotten those days, I have only
Forgotten how simply they seemed to occur . . .

It was difficult to write. The heart for it was faint. It was useless, as in Chekhov's crushing story, to try and tell someone of my child's death. I could hardly bring myself to mention it. You must remember, but it was precisely that which was terrible. In reality I tried to forget her and what had happened.

In a jeweler's window off Bond Street I had once seen an antique gold box about the size of a box of matches. It had a small drawer in which lay half a dozen ivory strips upon which riddles or questions were written in black enamel. Inserted in a slot they produced an answer in a narrow window on top of the box. *Qui nous console*—who consoles us—was one of the riddles. *Le temps* was the answer, a word which can mean either weather or time.

In the country there was both.

———

I woke on Christmas morning two or three years later. My father was born on this day. Eight decades back. Wearing a long fur coat I had bought secondhand in Southampton, I walked in the woods, the two of us did, the dog running ahead. At the weir the stream was frozen along the banks. In the light dusting of snow were the footprints of a wild duck.

We had lunch at the Lords', Sherry and Pam's—he was a painter, Fox's good friend; theirs was that rarity, a perfect marriage, his third, her second. His income was meager but he owned a house. Occasionally they argued. "You've never been poor!" he cried, furious.

"Darling, I didn't have the time," she said.

The clear winter light was streaming across the fields. There were views from every window of the house. Sherry's eighty-three-year-old mother was there also. She was a widow. I knew the story of her husband's death. His heart was failing. The family had gathered to see him and at the end of the afternoon had left for the day. He was alone with the nurse. There was a bottle of scotch over there, he told her, would she care to join him for a drink? They sat sipping from their glasses as the sun set and evening came on. He finished his and held out his glass. "What would you say to one for the road?" he asked and then lay back. I believe they were his last words.

During the week before New Year I made some lists, jotted things, really: Pleasures, those that remained to me; Ten Closest Friends; Books Read. I also thought of various people as you do at year's end. Did Not Make the Voyage: my mother's baby sister who died, I think, unnamed; George Cortada; Kelly; Joe Byron; Thomas Maynard, aged eight; Kay's miscarried child; Sumo's puppies . . .

Late in the day we walked on the deserted beach.

Afterwards I bathed, dressed, put on a white turtleneck, and, looking in the mirror, combed my hair. I had seen worse. Health, good. Hopes, fair.

Karyl Roosevelt and Dana, her son, came for drinks. She had been the most beautiful woman. Perhaps as a consequence her life had been devoted to men. Even afterwards she spoke of them with affection.

She'd been married to a very rich man. The first time they went to Europe they flew directly to Yugoslavia and boarded Marshal Tito's yacht. Tito, his sleeves rolled up, rowed her around a bay near Dubrovnik himself.

We drove to dinner at Billy's. Very few customers. Then back to the house before midnight, where we made a fire, drank toasts, and read aloud from favorite books. I read the last speech in Noël Coward's *Cavalcade*, the one in which the wife toasts her husband. They have lost both their sons in the war (1914–1918) and she drinks to them, to what they might have been, and to England.

Kay read from *Ebenezer Le Page*. Karyl, the last part of Joyce's "The Dead," where the snow is falling on all Ireland, also from *Anna Karenina, Humboldt's Gift,* and *The Wapshot Chronicle.* Dana read Robert Service, Stephen King, and Poe, something long and incomprehensible. Perhaps it was the drinks. "As the French say, *comment?*" Kay remarked.

The fire had burned to embers, the company was gone. We walked in the icy darkness with the old, limping dog. Nothing on the empty road, no cars, no sound, no lights. The year turning, cold stars above. My arm around her. Feeling of courage. Great desire to live on.

INDEX

picador.com

blog
videos
interviews
extracts